PENGUIN ⟨🐧⟩ CLASSICS

DE PROFUNDIS
AND OTHER PRISON WRITINGS

OSCAR FINGAL O'FLAHERTIE WILLS WILDE was born in Dublin in 1854, his father an eminent eye-surgeon and his mother a national poet who wrote under the pseudonym of 'Speranza'. He went to Trinity College, Dublin, and then to Magdalen College, Oxford, where he began to propagandize the new Aesthetic (or 'Art for Art's Sake') Movement. Despite winning a first and the Newdigate Prize for Poetry, Wilde failed to obtain an Oxford fellowship after his finals, and was forced to earn a living by lecturing and writing for periodicals. He published a largely unsuccessful volume of poems in 1881 and in the next year undertook a lecture-tour of the United States in order to promote the D'Oyly Carte production of Gilbert and Sullivan's comic opera *Patience*. After his marriage to Constance Lloyd in 1884, he tried to establish himself as a writer, but with little initial success. However, his three volumes of short fiction, *The Happy Prince* (1888), *Lord Arthur Savile's Crime* (1891) and *A House of Pomegranates* (1891), together with his only novel, *The Picture of Dorian Gray* (1891), gradually won him a reputation as a modern writer with an original talent, a reputation confirmed and enhanced by the phenomenal success of his Society Comedies – *Lady Windermere's Fan*, *A Woman of No Importance*, *An Ideal Husband* and *The Importance of Being Earnest*, all performed on the West End stage between 1892 and 1895.

Success, however, was short-lived. In 1891 Wilde had met and fallen in love with Lord Alfred Douglas. In 1895, when his success as a dramatist was at its height, Wilde brought an unsuccessful libel action against Douglas's father, the Marquess of Queensberry. Wilde lost the case and two trials later was sentenced to two years' imprisonment for acts of gross indecency. As a result of this experience he wrote *De Profundis*, his long confessional letter to Douglas, and *The Ballad of Reading Gaol*. He was released from prison in 1897 and went into an immediate self-imposed exile on the Continent. He died in Paris in ignominy in 1900.

COLM TÓIBÍN is the author of six novels, including *The Blackwater Lightship* (1999), *The Master* (2004) and *Brooklyn* (2009), and two story collections, *Mothers and Sons* (2006) and *The Empty Family* (2010). His essay collections are *Love in a Dark Time: Gay Lives from Wilde to Almodóvar* (2002), *All a Novelist Needs: Essays on Henry James* (2010) and *New Ways to Kill Your Mother: Writers and Their Families* (2012). He is Irene and Sidney Silverman Professor of the Humanities at Columbia University and a contributing editor at the *London Review of Books*.

OSCAR WILDE

De Profundis
and Other Prison Writings

Edited and with an introduction by
COLM TÓIBÍN

PENGUIN BOOKS

PENGUIN BOOKS

UK | USA | Canada | Ireland | Australia
India | New Zealand | South Africa

Penguin Books is part of the Penguin Random House group of companies
whose addresses can be found at global.penguinrandomhouse.com.

The text of the letters, and the accompanying notes, first published in
The Complete Letters of Oscar Wilde, edited by Merlin Holland and
Rupert Hart-Davis, and published in Great Britain, by Fourth Estate Ltd, 2000.
Letters and notes reprinted by permission of HarperCollins Publishers Ltd
This edition published in Penguin Classics 2013

019

Set in 10.25/12.25 PostScript Adobe SabonTypeset by Dinah Drazin
Printed in Great Britain by Clays Ltd, Elcograf S.p.A.

ISBN: 978-0-140-43990-8

www.greenpenguin.co.uk

MIX
Paper from
responsible sources
FSC® C018179

Penguin Random House is committed to a
sustainable future for our business, our readers
and our planet. This book is made from Forest
Stewardship Council® certified paper.

Contents

Chronology

1854 Oscar Fingal O'Flahertie Wilde born (he added 'Wills' in the 1870s) on 16 October at 21 Westland Row, Dublin.

1855 His family move to 1 Merrion Square in Dublin.

1857 Birth of Isola Wilde, Oscar's sister.

1858 Birth of Constance Mary Lloyd, Wilde's future wife.

1864 Wilde's father is knighted following his appointment as Queen Victoria's 'Surgeon Oculist' the previous year. Wilde attends Portora Royal School, Enniskillen.

1867 Death of Isola Wilde.

1871–4 At Trinity College, Dublin, reading Classics and Ancient History.

1874–8 At Magdalen College, Oxford, reading Classics and Ancient History ('Greats').

1875 Travels in Italy with his tutor from Dublin, J.P. Mahaffy.

1876 First poems published in *Dublin University Magazine*. Death of Wilde's father, Sir William Wilde.

1877 Further travels in Italy, and in Greece.

1878 Wins the Newdigate Prize for Poetry in Oxford with 'Ravenna'. Takes a double first from Oxford. Moves to London and starts to establish himself as a popularizer of Aestheticism.

1881 Meets Constance Lloyd. *Poems* published at his own expense; not well received critically.

1882 Lecture tour of North America, speaking on art, aesthetics and house decoration. Revised edition of *Poems* published.

1883 His first play, *Vera; or, The Nihilists*, performed in New York; it is not a success.

1884 Marries Constance Lloyd in London, honeymoon in Paris and Dieppe.

1885 Moves into 16 Tite Street, Chelsea. Cyril Wilde is born.

1886 Vyvyan Wilde born. Meets Robert Ross, to become his lifelong friend and, after his death, his literary executor. Ross might have been Wilde's first homosexual lover.

1887 Becomes the editor of *Lady's World: A Magazine of Fashion and Society*, and changes its name to *Woman's World*. Publication of 'The Canterville Ghost' and 'Lord Arthur Savile's Crime'.

1888 *The Happy Prince and Other Tales* published; on the whole well received.

1889 'Pen, Pencil and Poison' (on the forger and poisoner Thomas Griffiths Wainewright), 'The Decay of Lying' (a dialogue in praise of artifice over nature and art over mortality), 'The Portrait of Mr W. H.' (on the supposed identity of the dedicatee of Shakespeare's sonnets) all published.

1890 *The Picture of Dorian Gray* published in the July number of *Lippincott's Monthly Magazine*; fierce debate between Wilde and hostile critics ensues. 'The True Function and Value of Criticism' (later revised and included in *Intentions* as 'The Critic as Artist') published.

1891 Wilde's first meeting with Lord Alfred Douglas ('Bosie'). *The Duchess of Padua* performed in New York. 'The Soul of Man Under Socialism' and 'Preface to Dorian Gray' published in February and March in the *Fortnightly Review*. The revised and extended edition of *The Picture of Dorian Gray* published by Ward, Lock and Company in April. *Intentions* (collection of critical essays), *Lord Arthur Savile's Crime and Other Stories* and *A House of Pomegranates* (fairy-tales) published.

1892 *Lady Windermere's Fan* performed at St James's Theatre, London (February to July).

1893 *Salomé* published in French. *A Woman of No Importance* performed at Haymarket Theatre, London.

1894 *Salome* published in English with illustrations by Aubrey Beardsley; Douglas is the dedicatee. *The Sphinx*, a poem with illustrations by Charles Ricketts, published.

1895 *An Ideal Husband* opens at Haymarket Theatre in January; it is followed by the hugely successful *The Importance of Being Earnest* at St James's Theatre in February. On 28 February Wilde returns to his club, the Albemarle, to find a card from Douglas's father, the Marquess of Queensberry, inscribed: 'For Oscar Wilde posing as a somdomite [sic]'. Wilde quickly takes out an action accusing Queensberry of criminal libel. In April Queensberry appears at the Old Bailey and is acquitted, following a successful plea of justification on the basis that Wilde was guilty of homosexual behaviour. Wilde is immediately arrested, after ignoring his friends' advice to flee the country. He is tried twice at the Old Bailey (the first trial ending in a hung jury), and on 25 May sentenced to two years' imprisonment with hard labour for 'acts of gross indecency with other male persons'. In July he is sent to Wandsworth Prison. In November he is declared bankrupt, and shortly afterwards transferred to Reading Gaol.

1896 Death of Wilde's mother, Lady Jane Francesca Wilde ('Speranza').

1897 Wilde writes the long letter to Douglas that would be later entitled 'De Profundis'. In May Wilde is released from prison, and sails for Dieppe by the night ferry. He never returns to Britain.

1898 *The Ballad of Reading Gaol* published pseudonymously as by 'C.3.3', Wilde's cell-number in Reading Gaol. Wilde moves to Paris in February. Constance Wilde (who had by now changed her name to Holland) dies.

1899 Willie (b. 1852), Wilde's elder brother, dies.

1900 In January Queensberry dies. By July Wilde himself is ill with a blood infection. On 29 November he is received into the Roman Catholic Church, and dies of cerebral meningitis on 30 November in the Hôtel d'Alsace in Paris.

1905 An abridged version of *De Profundis*, edited by Robert Ross, published.

1908 The *Collected Works*, edited by Robert Ross, published.

Introduction

In 1895 in London the personal became political because an Irish playwright pushed his luck. Oscar Wilde, as the year opened, was the toast of London. He had powerful friends among the intellectual and political and social elite. He was slowly winning immense respect as a playwright and an artist, having won in the 1880s notoriety as a wit and social butterfly. He could do as he pleased. His plays were written quickly and effortlessly; he himself seemed to move in the same spirit between intimate family life and, when he became bored with that, a life in hotels and foreign places. He could mingle among the great and the good and then pleasurably spend time with young men from a different, mostly lower, social class. He could also continue his liaison with the young and beautiful Lord Alfred Douglas, also known as Bosie, whom he had met four years earlier, and try to ignore the protests of Douglas's father, the Marquess of Queensberry, who was sure that his son was being corrupted. He was at the height of his fame and his glory; he must have seemed untouchable. By May, however, he was in prison, abandoned by most of his friends, his reputation ruined, his name a byword for corruption and evil, the Marquess of Queensberry fully vindicated. Wilde's family life was destroyed, he was declared a bankrupt and he was about to serve a sentence whose severity was beyond his imagination.

In the years that followed, everybody who wrote about Oscar Wilde seemed to have known a different facet of him. W. B. Yeats, for example, remembered Wilde the married man towards the end of the 1880s.

He lived in a little house at Chelsea that the architect Godwin had decorated with an elegance that owed something to Whistler . . . I remember vaguely a white drawing-room with Whistler etchings, 'let into' white panels, and a dining-room all white, chairs, walls, mantelpiece, carpet, except for a diamond-shaped piece of red cloth in the middle of the table under a terracotta statuette . . . It was perhaps too perfect in its unity . . . and I remember thinking that the perfect harmony of his life there, with his beautiful wife and two young children, suggested some deliberate artistic composition.[1]

Oscar Wilde's younger son, Vyvyan, also remembered those years when his father was 'a real companion' to him and his brother, with 'so much of the child in his own nature that he delighted in playing our games . . . When he grew tired of playing he would keep us quiet by telling us fairy stories, or tales of adventure, of which he had a never-ending supply.'[2]

Among the children's writers whom Wilde admired, according to his son, was Robert Louis Stevenson, whose *The Strange Case of Dr Jekyll and Mr Hyde* appeared in 1886, the year of Vyvyan's birth. This was the time when, as Karl Miller wrote in his book *Doubles*, 'a hunger for pseudonyms, masks, new identities, new conceptions of human nature, declared itself'.[3] Thus Dr Jekyll could announce with full conviction: 'This, too, was myself' as he became 'a stranger in his own house'. Jekyll 'learned to recognise the thorough and primitive duality of man; I saw that, of the two natures that contended in the field of my consciousness, even if I could rightly be said to be either, it was only because I was radically both'.[4] Thus as Wilde set to work on the creation of both himself and his character Dorian Gray, he was following an example which was embedded in the spirit of the age.

London at around the time of the publication of Wilde's novel *The Picture of Dorian Gray* in 1891 was where many artists – including W. B. Yeats, George Bernard Shaw, Joseph Conrad and Henry James – allowed their doubled selves, and their work full of masked selves, secret agents, secret sharers and sexual secrets, to flourish and further multiply. Wilde in

London was both an Englishman and an Irishman, an aristo-
crat and an Irish patriot, a family man and a man who never
seemed to be at home, a dilettante and a dedicated artist.
Everywhere he went, he left behind in some attic of the mind
an opposite self, recently discarded.

Every man, W. B. Yeats pointed out during this same period,
has 'some one scene, some one adventure, some one picture
that is the image of his secret life'.[5] In 1909, Joseph Conrad
wrote his story 'The Secret Sharer', in which the captain of a
ship is confronted with his precise double: 'It was, in the night,
as though I had been faced by my own reflection in the depths
of a sombre and immense mirror.' Conrad's narrator refers to
the interloper as 'my second self'. No self in these years was
stable. In October 1894 Robert Louis Stevenson wrote: 'I am
a fictitious article and have long known it. I am read by jour-
nalists, by my fellow novelists and by boys.'[6] In August 1891,
while staying at the Marine Hotel in Kingstown in Ireland,
Henry James – described by his biographer Leon Edel as some-
one 'in search of, in flight from, something or other'[7] – had the
idea for his story 'The Private Life', in which the sociable writer
in the drawing room could at the same moment be found alone
as his other self working in his study. In those years the writer
was either two people, or he was nobody.

A writer's feelings could reflect this too. James both feared
and envied Oscar Wilde. He feared Wilde's Irishness while seek-
ing to disguise the fact that his own four grandparents were
of Irish origin or Irish birth; he feared Wilde's homosexuality,
while seeking to annihilate his own; he envied Wilde's sociabil-
ity, while seeking greater and greater solitude; and he envied
Wilde's audience, while bemoaning the dwindling of the income
from his own work.

In February 1895, when James's theatrical disaster *Guy
Domville* was taken off and replaced by Wilde's *The Importance
of Being Earnest*, James wrote to his brother: 'Oscar Wilde's
farce which followed "Guy Domville" is, I believe, a great suc-
cess – and with his two roaring successes running now at once
he must be raking in the profits.'[8] Wilde's wealth, however,
resided in the attic of James's imagination. In the real world, or

in the world which seemed real sometimes, Wilde was actually on the run from his creditors: 'I am already served with writs for four hundred pounds, rumours of prosperity having reached the commercial classes.'[9] Suddenly, he had managed to be rich and poor at the same time.

'Wilde,' Declan Kiberd has written, 'was the first major artist to discredit the romantic idea of sincerity and to replace it with the darker imperative of authenticity: he saw that in being true to a single self, a sincere man may be false to half a dozen other selves.'[10] This may seem accurate in retrospect, if we view Wilde's career as seamless, planned and fully thought out, as though it were a story or a work of art. If we view him in the few months before he went to prison, however, as he might have seemed to his contemporaries or indeed to himself, his life and his work appear rather more accidental and contradictory, dictated both by forces and feelings beyond his control and impelled by a set of actions and decisions which might easily have been different.

As George Bernard Shaw, who knew Wilde in the years of his fame as a playwright, wrote in 1938: 'It must not be forgotten that though by culture Wilde was a citizen of all civilised capitals, he was at root a very Irish Irishman, and, as such, a foreigner everywhere but in Ireland.'[11] Wilde's Irish background remains an essential ingredient in his career, just like Stevenson's Scottishness, James's New England origins or Conrad's Polish birth. Like his homosexuality, Wilde's Irishness left him an outsider in Oxford and London, but much of the time invisibly and ambiguously so. The English upper class he wrote about in his fiction and his plays was, as Karl Miller comments, 'a class exoticized, eroticised, by an outsider'.[12] Henry James shared Wilde's fascination with the manners and mores of this class. And all of these writers shared one essential ingredient with the people in whose country they had settled – a command of the English language. This operated as a sort of alibi for them, allowing them to shine on the page and the stage, allowing them immense possibilities for invention and disguise. The voyage from one self to another gave them their style; their style, in turn, offered them an easy intercourse with the English themselves. The problem lay in the middle.

Oscar Wilde's parents were also steeped in ambiguities; they were members of an Irish ruling class who had offered, through his father's work as an antiquarian and his mother's nationalism and poetry, their allegiance both to an Ireland of the past, before the English invasion, and to an Ireland of the future, which would be free of England. They belonged to a distinguished group of Irish Protestant aristocrats and bohemians who managed to remain a ruling class in Ireland and an amusing class in London, while seeking, directly or indirectly, the destruction of English power in Ireland.

This set of configured and ambiguous allegiances gave the members of this class enormous freedom and helped to sharpen their wit. They were capable of masquerading as eminent Victorians while having rich sexual lives, just as they were capable of managing their estates and servants and having their rents paid on time while preaching freedom.

Thus Lady Gregory, born in 1852, a leading figure in the Irish revival and a founder of the Abbey Theatre in Dublin, could begin her affair with the English poet Wilfred Scawen Blunt a year after her marriage in 1880 while modelling her dress and bearing on that of Queen Victoria; she could write seditious plays about Ireland while threatening her Irish tenants if they did not pay the rent. Thus W. B. Yeats, born in 1865, could write poems about unrequited love while pursuing an adventurous love life in London. So too the parents of Oscar Wilde: Sir William, born in 1815, could combine sexual licence with a knighthood and membership of the Dublin ruling class; Lady Wilde, born in 1821, could write editorials in nationalist newspapers calling for violent revolt against England and then happily move her salon to London after the death of her husband in 1876.

Oscar Wilde, born in 1854, loved referring to his mother as Lady Wilde. Studying at Oxford in his early twenties, he would have seemed a normal member of the upper classes, and indeed, from priggish letters written during those years, and from friendships with figures such as George Curzon, the future conservative politician and Viceroy of India, it is clear that he bore all the hallmarks of his class with pride and skill. His Irish identity was uncertain, and this very uncertainty meant that he could, while in England, insist on his own Irishness as though for the first time while learning to mimic his new friends' Englishness.

His heritage, unlike that of his English friends, however, was based on no firm set of morals and manners, no long-held convictions about privileges and rules. His heritage was protean and open to suggestion. He looked like the English ruling class; he could speak like them if it suited him; he enjoyed their company and he entertained them; but, as a writer, what he learned to do best was mock them; and when it came to a crisis he would fundamentally misunderstand them.

His homosexuality, like his Irishness, would also loosen his allegiances to shared principles, would assist further in undermining his loyalty to any set of values held by those who made the laws and those who obeyed them. Ford Madox Ford, who at one point used the same lawyer as Wilde, knew about Wilde's chameleon qualities and admired his ability, when the crisis came, to exude self-pity in enormous quantities while at the same time being able to see his own self-pity as a kind of play, or further self-dramatization:

He came into Humphreys's [his solicitor's] office . . . and before Humphreys could get words spoken, he had sunk into a chair, covered his face with his hands, and sobbingly deplored the excesses of his youth, his wasted talent, and his abhorred manhood. He spread himself in Biblical lamentation. But when Humphreys, coming round his table, was intent on patting him on the shoulder and telling him to cheer up and be a man . . . Wilde suddenly took his hands down from his face, winked jovially at [Humphreys] and exclaimed: 'Got you there, old fellow.'

In the same article, written in 1939, Ford recalls the visits of Oscar Wilde to his grandfather Ford Madox Brown. Wilde, once again, arrived as one of his own doubles:

Mr Wilde was a quiet individual who came every Saturday, for years, to tea with the writer's grandfather – Ford Madox Brown. Wilde would sit in a high-backed armchair, stretching out one hand a little towards the blaze of the wood fire on the hearth and talking of the dullest possible things to Ford Madox Brown, who . . . sat on the other side of the fire in another high-backed chair and, stretching out towards the flames his other hand, disagreed usually with Mr Wilde on subjects like that of the Home Rule for Ireland Bill or the Conversion of the Consolidated Debt.

Wilde, Ford wrote, continued these visits, 'as he said later, out of liking for the only house in London where he did not have to stand on his head'.[13]

All of these dualities clearly inspired the wit, the perfect patterning and the pure subversion in his best criticism and his best work for the theatre. They do not help, however, to explain the sheer badness of his poetry, which was full of pre-Raphaelite gloom, archaic phrasing, rarefied poetic diction and sentiments he did not mean. His dualities came in many guises, then: he was not only a married man who was homosexual, an Irishman in London, a wit who was also serious, but a limp and timid lyricist who wrote brave and modern plays.

None of these dualities, however, either caused or can fully explain his frame of mind and what happened to him in the winter and spring of 1895. On 3 January of that year, his play *An Ideal Husband* opened at the Haymarket Theatre in London to critical acclaim and great popularity. The Prince of Wales and the future prime minister Arthur Balfour were in attendance on the opening night. *The Importance of Being Earnest* was already written and was set to replace Henry James's failed play *Guy Domville* at the St James Theatre on 14 February.

At the beginning of January, Wilde was persuaded by his lover Lord Alfred Douglas to accompany him to Algeria, although he, in fact, wished to stay to oversee the rehearsals of his new play. As André Gide, who met them in Algiers, attested, their time in Algeria was interesting. All three of them found a pleasure and freedom not as easily or cheaply available in London or Paris. The reputation of Wilde and Douglas came before them. Gide wrote to his mother that Wilde was 'the most dangerous product of modern civilisation'; he seemed to Gide 'to have corrupted [Douglas] to the very marrow of his bones'. Wilde set about corrupting Gide too, or so Gide wrote much later, introducing him to an Arab boy and accompanying them to an apartment where Gide held in his 'bare arms that perfect, wild little body, so dark, so ardent, so lascivious'.[14] Later, as Gide told his mother (having left out the part about the Arab boy), they met up with Douglas, who had a boy called Ali in tow, who must have been only twelve or thirteen. Although Douglas 'returned incessantly, and with disgusting obstinacy to things I spoke of with only with the greatest embarrassment, an embarrassment that was increased by his total lack of it', Gide admitted that he found him 'absolutely charming'.[15]

Wilde wrote to his friend Robert Ross about the joys of hashish and the beautiful boys: 'We have been on an excursion into the mountains of Kabylia – full of villages peopled by fauns. Several shepherds fluted on reeds for us. We were followed by lovely brown things from forest to forest. The beggars here have profiles, so the problem of poverty is easily solved.'[16] It is likely that the excitement they found in Algeria, while wonderful in its way, was also deeply unsettling, making English rules and responsibilities seem even more absurd and worth ignoring.

Wilde began making his way back to England at the end of January. The ferry from Algeria to France was twenty hours late because of a storm; the outgoing journey had also been rough. From Marseilles Wilde travelled to Paris, where he visited the artist Edgar Degas before returning to London to attend final rehearsals and prepare for his opening night. In the shadows always was his family whom he did not see – his sons were at boarding school, but he stayed in hotels in any case, his wife uncertain of his whereabouts – and Lord Alfred Douglas's father, the Marquess of Queensberry, who wished to sever the connection between Wilde and his son. Wilde was anchorless, rudderless and increasingly famous. He dined out and stayed out late. There is no evidence that he read quietly in his hotel room. He was not producing any new work and letters written during this time are brief and hurried. When *The Importance of Being Earnest* opened, the *New York Times* commented: 'Oscar Wilde may be said to have at last, and by a single stroke, put his enemies under his feet.'[17] But it was not true. His enemies lay both within, among the warring factions of his unsettled self, and outside himself, as the Marquess of Queenberry became more determined to save his son.

Queensberry had bought a ticket for the opening night of his play. On 14 February, Wilde wrote to an unidentified correspondent: 'Bosie's father is going to make a scene tonight. I am going to stop him.'[18] A few days after the opening he wrote to Lord Alfred Douglas:

> the Scarlet Marquis made a plot to address the audience on the first night of my play! . . . he was not allowed to enter.
>
> He left a grotesque bouquet of vegetables for me! This of course makes his conduct idiotic, robs it of dignity.
>
> He arrived with a prize-fighter!![19] I had all Scotland Yard – twenty police – to guard the theatre. He prowled about for three hours, then left chattering like a monstrous ape.[20]

And there were other enemies too in the city where Wilde had reinvented himself: the young men, less rich and privileged than he, whom at this time he still considered his friends and whom he entertained lavishly. They would soon prove all too ready to blackmail him and inform Queensberry about his activities.

It cannot be overstated how much raw fame was attached to the author of two successful new plays running at the same time in London in these years. Nor can it be overemphasized how Wilde's highly charged time in Algeria and the stresses of travelling there and back had further upset his equilibrium. A hundred years later, his behaviour would have been perfectly understood as deriving from a mixture of jet lag and crazed celebrity. In 1895, there were so such understandings, nor terms to describe them.

Wilde, in any case, was already, when he received the famous calling card, someone on the run, someone whose judgement on any important matter would have been seriously impaired.

The card, left at the Albemarle Club, was dated 18 February, four days after his play's opening night, but he did not receive it until ten days later. It read: 'For Oscar Wilde posing somdomite [sic]' and it was from the Marquess of Queensberry.

The card had been handed first to the porter at the club, who had held it for Wilde. What would the author of 'The Decay of Lying' or *The Importance of Being Earnest* say about it? How would he reply? Wilde, as he carefully read the card, lost all the flippancy and clever carelessness which he paraded in print and on the stage. Instead, he became the son of Sir William Wilde, friend to the most powerful figures in the London of his day, and a distinguished writer whose opening nights were attended by the Prince of Wales. He was elated and exhausted, bubbling with success and fame. The mask was pulled back. The card did not amuse him, or cause him to respond as readers of his work might have expected – with laughter or disdain, mockery or insouciance. It caused him to adopt a new tone, one that was pompous and hurt and self-important. His letter to Robert Ross, written on that day, uses words like 'hideous' and 'ruined' and terms like 'criminal prosecution'. He had ceased to mock the ruling class as he strove now to present himself as an indignant member of it.

'His swelled head,' George Bernard Shaw later wrote, 'led him to believe that, as he himself put it, there was nothing he could not carry through successfully: a delusion which seems to have taken possession of him when his success as a playwright brought him plenty of money for the first time.'[21] The excitement of the previous two months had impaired his judgement; his status as aristocratic Irishman to whom London had pandered would not help him now as he sought to defend his good name, something about which he had been, both in his actions and his attitudes, extremely careless in the years leading up to 1895. 'It is his vanity that has brought all this disgrace upon him,' his brother Willie told W. B. Yeats at the time. 'They swung incense before him. They swung it before his heart.'[22] Wilde was one of the very few who did not realize that he was, as the trial began, the most vulnerable man in London.

*

It is only with the recent publication of the full transcript of the questioning of Wilde by the lawyer Edward Carson in Wilde's case against the Marquess of Queensberry[23] that we have an idea of precisely the sort of life he had been leading in the years before his trial: the time spent in restaurants and hotels with numerous young men from a lower social position, and the upper-class world he otherwise inhabited as a family man, famous author and frequenter of respectable clubs and drawing rooms. The transcript gives us a sense of the risks Wilde was taking in bringing the case in the first place.

Robert Ross advised him at the time not to bring an action. Frank Harris, another close friend, agreed. 'You are sure to lose it,' Harris is reported to have said to Wilde. 'You haven't a dog's chance and the English despise the beaten.' When Wilde had lunch at the Café Royal with Harris and George Bernard Shaw, he was urged by both to drop the case. 'You should go abroad,' Harris told him, 'and, as ace of trumps, you should take your wife with you.'[24] George Bernard Shaw, remembering that lunch, wrote in 1938 how Wilde 'miscalculated the force of the social vengeance he was unloosing on himself'.[25] Harris, meanwhile, claims that as the lunch came to an end 'Oscar seemed inclined to do as I proposed'. Then Lord Alfred Douglas arrived. 'At Oscar's request, I repeated my argument and to my astonishment Douglas got up at once, and cried with his little white venomous, distorted face: "Such advice shows you are no friend of Oscar's."'[26]

In his preface to Harris's book on Oscar Wilde, George Bernard Shaw makes clear that neither he nor his associates, including Harris, knew of Wilde's homosexuality as a matter of fact until Wilde was cross-examined in the case.[27] They knew of his decadence, of his flaunting a sort of sexual ambiguity, but they did not know that he was consorting with younger men of the lower classes nor that he had actually had sexual relations with Lord Alfred Douglas. In the preface to Harris's book, Shaw insists that the warning they gave to Wilde at the Café Royal was on the basis that a jury would not rule against a father who seemed to be protecting his own son's reputation.

Harris's subsequent blaming of Lord Alfred Douglas for forcing Wilde to sue for libel and, indeed, his description of Douglas's physiognomy at the time, deserve to be taken lightly and treated with care. It was easy with hindsight to demonize Douglas; but it was Wilde who sued and it was Wilde who chose to stay in London rather than flee to France when he had lost the case against the Marquess of Queensberry and when it became inevitable that the Crown would bring a criminal charge against him.

There is no simple, clear reason why Wilde chose to remain in London once his libel action against Queensberry had collapsed and it had become apparent that, as a result of information offered in the libel case, he would be arrested on charges of gross indecency with enough evidence to convict him. As the time grew near for the decision to be made, when there was still a possibility of catching a train and boat to France, he could not make up his mind. 'A half-packed suitcase lay on the bed, emblem of contradictory impulses,' Wilde's biographer Richard Ellmann writes. 'He was tired of action. Like Hamlet, as he understood that hero, he wished to distance himself from his plight, to be the spectator of his own tragedy . . . A man so concerned with his image disdained to think of himself as a fugitive, skulking in dark corners, instead of lording it in the limelight . . . Suffering was more becoming than embarrassment.'[28] Calling at Wilde's house, Yeats remembers Willie Wilde saying to him: 'If he is acquitted, he will stay out of England for a few years, and can then gather his friends about him once more – even if he is condemned he will purge his offence – but if he runs away he will lose every friend that he has.'[29] Yeats later heard, 'from whom I forget now', that Lady Wilde had told Oscar: 'If you stay, even if you go to prison, you will always be my son, it will make no difference to my affection, but if you go, I will never speak to you again.'[30] Wilde's family, it seemed, somehow saw their own destiny as rebels, as belonging to Irish history, in Oscar's martyrdom; they believed their honour was at stake. 'He is an Irish gentleman, and he will face the music,' his brother is reported to have said.[31] 'I have never doubted,'

Yeats continues in his own account, 'even for an instant, that he made the right decision, and that he owes to that decision half of his renown.'[32]

For Irish patriots of even the mildest hue, a prison sentence, especially one served in England, was a badge of honour and a cause for celebration. Willie Wilde was wrong, however, when he said that Wilde would lose every friend he had if he absconded. Most of his friends, including his wife, were English enough to favour his leaving. His refusal to do so was prompted not so much by the advice of his mother and brother, or his Irish disrespect for the law, or his prevarication, but by the fact that he had not the slightest idea what a prison sentence would entail. Prison, for him, remained an abstract thing until – after two devastating trials at the Old Bailey, in which young men whom he had trusted gave evidence against him and he was found guilty of 'acts of gross indecency with other male persons' – he was actually sentenced to two years in gaol with hard labour. He served those two years to the day.

'People not familiar with prisons had no idea what their procedures were,' Richard Ellmann comments. 'That is perhaps the only excuse for Henry James, who wrote to Paul Bourget that Wilde's sentence to hard labour was too severe, that isolation would have been more just.'[33] Wilde's misfortune was to serve his sentence just before prison conditions were officially changed by the 1898 Prison Act. Until that act was passed, the isolation to which all prisoners were subjected was harsher than anyone, including Wilde himself or Henry James, could imagine.

In isolation, Wilde slept on a plank bed with no mattress. He was allowed one hour's exercise a day, walking in Indian file in the yard with other prisoners but not allowed to communicate with them. He could not sleep, he was permanently hungry and he suffered from dysentry. For the first month, Wilde was tied to the treadmill six hours a day, making an ascent, as it were, of six thousand feet each day, with five minutes' rest after every twenty minutes. Towards the end of his sentence, when the regime had eased somewhat because of a change of governor at the gaol, the new incumbent, Major Nelson, remarked to

Robert Ross: 'He looks well. But like all men unused to man-
ual labour who receive a sentence of this kind, he will be dead
within two years.'[34]

In the outside world, Constance Wilde planned to take the
children to Ireland, but as Vyvyan recalls:

> the hue and cry after the Wilde family was just as bad, if not
> worse, in Ireland, the land of my father's birth; so our plans were
> changed. It was thought better, after all, that we should go and
> hide ourselves abroad [in Switzerland]. There at least we could
> live unmolested . . . My mother remained behind, to be of what
> assistance she could to my father, until she too was driven from
> her home by the entrance of the bailiff's men, and the subsequent
> sale of all the contents of the house. The sale was a scandal-
> ous piece of barefaced robbery . . . For months afterwards, my
> brother and I kept asking for our soldiers, our trains and other
> toys, and we could not understand why it upset our mother . .
> . It was only when I saw the catalogue, many years later, that I
> realised why my mother had been so upset. The sale consisted of
> 246 lots; number 237 was 'A large quantity of toys'; they realised
> thirty shillings.[35]

Neither Vyvyan nor his brother ever saw their father again.
Lady Wilde, the boys' grandmother, would die during the first
year of her son's imprisonment. Constance would die within a
year of his release.

In the meantime, Lord Alfred Douglas was in France, feeling
as sorry for himself as he did for Wilde, with no understanding
either of what a sentence of two years' hard labour would be
like. Wilde's prison sentence was bound to change his relation-
ship with Douglas. The affair between them, which had trans-
formed both of their lives, had always been tempestuous. While
their arguments and Douglas's tantrums, such as they were, are
well documented, their ordinary life together, the fierce attach-
ment between them and their love for each other, must be, much
of the time, taken for granted. In April and May 1895, however,
before he went to prison, Wilde had made his love for Douglas
absolutely clear to his friends and in a series of letters. He wrote

to his friends More Adey and Robert Ross, for example: 'Bosie is so wonderful. I think of nothing else. I saw him yesterday.'[36] A week later, he wrote that 'nothing but Alfred Douglas's daily visits quicken me into life'.[37] Douglas, in turn, corresponded with him from Paris: 'I continue to think of you day and night and send you all my love. I am always your own loving and devoted boy.'[38] Before he was sentenced, Wilde penned two last passionate and tender letters to Douglas in which he stated that 'Never has anyone in my life been dearer than you, never has any love been greater, more sacred, more beautiful' and 'O sweetest of all boys, most loved of all loved, my soul clings to your soul, my life is your life, and in all the worlds of pain and pleasure, you are my ideal of admiration and joy.'[39] He did not, indeed, could not, write to him again for nineteen months and it was during this time he began to rethink what had happened between them. The next letter is the one that came to be known as *De Profundis*.[40]

The writing of *De Profundis* during the final months of Wilde's sentence was only possible because of the gradual relaxation in the severity of the prison regime, beginning in July 1896 with the arrival of Major J. O. Nelson as governor of Reading Gaol. Wilde was later to praise Nelson as 'the most Christlike man I ever met'.[41] Under the previous regime, Wilde had been allowed to write to solicitors and the Home Office, and to a limited extent to friends, but his letters were inspected and the writing materials removed as he finished each letter. Now he was to be allowed pen and ink all the time, and while what he wrote was removed each evening, it was handed back to him in the morning. *De Profundis*, written in the form of a long letter, a clever stratagem devised by him and agreed to by Nelson, was never sent and thus remained his property. It took him three months, with much revision.

By this time, his love for Douglas had turned into a sort of bitterness, and the tone of his long letter manages to capture that bitterness as well as the extraordinary attachment he felt for Douglas. *De Profundis* is neither fair-minded nor consistent; it is, at times, greatly bloated in its comparisons and its rhetoric. But in the prose there is also, much of the time, a beautiful, calm eloquence; the balance comes in the way the sentences are constructed rather than in the quality of the humility or the accusations. There is a sense of urgency, of matters newly understood being said because there might not. be time or opportunity to say them in the future. Wilde's old skill at paradox and phrase-making is no longer there to amuse his audience or mock his betters but to kill his own pain and grief. He writes not as art, but as a desperately serious matter.

'The only beautiful things,' his character Vivian tells us in Wilde's essay 'The Decay of Lying' (1889), 'are the things that do not concern us.'[42] Eight years later, in his cry 'from the depths',[43] he wrote of what most deeply concerned him: 'If there be in it one single passage that brings tears to your eyes, weep as we weep in prison when the day no less than the night is set apart for tears' (p. 46). And then, in what is perhaps the most shocking sentence in the whole letter, he writes: 'The supreme vice is shallowness' (p. 46). Once upon a time it would have been the supreme virtue.

He accuses Douglas of distracting him from his art, of spending his money, of degrading him ethically, of constant scene-making, of deliberately and then thoughtlessly mistreating him. He goes over Douglas's bad behaviour in matters large and petty, often citing dates and places and details, but all delivered in a tone which is fluent and sweeping, full of carefully controlled emotional cadence and measured elegance. The change in his voice is astonishing, like a tenor becoming a baritone, with a new range and depth and a new attention to feeling, but the old skills and tricks with pitch and paradox are still in place, despite his circumstances; even perhaps because of them.

The letter cannot be read for its accurate account of their relationship nor taken at its word. While some of the accusations are valid, others are petty and foolish and untrue. But that is not the point. It was not written by an historian attempting to set the record straight. Nor can it be read, as Wilde's poems can be read, as efforts at the creation of a purely beautiful music. De Profundis has neither the informality of a personal letter nor the art of a piece of imaginative writing.

Its seductive, hurt and passionate tone places it in a different category. The letter remains Wilde's greatest piece of prose-writing because of the change it marks in his imaginative procedures. The high priest of flippancy and mocking laughter has set himself suddenly and shockingly against shallowness; he is desperately hurt and wounded, but he is still in command of his sentences, their structure and their sweep. In the dim light of the prison cell and with the memory of his suffering fresh, it was as though he sought a new sort of tension in his writing between breathlessness and breath-control. He writes long and highly wrought sentences, loving lists of adjectives and clever, Latinate diction and elaborate punctuation. To be followed by a pure, plain statement, full of the clipped sharp tone of the Anglo-Saxon.

'Of course I should have got rid of you,' he states at one point in the letter (p. 54). The reader will want to know why he did not, and the answer comes in the length and the complexity of Wilde's relationship with Douglas, in the very intimate and immediate tone of De Profundis itself, in the letters written to Douglas in May 1895 and in the fact that both of them, once Wilde was released, made an effort to live together and stay together, to the horror of both Constance Wilde and Douglas's family. De Profundis, then, despite everything, is a sort of love letter, even though it might not have been meant like that, nor indeed greatly welcomed by its recipient in time to come.

Wilde's problem, on his release, was akin to his problem on being arrested: the general lack of understanding of what such a prison sentence would be like and what damage it would cause. Some of his friends presumed that he would begin writing again, not realizing that something essential in him had been broken. In June 1897, he wrote to Frank Harris: 'The prisoner looks to liberty as an immediate return to all his ancient energy, quickened into more vital forces by long disuse. When he goes out, he finds he still has to suffer. His punishment, as far as its effects go, lasts intellectually and physically, just as it lasts socially. He still has to pay.'[44] In 'The Decay of Lying' he had criticized the writer Charles Reade for 'a foolish attempt to be modern, to draw public opinion to the state of our convict prisons' through his novels written with a social conscience.[45] Now, he himself, in two long and eloquent letters to the *Daily Chronicle* (pp. 188 and 201), made clear the levels of cruelty exercized in the prison system, what he had witnessed and what he had personally suffered. In his exile he had become a social reformer.

In June 1897, soon after his release, he began work on *The Ballad of Reading Gaol*, which he described to Laurence Housman in a letter of 22 August:

> I am occupied in finishing a poem, terribly realistic for me, and drawn from actual experience, a sort of denial of my own philosophy of art in many ways. I hope it is good, but every night I hear cocks crowing ... so I am afraid I may have denied myself, and would weep bitterly, if I had not wept away all my tears.[46]

Both Yeats and Richard Ellmann preferred those parts of the poem that told the story directly and dealt with the specific narrative. Yeats cut out the more abstract sections in his *Oxford Book of Modern Verse 1892–1935*. 'The *Ballad*,' Ellmann writes, 'is strongest when it concentrates on the trooper and prison conditions, weakest when it deals with capitalised abstractions like Sin and Death, and imports imagery from "The Rime of the Ancient Mariner". At its best the sharp details and colloquial language carry conviction.'[47]

Yeats himself made well-wrought poems with a single tone and a sharp finish; his style as a poet, even when he was at his most lyrical, was decisive and definitive. Wilde managed such a tone in *The Importance of Being Earnest*, with seamless patterning and no room for untidy diversions or parts of the plotting which were less than perfect. It was almost unimaginable, however, that he could have produced such a work in the summer of 1897.

He had previously written poems with elaborate verse and rhyme schemes, and he was, as the plots of his plays show, a great magpie with the work of other writers, to which he added an enormous fluency of his own. Rudyard Kipling's *Barrack-*

Room Ballads had appeared to great popularity in 1892. Now Wilde chose the ballad as his form – six-line stanzas with the last line often coming in a more startling and flat rhythm than the rolling rhythms of the previous five. The poem has none of the self-pity of *De Profundis*; there is instead a tone of terror which comes in some of the stanza-endings and then not in others. The variety in the narrative, moving from stanzas about the general plight of the condemned to the specific story of one man who is to be executed and back again, delivers moments of pure shock which would not be there were the poem more singly focused. Wilde himself realized that it was not a perfect work of art. He wrote to Robert Ross in October 1897 about his misgivings: 'The poem suffers under the difficulty of a divided aim in style. Some is realistic, some is romantic; some poetry, some propaganda. I feel it keenly, but as a whole I think the production is interesting.'[48]

The poem was published in February 1898 under Wilde's Reading prison number, 'C.3.3', but the seventh edition, in 1899, had his name in brackets under the number. The first six editions sold five thousand copies in England within three months of publication. In 1954 when Vyvyan Holland, as he was called after his father's disgrace when the family fled to the Continent, wrote his memoir *Son of Oscar Wilde*, he remarked that he did not see a copy of the poem until he went to Cambridge in 1905. Until then he had not even known of its existence. 'I do not think that my mother ever saw it at all. The conspiracy of silence around my father was very efficient and I doubt whether anyone would have called her attention to it.'[49] But he was mistaken; she merely kept it hidden from her children. On 19 February 1898, Constance wrote to her brother: 'I am frightfully upset by this wonderful poem of Oscar's . . . It is frightfully tragic and makes one cry.'[50] A month before she died, she wrote about the poem again to her friend Carlos Blacker: 'if you do see [Oscar] tell him I think *The Ballad* exquisite, and I hope that the great success it has had in London at all events will urge him on to write more.'[51] Wilde himself died two years later, in November 1900. *The Ballad of Reading Gaol* was his last work.

Had Wilde died peacefully in his bed in the opening months of 1895 before bringing a case again Lord Alfred Douglas's father, before serving his sentence, he would still be a great playwright. His work, especially *The Importance of Being Earnest*, would be as central in our repertoire as it is now. The man who suffered would not have come to light; the mind which created and the art he made would have been everything. What happened to him over the next five years has changed our response to his work, however. His name became a byword for martyrdom, for the fall from grace, for the gap between the salon and the prison cell which he made seem both so narrow and so wide. His plays would have survived without his notoriety, and yet when we watch them we cannot erase the knowledge that such cleverness led to prison. We hold our breath at his cheek; the laughter he provokes has a dark and unsettling edge.

Such cleverness placed under the pressure of suffering also led directly to Wilde's greatest poem, and one of the greatest ballads written in the language, *The Ballad of Reading Gaol*; it also led to the astonishing and enticing cadences of *De Profundis*, and the reforming, steely eloquence of his letters to the *Daily Chronicle*, letting the wider world know what the narrow world of the prison did to its inmates. The man who had revelled in duality became in these writings quite singular, and all the more interesting and intriguing for that. He moved from being a writer of the 1890s to becoming our contemporary by adding in his work from prison new, strange and deeply affecting aspects to his old duality, a new mask which came to look more like a face than any which he had worn before.

Colm Tóibín, 2013

NOTES

1   W.B. Yeats, *Autobiographies* (London: Macmillan, 1956), pp. 134–5.
2   Vyvyan Holland, *Son of Oscar Wilde* (originally published 1954), new edition with a foreword by Merlin Holland (Oxford: Oxford University Press, 1988), pp. 52–3.

3   Karl Miller, *Doubles: Studies in Literary History* (Oxford: Oxford University Press, 1987), p. 209.

4   Quoted in ibid., pp. 211–12.

5   Quoted in ibid., p. 222.

6   Letter to Sidney Colvin, 6 October 1894, quoted in ibid., p. 215.

7   Quoted in ibid., p. 199.

8   Quoted in Colm Tóibín, *Love in a Dark Time: Gay Lives from Wilde to Almodóvar* (London: Picador, 2002), p. 42.

9   Quoted in ibid., p. 43.

10   Declan Kiberd, *Inventing Ireland: The Literature of the Modern Nation* (London: Jonathan Cape, 1995), p. 38.

11   Quoted in Frank Harris, *Oscar Wilde* (London: Constable & Co., 1938), p. xlviii.

12   Miller, *Doubles*, p. 225.

13   Ford Madox Ford, 'Memories of Oscar Wilde' *Saturday Review of Literature*, vol. 20, no. 5, (27 May 1939), pp. 15 and 3.

14   Quoted in Tóibín, *Love in a Dark Time*, p. 40.

15   Ibid.

16   Oscar Wilde, *The Complete Letters of Oscar Wilde*, ed. Merlin Holland and Rupert Hart-Davis (London: Fourth Estate, 2000), p. 629.

17   Quoted in Richard Ellmann, *Oscar Wilde* (Harmondsworth: Penguin, 1987), p. 406.

18   Wilde, *Letters*, p. 632.

19   The Marquess of Queensberry, known for his love of boxing, is best remembered for the Queensberry Rules, the code of conduct on which modern boxing is based.

20   Wilde, *Letters*, p. 632.

21   Quoted in Harris, *Oscar Wilde*, p. xli.

22   Quoted in Yeats, *Autobiographies*, p. 289.

23   See Merlin Holland, *Irish Peacock and Scarlet Marquess: The Real Trial of Oscar Wilde* (London: Fourth Estate, 2003). See also H. Montgomery Hyde, *The Trials of Oscar Wilde* (London: William Hodge & Co., 1948).

24   Harris, *Oscar Wilde*, p. 139.

25   Quoted in ibid., p. 142.

26   Ibid., p. 143.

27   Ibid., p. xxviiii.

28   Ellmann, *Oscar Wilde*, p. 429.

29   Quoted in Yeats, *Autobiographies*, p. 289.

30   Ibid.

31   Quoted in Joy Melville, *Mother of Oscar: The Life of Jane Francesca Wilde* (London: John Murray, 1994), p. 260.

32   Yeats, *Autobiographies*, p. 289.

33   Ellmann, *Oscar Wilde*, p. 474.

34   Quoted in ibid., p. 490.

35   Holland, *Son of Oscar Wilde*, pp. 61–2.

36   Wilde, *Letters*, p. 642.

37   Ibid., p. 644.

38   Quoted in Tóibín, *Love in a Dark Time*, p. 62.

39   Wilde, *Letters*, pp. 650–52.

40   For the history of its posthumous publication by Robert Ross, see note 1 on p. 243.

41   Quoted in Ellmann, *Oscar Wilde*, p. 476.

42   Richard Ellmann (ed.), 'The Decay of Lying', in *The Artist as Critic: Critical Writings of Oscar Wilde* (Chicago: University of Chicago Press, 1968), p. 300.

43   *De Profundis* translates as 'from the depths', the title taken by Robert Ross (see note 40 above) from the opening of the penitential Psalm 130: 'From the depths I have cried out to you, O Lord'.

44   Wilde, *Letters*, p. 896.

45   Ellmann (ed.), 'The Decay of Lying', p. 300.

46   Wilde, *Letters*, p. 928.

47   Ellmann, *Oscar Wilde*, p. 500.

48   Wilde, *Letters*, p. 956.

49   Holland, *Son of Oscar Wilde*, p. 133.

50   Quoted in Wilde, *Letters*, p. 1022, note 4.

51   Ibid., p. 1035, note 1.

Further Reading

Ellmann, Richard, *Oscar Wilde* (Penguin: Harmondsworth, 1987)

Harris, Frank, *Oscar Wilde* (London: Constable & Co., 1938)

Holland, Merlin, *Irish Peacock and Scarlet Marquess: The Real Trial of Oscar Wilde* (London: Fourth Estate, 2003)

Holland, Vyvyan, *Son of Oscar Wilde* (Oxford: Oxford University Press, 1988)

Hyde, H. Montgomery, *The Trials of Oscar Wilde* (London: William Hodge & Co., 1948)

Kiberd, Declan, *Inventing Ireland: The Literature of the Modern Nation* (London: Jonathan Cape, 1995)

Melville, Joy, *Mother of Oscar: The Life of Jane Francesca Wilde* (London: John Murray, 1994)

Miller, Karl, *Doubles: Studies in Literary History* (Oxford: Oxford University Press, 1987)

O'Sullivan, Vincent, *Aspects of Wilde* (London: Constable, 1936)

Tóibín, Colm, *Love in a Dark Time: Gay Lives from Wilde to Almodóvar* (London: Picador, 2002)

Wilde, Oscar, *The Artist as Critic: Critical Writings of Oscar Wilde*, ed. Richard Ellmann (Chicago: University of Chicago Press, 1968)

— *The Complete Works of Oscar Wilde* (Glasgow: HarperCollins, 1994)

— *The Complete Letters of Oscar Wilde*, ed. Merlin Holland and Rupert Hart-Davis (London: Fourth Estate, 2000)

Yeats, W. B., *Autobiographies* (London: Macmillan, 1956)

Note on the Text

The text of the letters, and their accompanying notes, included in this edition is based on *The Complete Letters of Oscar Wilde*, edited by Merlin Holland and Rupert Hart-Davis (London: Fourth Estate, 2000).

The editors of *The Complete Letters* approached Wilde's text with the aim of clarifying only those elements that would otherwise have made it difficult to read and enjoy. Although Wilde's spelling was generally good, he often misspelled proper names, and so these have been corrected. Elsewhere original spellings have been retained, including '-ise' word endings. Wilde's use of capitals was sometimes erratic – he liked to use an initial capital for words beginning T and H, for instance – and has therefore been standardized. Underlined words have been printed in italics, as have foreign words and the titles of works, following the usual convention.

Preserving Wilde's punctuation, consisting of short dashes for almost every kind of stop, would likewise have made the text hard to read and so it has been replaced by normal punctuation. Some standardization has also been employed at the top of each letter, with the date always shown on the left and the address on the right. Where Wilde omitted the date or place of writing, the most likely possibility has been suggested in square brackets, with doubtful dates preceded by a query.

The manuscripts containing Wilde's letters are located in various libraries and private collections around the world; full details of the current location of Wilde's prison writings can be found in *The Complete Letters*.

DE PROFUNDIS
AND OTHER LETTERS

Letters of
March 1895–March 1897

To Ada Leverson

[*Circa 11 March 1895*][1]

My dear Friend,

A thousand thanks. For a week I go away with Bosie: then return to fight with panthers.[2]

  Oscar

Kind regards to dear Ernest.

To Constance Wilde

[? *5 April 1895*][3]

Dear Constance,

Allow no one to enter my bedroom or sittingroom – except servants – today. See no one but your friends. Ever yours

  Oscar

To the Editor of the Evening News

5 April 1895[4]   *Holborn Viaduct Hotel*

It would have been impossible for me to have proved my case without putting Lord Alfred Douglas in the witness-box against his father.

Lord Alfred Douglas was extremely anxious to go into the box, but I would not let him do so.

Rather than put him in so painful a position I determined to retire from the case, and to bear on my own shoulders whatever ignominy and shame might result from my prosecuting Lord Queensberry.[5]

Oscar Wilde

To Lord Alfred Douglas

[*5 April 1895*]   [*Cadogan Hotel*]

My dear Bosie,

I will be at Bow Street Police Station tonight – no bail possible I am told. Will you ask Percy, and George Alexander, and Waller,[6] at the Haymarket, to attend to give bail.[7]

Would you also wire Humphreys to appear at Bow Street for me. Wire to 41 Norfolk Square, W.

Also, come to see me. Ever yours

Oscar

To Ada and Ernest Leverson

9 April 1895   *HM Prison, Holloway*

Dear Sphinx and Ernest,

I write to you from prison, where your kind words have reached
me and given me comfort, though they have made me cry, in
my loneliness. Not that I am really alone. A slim thing, gold-
haired like an angel, stands always at my side. His presence
overshadows me. He moves in the gloom like a white flower.

With what a crash this fell! Why did the Sibyl say fair things?[8]
I thought but to defend him from his father: I thought of noth-
ing else, and now—

I can't write more. How good and kind and sweet you and
Ernest are to me.

Oscar

To an Unidentified Correspondent[9]

15 April 1895   *HM Prison, Holloway*

My dear kind good sweet friend,

What can I say to you? How can I thank you? I cannot express
anything adequately. I am dazed with horror. Life has at last
become to me as real as a dream.

What more hideous things may crawl out to cry against me
I don't know. I hardly care, I think, for sometimes there is sun-
light in my cell, and every day someone whose name is Love
comes to see me, and weeps so much through prison-bars that it
is I who have to comfort him.[10]

With my deepest affection, my most sincere gratitude, ever
yours

Oscar

To R. H. Sherard

16 April 1895   *HM Prison, Holloway*

My dear Robert,

You good, daring reckless friend! I was delighted to get your letter, with all its wonderful news. For myself, I am ill – apathetic. Slowly life creeps out of me. Nothing but Alfred Douglas's daily visits quicken me into life, and even him I only see under humiliating and tragic conditions.

Don't fight more than six duels a week! I suppose Sarah[11] is hopeless; but your chivalrous friendship – your fine, chivalrous friendship – is worth more than all the money in the world. Ever yours

    Oscar

To Ada Leverson

23 April 1895   *HM Prison, Holloway*

My dear Sphinx,

I have just had a charming note from you, and a charming note from Ernest. How good you both are to me!

Willie has been writing me the most monstrous letters. I have had to beg him to stop.

Today Bosie comes early to see me. My counsel seem to wish the case to be tried at once. I don't, nor does Bosie. Bail, or no bail, I think we had better wait.

[*Later*] I have seen counsel, and Bosie. I don't know what to do. My life seems to have gone from me. I feel caught in a terrible net. I don't know where to turn. I care less when I think that he is thinking of me. I think of nothing else. Ever yours

    Oscar

To Lord Alfred Douglas

Monday Evening [29 April 1895][12]   *HM Prison, Holloway*

My dearest boy,

This is to assure you of my immortal, my eternal love for you. Tomorrow all will be over. If prison and dishonour be my destiny, think that my love for you and this idea, this still more divine belief, that you love me in return will sustain me in my unhappiness and will make me capable, I hope, of bearing my grief most patiently. Since the hope, nay rather the certainty, of meeting you again in some world is the goal and the encouragement of my present life, ah! I must continue to live in this world because of that.

Dear —[13] came to see me today. I gave him several messages for you. He told me one thing that reassured me: that my mother should never want for anything. I have always provided for her subsistence, and the thought that she might have to suffer privations was making me unhappy. As for you (graceful boy with a Christ-like heart), as for you, I beg you, as soon as you have done all that you can, leave for Italy and regain your calm, and write those lovely poems which you do with such a strange grace. Do not expose yourself to England for any reason whatsoever. If one day, at Corfu or in some enchanted isle, there were a little house where we could live together, oh! life would be sweeter than it has ever been. Your love has broad wings and is strong, your love comes to me through my prison bars and comforts me, your love is the light of all my hours. Those who know not what love is will write, I know, if fate is against us, that I have had a bad influence upon your life. If they do that, you shall write, you shall say in your turn, that it is not so. Our love was always beautiful and noble, and if I have been the butt of a terrible tragedy, it is because the nature of that love has not been understood. In your letter this morning you say something which gives me courage. I must remember it. You write that it is my duty to you and to myself to live in spite of everything. I think that is true. I shall try and I shall do it. I want you to keep Mr Humphreys informed of your movements so that when he comes he can tell me what you are doing. I believe solicitors are allowed to see the prisoners fairly often. Thus I could communicate with you.

I am so happy that you have gone away! I know what that must have cost you. It would have been agony for me to think that you were in England when your name was mentioned in court. I hope you have copies of all my books. All mine have been sold. I stretch out my hands towards you. Oh! may I live to touch your hair and your hands. I think that your love will watch over my life. If I should die, I want you to live a gentle peaceful existence somewhere, with flowers, pictures, books, and lots of work. Try to let me hear from you soon. I am writing you this letter in the midst of great suffering; this long day in court has exhausted me. Dearest boy, sweetest of all young men, most loved and most loveable. Oh! wait for me! wait for me! I am now, as ever since the day we met, yours devoutly and with an immortal love

    Oscar

To Ada Leverson

3 May 1895   HM Prison, Holloway

Dear and wonderful Sphinx,

If I do not get bail today will you send me some books?[14] I would like some Stevensons – *The Master of Ballantrae* and *Kidnapped*. Now that he[15] is away I have no one who brings me books, so I come to you, for you and Ernest are so good to me that I am glad to think that I never can repay you. Life is not long enough to allow of it. Always, always, I shall be in your debt.

Your letter cheered me very much. I do hope to see you soon. I have had no letter as yet today from Fleur-de-Lys. I wait with strange hunger for it.

My warmest thanks to Ernest. Always yours in gratitude and affection

Oscar

To Ada Leverson

[4 or 5 May 1895]   [HM Prison, Holloway]

My dear Sphinx,

Ernest's Shakespeare has arrived safe, and I hear your books are below. I hope I shall be allowed to have them, as Sunday is such a long day here.

I had two letters from Jonquil[16] today – to make up – and I saw Frank Harris. He was very pleasant and I think will be able to help in the way of the press. I have just written to Calais to say how sweet you and Ernest are to me. I believe I come out on Tuesday next. I must see you, of course. Ever with great affection yours

Oscar

To Ada Leverson

6 May 1895   HM Prison, Holloway

My dear Sphinx,

I have not had a line today from Fleur-de-Lys. I suppose he is at Rouen. I am so wretched when I don't hear from him, and today I am bored, and sick to the death of imprisonment.

I am reading your books, but I want to be out, and with people I love. The days seem endless.

Your kindness and Ernest's make things better for me. I go on trespassing on it more and more. Oh! I hope all will come well, and that I can go back to Art and Life. Here I sicken in inanition. Ever with great affection yours

Oscar

Letter from Bosie, at Rouen, just arrived. Please wire my thanks to him. He has cured me of sorrow today.

To Ada Leverson

[? *Early May 1895*]   [? *146 Oakley Street*][17]

My dear Sweet Kind Friend,

I have no words to thank you for all you do for me, but for you and Ernest Bosie and I have deepest love.

I hope to be in better spirits tonight. Your sweetness last night was wonderful. Your flowers are like him – your sending them like yourself. Dear, dear Friend, tonight I see you at 7.45. Ah! you are good and gentle and wonderful. Always devotedly yours

Oscar

To Lord Alfred Douglas

[*May 1895*][18]   [? *2 Courtfield Gardens*][19]

As for you, you have given me the beauty of life in the past, and in the future if there is any future. That is why I shall be eternally grateful to you for having always inspired me with adoration and love. Those days of pleasure were our dawn. Now, in anguish and pain, in grief and humiliation, I feel that my love for you, your love for me, are the two signs of my life, the divine sentiments which make all bitterness bearable. Never has anyone in my life been dearer than you, never has any love been greater, more sacred, more beautiful . . .[20]

Dear boy, among pleasures or in prison, you and the thought of you were everything to me. Oh! keep me always in your heart; you are never absent from mine. I think of you much more than of myself, and if, sometimes, the thought of horrible and infamous suffering comes to torture me, the simple thought of you is enough to strengthen me and heal my wounds. Let destiny, Nemesis, or the unjust gods alone receive the blame for everything that has happened.

Every great love has its tragedy, and now ours has too, but to have known and loved you with such profound devotion, to have had you for a part of my life, the only part I now consider beautiful, is enough for me. My passion is at a loss for words, but you can understand me, you alone. Our souls were made for one another, and by knowing yours through love, mine has transcended many evils, understood perfection, and entered into the divine essence of things.

Pain, if it comes, cannot last for ever; surely one day you and I will meet again, and though my face be a mask of grief and my body worn out by solitude, you and you alone will recognise the soul which is more beautiful for having met yours, the soul of the artist who found his ideal in you, of the lover of beauty to whom you appeared as a being flawless and perfect. Now I think of you as a golden-haired boy with Christ's own heart in you. I know now how much greater love is than everything else. You have taught me the divine secret of the world.

[NB: this letter is incomplete]

To Lord Alfred Douglas

[20 May 1895][21]   [? 2 Courtfield Gardens]

My child,

Today it was asked to have the verdicts rendered separately. Taylor is probably being judged at this moment, so that I have been able to come back here. My sweet rose, my delicate flower, my lily of lilies, it is perhaps in prison that I am going to test the power of love. I am going to see if I cannot make the bitter waters sweet by the intensity of the love I bear you. I have had moments when I thought it would be wiser to separate. Ah! moments of weakness and madness! Now I see that that would have mutilated my life, ruined my art, broken the musical chords which make a perfect soul. Even covered with mud I shall praise you, from the deepest abysses I shall cry to you. In my solitude you will be with me. I am determined not to revolt but to accept every outrage through devotion to love, to let my body be dishonoured so long as my soul may always keep the image of you. From your silken hair to your delicate feet you are perfection to me. Pleasure hides love from us but pain reveals it in its essence. O dearest of created things, if someone wounded by silence and solitude comes to you, dishonoured, a laughing-stock to men, oh! you can close his wounds by touching them and restore his soul which unhappiness had for a moment smothered. Nothing will be difficult for you then, and remember, it is that hope which makes me live, and that hope alone. What wisdom is to the philosopher, what God is to his saint, you are to me. To keep you in my soul, such is the goal of this pain which men call life. O my love, you whom I cherish above all things, white narcissus in an unmown field, think of the burden which falls to you, a burden which love alone can make light. But be not saddened by that, rather be happy to have filled with an immortal love the soul of a man who now weeps in hell, and yet carries heaven in his heart. I love you, I love you, my heart is a rose which your love has brought to bloom, my life is a desert fanned by the delicious breeze of your breath, and whose cool springs are your eyes; the imprint of your little feet makes valleys of shade for me, the odour of your hair is like myrrh, and wherever you go you exhale the perfumes of the cassia tree.

Love me always, love me always. You have been the supreme, the perfect love of my life; there can be no other.

I decided that it was nobler and more beautiful to stay. We could not have been together. I did not want to be called a coward or a deserter. A false name, a disguise, a hunted life, all that is not for me, to whom you have been revealed on that high hill where beautiful things are transfigured.

O sweetest of all boys, most loved of all loves, my soul clings to your soul, my life is your life, and in all the worlds of pain and pleasure you are my ideal of admiration and joy.

Oscar

To Robert Ross

10 March 1896   [*HM Prison, Reading*][22]

My dear Robbie,

I want you to have a letter written at once to Mr Hargrove, the solicitor, stating that as my wife has promised to settle one third on me in the case of her predeceasing me I do not wish any opposition to be made to her purchasing my life-interest.[23] I feel that I have brought such unhappiness on her and such ruin on my children that I have no right to go against her wishes in anything. She was gentle and good to me here, when she came to see me.[24] I have full trust in her. Please have this done *at once*, and thank my friends for their kindness. I feel I am acting rightly in leaving this to my wife.

Please write to Stuart Merrill in Paris, or Robert Sherard, to say how gratified I was at the performance of my play: and have my thanks conveyed to Lugné-Poë; it is something that at a time of disgrace and shame I should be still regarded as an artist. I wish I could feel more pleasure: but I seem dead to all emotions except those of anguish and despair. However, please let Lugné-Poë know that I am sensible of the honour he has done me. He is a poet himself. I fear you will find it difficult to read this, but as I am not allowed writing materials I seem to have forgotten how to write: you must excuse me.

Thank More for exerting himself for books: unluckily I suffer from headaches when I read my Greek and Roman poets, so they have not been of much use, but his kindness was great in getting them sent.[25] Ask him to express also my gratitude to the lady who lives at Wimbledon.[26] Write to me please in answer to this, and tell me about literature – what new books etc.: also about Jones's play and Forbes-Robertson's management:[27] about any new tendency in the stage of Paris or London. Also, try and see what Lemaître, Bauër, and Sarcey[28] said of *Salomé* and give me a little résumé: please write to Henri Bauër and say I am touched at his writing nicely.[29] Robert knows him. It was sweet of you to come and see me:[30] you must come again next time. Here I have the horror of death with the still greater horror of living: and in silence and misery [*some lines cut out by prison officials*] but I won't talk more of this. I always remember you with deep affection. Ever your friend

O. W.

I wish Ernest would get from Oakley Street my portmanteau, fur coat, clothes, and the books of *my own writing* I gave my dear mother. Ask Ernest in whose name the burial-ground of my mother was taken.[31] Goodbye.

To Robert Ross

Saturday, [30 May 1896][32]   [*HM Prison, Reading*]

Dear Robbie,

I could not collect my thoughts yesterday, as I did not expect you till today. When you are good enough to come and see me will you always fix the day? Anything sudden upsets me.

You said that Douglas was going to dedicate a volume of poems to me. Will you write at once to him and say he must not do anything of the kind. I could not accept or allow such a dedication. The proposal is revolting and grotesque.[33] Also, he has unfortunately in his possession a number of letters of mine. I wish him to at once hand all these without exception over to you; I will ask you to seal them up. In case I die here you will destroy them. In case I survive I will destroy them myself. They must not be in existence. The thought that they are in his hands is horrible to me, and though my unfortunate children will never of course bear my name, still they know whose sons they are and I must try and shield them from the possibility of any further revolting disclosure or scandal.

Also, Douglas has some things I gave him: books and jewellery. I wish these to be also handed over to you – for me. Some of the jewellery I know has passed out of his possession under circumstances unnecessary to detail, but he has still some, such as the gold cigarette-case, pearl chain and enamelled locket I gave him last Christmas. I wish to be certain that he has in his possession nothing that I ever gave him. All these are to be sealed up and left with you. The idea that he is wearing or in possession of anything I gave him is peculiarly repugnant to me. I cannot of course get rid of the revolting memories of the two years I was unlucky enough to have him with me, or of the mode by which he thrust me into the abyss of ruin and disgrace to gratify his hatred of his father and other ignoble passions. But I will not have him in possession of my letters or gifts. Even if I get out of this loathsome place I know that there is nothing before me but a life of a pariah – of disgrace and penury and contempt – but at least I will have nothing to do with him nor allow him to come near me.

So will you write at once to him and get these things: until I know they are in your possession I will be more miserable than usual. It is I know an ungracious thing to ask you to do, and he will perhaps write to you in terms of coarse abuse, as he did to Sherard when he was prevented publishing more of my letters, but I earnestly beg of you not to mind. *As soon* as you have received them please write to me, and make part of your letter just like your other, with all its interesting news of literature and the stage. Let me know why Irving leaves Lyceum etc.,[34] what he is playing: what at each theatre: who did Stevenson criticise severely in his letters:[35] anything that will for an hour take my thoughts away from the one revolting subject of my imprisonment.

In writing to Douglas you had better quote my letter fully and frankly, so that he should have no loophole of escape. Indeed he cannot possibly refuse. He has ruined my life – that should content him.[36]

I am deeply touched by the Lady of Wimbledon's kindness. You are very good to come and see me. Kind regards to More, whom I would so like to see.

O. W.

Has anything come of Carlos Blacker and Newcastle?[37] The trial. The Sphinx has some letters of D's to me: they should be returned to him at once, or destroyed.

O. W.

To the Home Secretary[38]

2 July 1896   *HM Prison, Reading*

To the Right Honourable Her Majesty's Principal Secretary of State for the Home Department.

The Petition of the above-named prisoner humbly sheweth that he does not desire to attempt to palliate in any way the terrible offences of which he was rightly found guilty, but to point out that such offences are forms of sexual madness and are recognised as such not merely by modern pathological science but by much modern legislation, notably in France, Austria, and Italy, where the laws affecting these misdemeanours have been repealed, on the ground that they are diseases to be cured by a physician, rather than crimes to be punished by a judge. In the works of eminent men of science such as Lombroso and Nordau,[39] to take merely two instances out of many, this is specially insisted on with reference to the intimate connection between madness and the literary and artistic temperament, Professor Nordau in his book on 'Degenerescence' published in 1894 having devoted an entire chapter to the petitioner as a specially typical example of this fatal law.

The petitioner is now keenly conscious of the fact that while the three years preceding his arrest were from the intellectual point of view the most brilliant years of his life (four plays from his pen having been produced on the stage with immense success, and played not merely in England, America, and Australia, but in almost every European capital, and many books that excited much interest at home and abroad having been published), still that during the entire time he was suffering from the most horrible form of erotomania, which made him forget his wife and children, his high social position in London and Paris, his European distinction as an artist, the honour of his name and family, his very humanity itself, and left him the helpless prey of the most revolting passions, and of a gang of people who for their own profit ministered to them, and then drove him to his hideous ruin.

It is under the ceaseless apprehension lest this insanity, that displayed itself in monstrous sexual perversion before, may now extend to the entire nature and intellect, that the petitioner writes this appeal which he earnestly entreats may be at once considered. Horrible as all actual madness is, the terror of madness is no less appalling, and no less ruinous to the soul.

For more than thirteen dreadful months now, the petitioner has been subject to the fearful system of solitary cellular confinement: without human intercourse of any kind; without writing materials whose use might help to distract the mind: without suitable or sufficient books, so essential to any literary man, so vital for the preservation of mental balance: condemned to absolute silence: cut off from all knowledge of the external world and the movements of life: leading an existence composed of bitter degradations and terrible hardships, hideous in its recurring monotony of dreary task and sickening privation: the despair and misery of this lonely and wretched life having been intensified beyond words by the death of his mother, Lady Wilde, to whom he was deeply attached, as well as by the contemplation of the ruin he has brought on his young wife and his two children.

By special permission the petitioner is allowed two books a week to read: but the prison library is extremely small and poor: it hardly contains a score of books suitable for an educated man: the books kindly added at the prisoner's request he has read and re-read till they have become almost meaningless to him: he is practically left without anything to read: the world of ideas, as the actual world, is closed to him: he is deprived of everything that could soothe, distract, or heal a wounded and shaken mind: and horrible as all the physical privations of modern prison life are, they are as nothing compared to the

entire privation of literature to one to whom Literature was
once the first thing of life, the mode by which perfection could
be realised, by which, and by which alone, the intellect could
feel itself alive.

It is but natural that living in this silence, this solitude, this
isolation from all human and humane influences, this tomb
for those who are not yet dead, the petitioner should, day and
night in every waking hour, be tortured by the fear of absolute
and entire insanity. He is conscious that his mind, shut out arti-
ficially from all rational and intellectual interests, does
nothing, and can do nothing, but brood on those forms of
sexual perversity, those loathsome modes of erotomania, that
have brought him from high place and noble distinction to the
convict's cell and the common gaol. It is inevitable that it should
do so. The mind is forced to think, and when it is deprived of
the conditions necessary for healthy intellectual activity, such
as books, writing materials, companionship, contact with the
living world, and the like, it becomes, in the case of those
who are suffering from sensual monomanias, the sure prey of
morbid passions, and obscene fancies, and thoughts that defile,
desecrate and destroy. Crimes may be forgotten or forgiven,
but vices live on: they make their dwelling house in him who
by horrible mischance or fate has become their victim: they are
embedded in his flesh: they spread over him like a leprosy: they
feed on him like a strange disease: at the end they become an
essential part of the man: no remorse however poignant can
drive them out: no tears however bitter can wash them away:
and prison life, by its horrible isolation from all that could
save a wretched soul, hands the victim over, like one bound
hand and foot, to be possessed and polluted by the thoughts
he most loathes and so cannot escape from.

For more than a year the petitioner's mind has borne this. It
can bear it no longer. He is quite conscious of the approach of
an insanity that will not be confined to one portion of the nature
merely, but will extend over all alike, and his desire, his prayer is
that his sentence may be remitted now, so that he may be taken
abroad by his friends and may put himself under medical care
so that the sexual insanity from which he suffers may be cured.

He knows only too well that his career as a dramatist and writer is ended, and his name blotted from the scroll of English Literature never to be replaced: that his children cannot bear that name again, and that an obscure life in some remote country is in store for him: he knows that, bankruptcy having come upon him, poverty of a most bitter kind awaits him, and that all the joy and beauty of existence is taken from him for ever: but at least in all his hopelessness he still clings to the hope that he will not have to pass directly from the common gaol to the common lunatic asylum.

Dreadful as are the results of the prison system – a system so terrible that it hardens their hearts whose hearts it does not break, and brutalises those who have to carry it out no less than those who have to submit to it – yet at least amongst its aims is not the desire to wreck the human reason. Though it may not seek to make men better, yet it does not desire to drive them mad, and so, earnestly does the petitioner beg that he may be allowed to go forth while he has still some sanity left: while words have still a meaning, and books a message: while there is still some possibility that, by medical science and humane treatment, balance may be restored to a shaken mind and health given back to a nature that once knew purity: while there is still time to rid the temperament of a revolting madness and to make the soul, even for a brief space, clean.

Most earnestly indeed does the petitioner beg the Home Secretary to take, if he so desires it, the opinion of any recognised medical authorities on what would be the inevitable result of solitary confinement in silence and isolation on one already suffering from sexual monomania of a terrible character.

The petitioner would also point out that while his bodily health is better in many respects here than it was at Wandsworth, where he was for two months in the hospital for absolute physical and mental collapse caused by hunger and insomnia, he has, since he has been in prison, almost entirely lost the hearing of his right ear through an abscess that has caused a perforation of the drum. The medical officer here has stated that he is unable to offer any assistance, and that the hearing must go entirely. The petitioner, however, feels sure that under the care of a specialist abroad his hearing might be preserved to him. He was assured by Sir William Dalby,[40] the great aurist, that with proper care there was no reason at all why he should lose his hearing. But though the abscess has been running now for the entire time of his imprisonment, and the hearing getting worse every week, nothing has been done in the way even of an attempted cure. The ear has been syringed on three occasions with plain water for the purpose of examination, that is all. The petitioner is naturally apprehensive lest, as often happens, the other ear may be attacked in a similar way, and to the misery of a shattered and debilitated mind be added the horrors of complete deafness.

His eyesight, of which like most men of letters he had always been obliged to take great care, has also suffered very much from the enforced living in a whitewashed cell with a flaring gas-jet at night: he is conscious of great weakness and pain in the nerves of the eyes, and objects even at a short distance become blurred. The bright daylight, when taking exercise in the prison-yard, often causes pain and distress to the optic nerve, and during the past four months the consciousness of failing eyesight has been a source of terrible anxiety, and should his imprisonment be continued, blindness and deafness may in all human probability be added to the certainty of increasing insanity and the wreck of the reason.

There are other apprehensions of danger that the limitation of space does not allow the petitioner to enter on: his chief danger is that of madness, his chief terror that of madness, and his prayer that his long imprisonment may be considered with its attendant ruin a sufficient punishment, that the imprisonment may be ended now, and not uselessly or vindictively prolonged till insanity has claimed soul as well as body as its prey, and brought it to the same degradation and the same shame.

Oscar Wilde[41]

To the Home Secretary[42]

4 July 1896   HM Prison, Reading

To the Right Honourable Her Majesty's Principal Secretary of
State for the Home Department.

The Petition of the above-named prisoner humbly sheweth that
the petitioner has been informed by the Governor of the Prison
that Mr More Adey is anxious to see him on behalf of Mrs
Oscar Wilde with reference to coming to some agreement with
regard to the guardianship, education, and future of their chil-
dren, and also with regard to financial arrangements connected
with their marriage-settlements, which in consequence of the
petitioner's bankruptcy require serious consideration.

The petitioner is naturally anxious to meet his wife's wishes,
whatever they may be, in every possible way. But while per-
fectly ready to see Mr Adey on her behalf would earnestly beg
that the interview be in the Solicitors' Room and for the space
of one hour, and not in the cage for half-an-hour and in pres-
ence of a warder.[43]

It would be impossible to discuss delicate and private matters
from behind a cage and with a warder present. Mr Adey has
no doubt written instructions of some kind from Mrs Wilde,
who is now in Germany, which the petitioner should see or
be made acquainted with. The petitioner has full confidence
in Mr Adey and would gladly avail himself of his advice. In a
matter so important as the guardianship and education of his
children an hour is but barely sufficient time even for scant
consideration. There are also difficult financial matters that
require settlement. The petitioner has also to settle the ques-
tion of his having access to his children, and other still more
domestic questions. Hurried interviews from behind a cage in
a warder's presence are necessarily of a painful and distressing
character: the petitioner is anxious that he should be able to
have this important business interview, so vital for his wife and

children, under conditions that allow of judgment, reflection, and, if possible, wise and rational decision.

Oscar Wilde

To R. H. Sherard

Wednesday [26 August 1896][44]   [*HM Prison, Reading*]

My dear Robert,

The Governor has told me that you have written to ask to see me. It is most kind and affectionate of you, but an order has already been sent to More Adey and Arthur Clifton (whom I have not seen yet) and, as you know, I am only allowed two visitors. I did not think there would have been any chance of your being in town. I hope you are well and writing a great deal. I often think of you and of our uninterrupted friendship, of twelve years' standing, and while I bitterly regret the sorrow that I have brought on you and others of my friends, I remember with pride and gratitude your chivalry and courage on my behalf. Should the end of my terrible punishment ever come, you are one of the few people I would like to see, and be with from time to time.

Please remember me very kindly to George Ives.[45] I was greatly touched at hearing of his desire to come and see me. In the terrible solitude and silence in which one lives a message or a memory means a great deal. I hope he is hard at work writing books. I am very glad you know him. He is such a good fellow and so clever.

Should you have anything special to communicate to me – something separate from the sympathy and affection you have, I know, for me – More Adey, who is to write to me in the course of the next fortnight, will communicate it in his letter. He has to write to me on business.

I was so disappointed at not seeing you that I have been allowed as a favour to write this letter to you. Pray remember me to any of my friends who may ask after me, and believe me, dear Robert, sincerely yours

    Oscar

More Adey to Oscar Wilde[46]

23 September 1896

Robbie is still at the sea, with his brother and mother, who has taken a house there for him. She sends you kind messages saying she often thinks of you and prays for your welfare. Robbie is going on well, the doctors say, but he suffers a great deal from dyspepsia which affects his spirits very much. You know how much he thinks of and feels for you. He looks very ill still. He had his hair cut very short while he was at his worst and, owing to his continued weakness, it has not yet grown again and is very thin. This makes him look different. He has had a photograph taken which I hope to have an opportunity of showing you before long. He amuses himself by reading Dickens and has become quite enthusiastic over *Barnaby Rudge* and *Our Mutual Friend* etc. They just serve to amuse him without tiring his head.

    Miss Schuster says 'Could not Mr Wilde now write down some of the lovely tales he used to tell me? Remind him of one about a nursing-sister who killed the man whom she was nursing. And there was one about the two souls on the banks of the Nile. Were there time I could mention others, but I think the mere reminder of some of his tales may set his mind in that direction and stir the impulse to write. He told me also a beautiful play (just two years ago) that he has not written, about a husband, a wife and her lover, with a plot rather in the style of *Frou-frou*.'[47]

    Perhaps you could jot down the plots of some of those splendid stories you told us from time to time; Robbie knows more than I do, but I remember the Moving Sphere story, and the one about the Problem and the Lunatic.[48] To make a little résumé from memory of what you have already invented might put you in the vein for fresh invention.

Poor Miss Schuster has to leave her beautiful house. She cannot manage to keep it on now that her mother is dead. She is expecting Lady Brooke [the Ranee of Sarawak][49] to stay with her in October. Lady Brooke has been with your wife during the last nine months. I will try to see her, or if that is impossible, will learn from Miss Schuster all about your children, and will then try to obtain permission to visit you to tell you all about them. I should ask for permission towards the middle or end of October.

Acting on advice I have just written to the Home Secretary, undertaking, if you are released before May, to accompany you abroad at once, and promising that you will remain there until after the end of May. I hope I did right.

I have also written to your wife saying you are better, as I gave her a very bad account of you after I saw you in July. I think it would be well if you obtained leave to write to her; if you were inclined to consent to her appointing a guardian of whom you approved for your children in case of her death it would be well to tell her so, but I think a letter to her in any case would be a good thing.

If you should hear of anything that I have done on your behalf without your knowledge of which you do not approve, I trust you will repudiate it in as strong terms as you please. If you should have changed your mind about the clothes, let me know when you write, otherwise I will order you a travelling suit from your tailors Doré. I think on the whole my suggestion was the better one, but it really does not matter if you prefer my getting them at Doré's. I shall not go abroad until I am quite certain I cannot be of any use to you here. I hope you do not think I have any feeling against Sherard. I am on perfectly friendly terms with all your friends and get on particularly well with Sherard. I merely object to his frightful indiscretion, which is a positive mania with him and, contrary to his affectionate intentions, does you harm.

[NB: this fragment of a longer letter survives only in draft form]

To More Adey

Friday [25 September 1896]   [*HM Prison, Reading*]

My dear More,

I was greatly delighted to get your letter. I was afraid that Bobbie[50] might have been ill, and that that was the cause of the delay. It was a real pleasure to hear from him at such length, and to see his old wit and pleasant satire running through his budget: I do hope he will be quite well soon. Please thank his mother for her kind messages. I am very glad she has been spared to watch over Bobbie in his illness.

I thank you very much for writing to the Home Secretary.[51] I do hope it will have some effect. But pity seems to beat in vain at the doors of officialism; and power, no less than punishment, kills what else were good and gentle in a man: the man without knowing it loses his natural kindliness, or grows afraid of its exercise. Still, I hope something may be done. I admit that I look forward with horror to the prospect of another winter in prison: there is something terrible in it: one has to get up long before daybreak and in the dark-cold cell begin one's work by the flaring gas-jet; through the small barred window only gloom seems to find an entrance: and days often go over without one's being once even in the open air: days on which one stifles: days that are endless in their dull monotony of apathy or despair. If I could be released before the winter comes, it would be everything. On November 19th I will have had eighteen months of this black loathsome life: perhaps then something may be done. I know you will do your best: I have no words for my sense of your great wonderful kindness to me.

With regard to my children, I feel that for their own sake as well as for mine they should not be bred up to look on me with either hatred or contempt: a guardian amongst my wife's relations would be for this reason impossible. Of course I would like Arthur Clifton if he would undertake the charge. And so, would you ask Arthur to be my solicitor now: Humphreys is of course of no use: though paid an enormous fee through Leverson he never once came to see me about my Bankruptcy: so I was allowed to become insolvent when there was no reason.[52] If Arthur will be my solicitor he can on application to the Home Secretary come and see me in the Solicitors' Room here for one hour without the presence of a warder, and with him I could discuss the whole affair, and then write to my wife on the whole subject. I would feel quite safe if Arthur was my children's guardian. And as a solicitor his advice would be of great service. If he could come within the next fortnight it would be a great thing.[53]

I was greatly touched by the extract from the letter of the Lady of Wimbledon. That she should keep a gracious memory of me, and have trust or hope for me in the future, lightens for me many dreadful hours of degradation or despair. I have tried to remember and write down the *Florentine Tragedy*:[54] but only bits of it remain with me, and I find that I cannot invent: the silence, the utter solitude, the isolation from all humane and humanising influences, kill one's brain-power: the brain loses its life: becomes fettered to monotony of suffering. But I take notes of books I read, and copy lines and phrases in poets: the mere handling of pen and ink helps me: the horror of prison is the horror of complete brutalisation: that is the abyss always in front of one, branding itself on one's face daily, and the faces of those one sees. I cling to my notebook: it helps me: before I had it my brain was going in very evil circles.

I am so glad you are friends with Robert Sherard: I have no doubt he is very indiscreet, but he is very true, and saved my letters from being published. I know there was nothing in them but expressions of foolish, misplaced, ill-requited, affection for one of crude and callous nature, of coarse greed, and common appetites, but that is why their publication would have been so shameful. The gibbet on which I swing in history now is high enough. There is no need that he of all men should for his own vanity make it more hideous.

I am so glad Pierre Louÿs has made a great name for himself.[55] He was most cultivated, refined, and gentle. Three years ago he told me I would have to choose between his friendship and my fatal connection with A. D. I need hardly say I chose at once the meaner nature and the baser mind. In what a mire of madness I walked! . . .[56] From your silence I see he still refuses to return my presents and letters . . . It is horrible he should still have the power to wound me and find some curious joy in doing so . . . I won't write about him any more today. He is too evil, and there is a storm outside . . .

Poor Aubrey:[57] I hope he will get all right. He brought a strangely new personality to English art, and was a master in his way of fantastic grace, and the charm of the unreal. His muse had moods of terrible laughter. Behind his grotesques there seemed to lurk some curious philosophy . . .

As for my clothes, my fur coat is all I need really; the rest I can get abroad. Don't bother yourself. I hope Arthur will come and bring me good news of you and Robbie. Ever yours

    Oscar

To the Home Secretary[58]

10 November 1896   *HM Prison, Reading*

To the Right Honourable Her Majesty's Principal Secretary of State for the Home Department.

The Petition of the above-named prisoner humbly sheweth that in the month of June last the petitioner, having been at that time a prisoner for more than a year, addressed to the Secretary of State a petition praying for his release on the grounds chiefly of mental health.

That the petitioner has received no answer to his petition, and would earnestly beg that it be taken into consideration, as on the 19th inst. the petitioner will have completed eighteen months of solitary confinement, a sentence of terrible severity in any case, and, in the case of the petitioner, rendered all the more difficult to bear, as it has been inflicted for offences which are in other countries of Europe more rightly recognised as tragic forms of madness coming chiefly on those who over-tax their brain, in art or science.

Some alleviations have been granted to the petitioner since the date of his former petition: his ear, that was in danger of total deafness, is now attended to daily: spectacles have been provided for the protection of his eyes: he is allowed a manuscript-book to write in, and out of a list of books, selected by himself and approved of by the Prison Commissioners, a few have been added to the Prison Library: but these alleviations, for which the petitioner is naturally very grateful, count for but little in relieving the terrible mental stress and anguish that the silence and solitude of prison-life intensify daily.

Of all modes of insanity – and the petitioner is fully con-scious now, too conscious it may be, that his whole life, for the two years preceding his ruin, was the prey of absolute madness – the insanity of perverted sensual instinct is the one most domi-nant in its action on the brain. It taints the intellectual as well as the emotional energies. It clings like a malaria to soul and body alike. And while one may bear up against the monotonous hardships and relentless discipline of an English prison: endure with apathy the unceasing shame and the daily degradation: and grow callous even to that hideous grotesqueness of life that robs sorrow of all its dignity, and takes from pain its power of purification; still, the complete isolation from everything that is humane and humanising plunges one deeper and deeper into the very mire of madness, and the horrible silence, to which one is, as it were, eternally condemned, concentrates the mind on all that one longs to loathe, and creates those insane moods from which one desires to be free, creates them and makes them permanent.

Under these circumstances the petitioner prays for his release on the expiration of his term of eighteen months' confinement, or at any rate before Christmas comes. Some friends have promised to take him abroad at once, and to see that he has the treatment and care that he requires. There is of course before him no public life: nor any life in literature any more: nor joy or happiness of life at all. He has lost wife, children, fame, honour, position, wealth: poverty is all that he can look forward to: obscurity all that he can hope for: yet he feels that, if released now, somewhere, unknown, untormented, at peace, he might be able to recreate the life of a student of letters, and find in literature an anodyne from pain, first, and afterwards a mode by which sanity and balance and wholesomeness might be restored to the soul. But the solitary confinement, that breaks one's heart, shatters one's intellect too: and prison is but an ill physician: and the modern modes of punishment create what they should cure, and, when they have on their side Time with its long length of dreary days, they desecrate and destroy whatever good, or desire even of good, there may be in a man.

To be at length, after these eighteen months of lonely sorrow and despair, set free, for whatever brief space of time health of mind or body may allow, is the earnest prayer of the petitioner.

Oscar Wilde

To Robert Ross[59]

[*November 1896*]   [*HM Prison, Reading*]

[...] France by Lina Munte. Could nothing be done, in improving the company and getting fees? I would be quite ready to give for the time the complete acting rights of *Salomé* to Lugné-Poë. I think Robert Sherard might help with advice. Or Stuart Merrill.

(6) I brought out *Salomé* at my own expense with the Librairie de l'Art Indépendant. So it is mine. I have had no accounts from them of any kind. I wonder would not a new edition be advisable as it is being played? This might be arranged for, and some fees or money got. Sherard or Merrill will do it I am sure.

(7) To these purely business matters perhaps More Adey will kindly reply. His letter dealing purely with business I will be allowed to receive. It will not, I mean, interfere with your

literary letter, with regard to which the Governor has just now read me your kind message.

For myself, dear Robbie, I have little to say that can please you. The refusal to commute my sentence has been like a blow from a leaden sword. I am dazed with a dull sense of pain. *I* had fed on hope, and now Anguish, grown hungry, feeds her fill on *me* as though she had been starved of her proper appetite. There are, however, kinder elements in this evil prison air than there were before: sympathies have been shown to me, and I no longer feel entirely isolated from humane influences, which was before a source of terror and trouble to me. And I read Dante, and make excerpts and notes for the pleasure of using a pen and ink. And it seems as if I were better in many ways. And I am going to take up the study of German: indeed this seems to be the proper place for such a study. There is a thorn, however – as bitter as that of St Paul, though different – that I must pluck out of my flesh in this letter.[60] It is caused by a message you wrote on a piece of paper for me to see. I feel that if I kept it secret it might grow in my mind (as poisonous things grow in the dark) and take its place with other terrible thoughts that gnaw me . . .[61] Thought, to those that sit alone and silent and in bonds, being no 'winged living thing', as Plato feigned it,[62] but a thing dead, breeding what is horrible, like a slime that shows monsters to the moon.

I mean, of course, what you said about the sympathies of others being estranged from me, or in danger of being so, by the deep bitterness of the feelings I expressed about Alfred Douglas: and I believe that my letter was lent and shown to others with the part about him cut out by a pair of scissors.[63] Now I don't like my letters shown about as curiosities: it is most distasteful to me: I write to you freely as to one of the dearest friends I have, or have ever had: and, with a few exceptions, the sympathy of others touches me, as far as its loss goes, very little. No man of my position can fall into the mire of life without getting a great deal of pity from his inferiors; and I know that when plays last too long, spectators tire. *My* tragedy has lasted far too long: its climax is over: its end is mean; and I am quite conscious of the fact that when the end *does* come

I shall return an unwelcome visitant to a world that does not want me; a *revenant*, as the French say, as one whose face is grey with long imprisonment and crooked with pain. Horrible as are the dead when they rise from their tombs, the living who come out from tombs are more horrible still.

Of all this I am only too conscious. When one has been for eighteen terrible months in a prison cell, one sees things and people as they really are. The sight turns one to stone. Do not think that I would blame *him* for my vices. He had as little to do with them as I had with his. Nature was in this matter a stepmother to each of us. I blame him for not appreciating the man he ruined. An illiterate millionaire would really have suited him better. As long as my table was red with wine and roses, what did he care? My genius, my life as an artist, my work, and the quiet I needed for it, were nothing to him when matched with his unrestrained and coarse appetites for common profligate life: his greed for money: his incessant and violent scenes: his unimaginative selfishness. Time after time I tried, during those two wasted weary years, to escape, but he always brought me back, by threats of harm to himself chiefly. Then when his father saw in me a method of annoying his son, and the son saw in me the chance of ruining his father, and I was placed between two people greedy for unsavoury notoriety, reckless of everything but their own horrible hatred of each other, each urging me on, the one by public cards and threats, the other by private, or indeed half-public scenes, threats in letters, taunts, sneers . . . I admit I lost my head. I let him do what he wanted. I was bewildered, incapable of judgment. I made the one fatal step. And now . . . I sit here on a bench in a prison cell. In all tragedies there is a grotesque element. He is the grotesque element in mine. Do not think I do not blame myself. I curse myself night and day for my folly in allowing him to dominate my life. If there was an echo in these walls it would cry 'Fool' for ever. I am utterly ashamed of my friendship with him. For by their friendships men can be judged. It is a test of every man. And I feel more poignant abasement of shame for my friendship with Alfred Douglas . . . fifty thousand times more . . . than I do, say, for my connection with Charley

Parker[64] of which you may read a full account in my trial. The former is to me a daily source of mental humiliation. Of the latter I never think. It troubles me not. It is of no importance . . . Indeed my entire tragedy sometimes seems to me grotesque and nothing else. For as a result of my having suffered myself to be thrust into the trap Queensberry had laid for me – the trap he openly betted in the Orleans Club he would lure me into – as a result of that, the father ranks in history with the good parents of moral tales: the son with the Infant Samuel: and I, in the lowest mire of Malebolge,[65] sit between Gilles de Retz and the Marquis de Sade.[66] In certain places no one, except those actually insane, is allowed to laugh: and, indeed, even in their case it is against the regulations for conduct: otherwise I think I would laugh at that . . . For the rest, do not let Alfred Douglas suppose that I am crediting him with unworthy motives. He really had no motives in his life at all. Motives are intellectual things. He had passions merely. And such passions are False Gods that *will* have victims at all costs, and in the present case have had one wreathed with bay. He himself cannot but choose to feel *some* remorse. That he should really realise what he has done would be a burden too heavy for him to bear. But he must sometimes think of it. So in your letter tell me how he lives, what his occupations are, his mode of life.

And so now I have in my letter plucked the thorn out. That little scrawled line of yours rankled terribly. I *now* think merely of you getting quite well again, and writing at last the wonderful story of the little restaurant with the strange dish of meat served to the silent clients.[67] Pray remember me, with my thanks, to your dear mother, and also to Aleck. The gilded Sphinx is I suppose wonderful as ever. And send from me all that in my thoughts and feelings is good, and whatever of remembrance and reverence she will accept, to the Lady of Wimbledon, whose soul is a sanctuary for those who are wounded, and a house of refuge for those in pain. Do not show this letter to others, nor discuss what I have written, in your answer. Tell me about that world of shadows I loved so much. And about his life and soul tell me also. I am curious of the thing that stung me: and in my pain there is pity.

Oscar

To More Adey

Wednesday Evening, 16 December [*1896*]   [*HM Prison,
                                                              Reading*]

My dear More,

I have received a letter from Mr Hargrove informing me that
the Official Receiver has determined to sell half of my interest
to my friends, and that under these circumstances, unless your
offer is at once withdrawn, my wife's offer[68] contained in the
letters handed to Arthur Clifton will be withdrawn too.

I feel that I had better trust myself entirely to your judgment,
and I am now of opinion that your course was a wise one. I
know you and others have carefully considered the whole case,
and my wife's proposal that in case of my surviving her I was to
have £150 a year was, I think, a cruel and heartless one, and as
inconsiderate of the children's interest as of my existence.

What Hargrove's next move will be I do not know. If my wife
leaves me absolutely without a penny I can only trust that for a
year at any rate I will be looked after, and I may be able to write
again. Business matters, such as the present, of course upset me,
and make me weak in mind and body, with the hysteria of shat-
tered nerves, sleeplessness, and the anguish in which I walk; but
Art is different. *There* one makes one's own world. It is with
shadows that one weeps and laughs. A mirror will give back to
one one's own sorrow. But Art is not a mirror, but a crystal. It
creates its own shapes and forms.

(2) It would be a great thing for me to see you (or Arthur
Clifton) some time next month, and at intervals, on my affairs.
I hope permission will be granted.[69] I suggested, on the last
occasion, *Arthur*, as through his being a *solicitor* I felt it gave
some chance of the interview being *private*. You remember how
abortive and painful and useless was my interview with you,
with the Prison Officer seated between us to note the subject
and character of our conversation; I could not discuss anything
with you to any purpose, and finally cut short the interview. I

was unable to go through with it. I would sooner see *you*, as you are more thoroughly acquainted with all the various difficulties in my way. Were the matter in the hands of the Governor I would have no fear of the result. *But the matter is entirely one for the Commissioners.* In case they prove obdurate, would your solicitor, Mr Holman, act for me, if Mr Hargrove tries to force legal proceedings? Nothing would induce me to see Humphreys. His advice would, I think, be worthless. This, for your consideration. His fees to be managed through Leverson.

(3) With regard to the books, there has been a little misunderstanding. The list was sent to you that you should add whatever *new* books *you* could think of, such as Stevenson's memoirs etc.:[70] books published since my imprisonment. To save time and trouble, it was considered more politic to have no further delay. So *my* list will have to suffice. And, indeed, will be a very great boon to me – of incalculable service – even Ollendorff[71] priceless: I find that to study a language one had forgotten is a good mental tonic: the mere mechanical side having its value. Of the kindness of my good friend Arthur[72] Humphreys, the publisher, I cannot trust myself to write. It is a very dear remembrance on his part of a pleasant literary friendship. Give him my warmest thanks. When I read Walter Pater I shall have two friends to think of. The books, however, remain behind. They are sentenced to perpetual imprisonment. But they may soothe and heal other troubled minds and breaking hearts. Those not on Humphreys's really lavish list, pray provide. Perhaps in February a few *new* books may be got. But these are, now, more than most welcome. I wait them eagerly.[73]

(4) I feel that my wife does not realise my mental state, or the suffering, both mental and physical, she is inflicting on me. I wish she could be brought to see that she should let me alone now for the next five months. When I reflect that the only two people who have, since my imprisonment, tried to distress me by terrible letters are my wife and Lord Queensberry, I feel fixed on some shrill pinnacle of horror. Lady Brooke has influence with my wife. Could she be asked from me to suggest to my wife not to trouble me or distress me any more till my release? We were great friends once.

(5) As my affairs are apparently being wound up I am anxious that the French translator of my novel should be considered.[74] I was under the impression that the French copyright was mine. It seems that, *subject to a ten per cent royalty*, it is Ward & Lock's. Of course, their having it is absurd. But I am entitled to ten per cent on every copy sold, which of course should go to the translator. Would you see Kernahan, the author, who is one of Ward & Lock's readers, and a friend of mine. The nominal sum of £10 was paid for the French rights to Humphreys: but it is monstrous that Ward & Lock should be making money before the translator is paid. The French are so nice to me, I am horrified at the position of the translator. I propose to refund the £10, through Leverson, and then to have the translator considered. His honorarium should be not less than £50. If I, through Leverson, have half of this paid, would Ward & Lock pay the rest? Also what of my ten per cent?

(6) The French rights of all my plays are mine. The mischief of *Lady Windermere's Fan* has been done.[75] I suppose there is no use bothering.

(7) A matter of great seriousness was alluded to by Arthur Clifton, and written about by Robbie, to me: but in both cases with such delicacy that it is still quite unintelligible to me. I refer to my feelings with regard to Alfred Douglas. I have not mentioned the subject to anyone but Robbie: I am horrified to think that newspapers should busy themselves with it: I don't know what they say, or who writes the things. Eighteen months ago I asked Robert Sherard to stop the publication of any more of my letters: since then, I have said nothing to him on the matter. If *he* writes on me, pray beg him *from me* never to mention in conjunction with mine that ill-omened and most unfortunate name, so fatal to me and to my house. Also, I would *like you* to see all my letters to Robbie. I find that I accused him of a mutilation, done here under the old régime, without my knowledge. I am very sorry. I have been unjust to Robbie. In this life we lead, we become ungracious. Tell him all this.

(8) In case of my copyrights being sold I hope the Receiver will let me know what terms are offered. There are some I consider of value still: *Dorian Gray*, *Lady Windermere*, *The Importance*

of Being Earnest, have still money-making chances. I fear it is only by putting *all* my troubles on to your shoulders that I can show you my gratitude to you and my trust in you. In such a strange plight Fate places one. Ever yours

Oscar

To Messrs Stoker and Hansell

31 December 1896   *HM Prison, Reading*

Gentlemen,

I hereby authorise you to act as my solicitors in reference to my family affairs, both with regard to my life interest in my wife's estate, and also to the guardianship of my children, and I request you to inform Messrs Hargrove & Son, 16 Victoria Street, Westminster Abbey, SW, that I desire that any communication which they may have to make to me should be made to me through you.

I believe I am correct in stating that the general outlines of the matter at issue have been communicated, by or through Mr More Adey, to you, but I am anxious, for your guidance and satisfaction, as well as for my own, that my own wishes and views should be clearly conveyed to you under my own hand.

I feel that it is quite right that the guardianship of the children should be vested in my wife, and that she should have the right to appoint guardians for them in case of her decease. In the latter case I think I should be allowed access to them 'at reasonable intervals on occasions approved of by the guardians'. In the former case I would be ready to leave the matter to my wife, and to engage not to make any attempt to see the children against her wishes, or to communicate with them in any way except through her. I agree readily to their bearing another name than mine: the name, in fact, she has chosen which is an old family name on her side.[76] I would not myself wish to reside in the same town with them. I propose to live, if I live anywhere, in Brussels. I have written all this to my wife, and I have also conveyed it to Mr Hargrove.

With regard to money affairs, the offer made to me by my wife of £150 a year is, of course, extremely small. I certainly hoped that £200 would have been fixed on. I understand that my wife alleges as one of the reasons for £150 being selected that she wishes to pay off a debt of £500 due from me to her brother Mr Otho Lloyd, at the rate of £50 a year. I think, with Mr Adey, that I should have the £200 if that debt should be paid off by me. However, I do not wish to haggle over the terms, though of course I think them small. The income under our marriage settlement is about £1000 a year, and on the death of Mrs Wilde's mother some addition will accrue.

With regard to my life interest I sincerely hope that half at least will be purchased for me. My wife does not realise that in case of my surviving her and living to any advanced age it would really be bad for my children to have an unfortunate father living in penury, and perhaps forced to make application for assistance to them. Such a state of things would be in every way undesirable and unseemly. In the case of my surviving my wife I wish to be placed above any necessity of troubling my children for my support. I was in hopes that at least half the interest would by this time have been secured, but I have been misled by Mr Hargrove's letter, which I enclose. As regards the other half, if it also could be got for me it would enable me to resettle it at once on the children as a proof of the affection I have for them and the genuineness of the position I am taking up with regard to their future welfare.

I should mention that my wife came to see me at Wandsworth prison and wrote to me a very touching and affectionate letter then (October year last).[77] She also on the death of my mother, Lady Wilde, came to break the news to me here in person[78] and displayed great tenderness and affection, but it is now nearly a year since I have seen her, and the long absence, combined with influences hostile to me personally surrounding her, has made her take up a certain stand with regard to my life interest and my income during her life. She is quite aware of the deep affection existing between me and my sons, and in her last letter (November 21) expresses her hope that 'when they

are older they may be proud to acknowledge me as their father'
and that I may win back the intellectual position I have lost;
with other gracious wishes. Mr Hargrove in one of his letters
stated that the proposed £150 a year would be forfeited on my
breaking any of the conditions attached to it. This is, I admit,
a painful and humiliating position for me to look forward to. I
think my solemn agreement should be sufficient. The happiness
of my children is my sole object and desire.

Would you kindly ask Mr More Adey to use all his efforts to
see me here *himself*. I have much to talk to him about. Also tell
him that I *quite* understand that the books were a present from
my friend Mr Humphreys the publisher. Also that Mr Alex-
ander holds no French rights at all in *Lady Windermere's Fan*
(one of my comedies) but that I am glad he should act for me.

I hope you will allow me to express in conclusion my thanks
to you for undertaking this delicate and difficult matter for me.
It relieves me of a great deal of the mental anxiety and distress
incident on my condition, and intensified by Mr Hargrove's
violent and harsh letters. I remain yours faithfully

    Oscar Wilde

To More Adey

18 February 1897   [*HM Prison, Reading*]

My dear More,

The Governor has kindly allowed me to see your letter, and to
answer it at once.

(1) With what pleasure I have read it I need not say. On
Saturday the 27th I hope to see you with Robbie and Ernest
Leverson. The interview, by special permission, is to be of
an hour's duration and in a private room. A warder will be
present, but this need not incommode us. The visiting order is
for three. We shall then surely be able to discuss all business
matters. Business with you, seriousness with Ernest, nonsense
with Robbie.

(2) I enclose the authorisation for Lugné-Poë. Pray thank him from me for his kindness. To be represented by so distinguished a poet charms me.

(3) With regard to what I will call the 'deposit-fund', that is a sum of money left for my disposal, not for the paying of my debts, but for my own help, and support, and the help of those I love, like my mother, there will, I feel sure, be, after what has been expended on my dear mother, a certain sum left, perhaps not small. Out of this I propose to pay in instalments at first my debts of honour, after I have seen that enough is forthcoming to give me at least eighteen months of free life to collect myself. To Charles Wyndham,[79] to take merely one instance out of alas! too many, I owe £300 for literary work never done: my trial of course prevented it. I must pay him half, if possible. But I want to do it myself when I go out of prison. Also with regard to Miss Napier, the money was advanced to my wife (£50) and I will pay it myself when I go out. I forget if Mrs Napier[80] lent my wife anything. The debt of £50 to my old friend please have paid at once *from me* through Ernest Leverson. I am sure Ernest will see that I must begin by paying half to people and then gradually all. Of this when we meet. It is only a week off. I may say that I would like to wait and see what my wife proposes to do before I come forward as having kind and generous friends. She has no right to take technical advantage of our marriage-settlement to leave me without anything.

(4) I told you I was going to write to Alfred Douglas. I am still at work at the letter.[81] It is the most important letter of my life, as it will deal ultimately with my future mental attitude towards life, with the way in which I desire to meet the world again, with the development of my character: with what I have lost, what I have learned, and what I hope to arrive at. At last I see a real goal towards which my soul can go simply, naturally, and rightly. Before I see you and Robbie I must finish the letter, that you may understand what I have become, or rather desire to become in nature and aim. My whole life depends on it. I will send the letter to Robbie, who must read it carefully and *copy it out carefully* every word, for me. Then you, having read it and seen that it is copied rightly, will send it for me to A. D. I

don't know his address. I hope to have it finished by Tuesday.

To dear Frank Harris my kindest regards and thanks. To you always my best of thanks and gratitude

Oscar Wilde

To More Adey

8 *March 1897*   *HM Prison, Reading*

My dear More,

I am very much obliged to you for your letter, which the Governor has kindly allowed me to have and to answer. My business is I know unpleasant, but then it was not for pleasure that you took its burden on you, so I will write quite frankly to you.

Your news has distressed me a good deal. The claims of my own trustees and my brother-in-law would of course be easily withdrawn, and I thought I could, if the Queensberry debt was paid, as it should have been, by the Queensberry family, have made an effort at any rate to pay off my own personal creditors, who are really very few in number. I see, however, that this cannot be. I will now have to think of how to retain or buy my interest in my books and plays. I do not think they will be valued high. As £150 has been already been paid to Humphreys who did nothing to help me (beyond of course forcing me to put in two appearances at the Bankruptcy Court where one would have been sufficient and engaging their own relative Mr Grain[82] to appear as counsel where no counsel was required) I am reluctant to even write to them. I am very anxious however to know how I can be kept informed of the state of things, so that if my copyrights are to be sold I may have a chance of bidding for them. I am also anxious about my claim to the place in Ireland: it is now in utter rack and ruin, but I am reluctant to see it pass to a stranger: could Mr Holman, already in touch with the Receiver, let you know if anything happens? In the case of my brother's death, without male issue, the Irish property should fetch something: £4000 or £5000 at least.

As regards the Queensberry family, I of course feel very strongly about their allowing me to be made bankrupt by their father for the costs of the trial, and for such an absolutely contemptible sum; less than half, as I told you, of what in three wasted summer months I spent on Bosie at Goring – less than one half! Their idea that it would be a sort of 'score' off their father not to pay him his paltry claim showed how utterly blind they were to my feelings. As for Queensberry, I suppose nobody ever had such intense pleasure of a low order at such a low cost as he had. It was in the cheapest of markets that he bought his triumph. Indeed it was the only occasion in his life that he found his pleasures economical. To send a man like myself to prison for £900, and then to take him out and make him an insolvent for £700 more, was a piece of good fortune he never looked for. As regards my own debts, they were hardly anything. Their letting their father triumph a second time over me, rather than pay so petty, so abject a sum as £700, cut me very deeply. And people who live in the world of action don't understand that there is another world in which they who are not free live: a world in which nothing happens but emotions, and in which consequently emotions have a power, a proportion, a permanence that is beyond the possibility of description.

I was told, on Percy's behalf, that he had laid aside the sum of £600 for me, as the equivalent of his father's costs, to be used I suppose in buying back for me the property the Bankruptcy Receiver had seized, and possibly in other ways. I conveyed to him my thanks. I consider Percy a very good-hearted fellow, kind and considerate. I would very much like to see him again some time. He should of course have paid the costs, and left me then if necessary to settle my other debts. But he, I have no doubt, acted under advice. If he had realised matters a little more he would have seen that he merely doubled his father's delight and exultation by not interfering to prevent my insolvency. It was the only thing Queensberry was afraid of. He need not have been . . .[83] With regard to the whole question the Queensberry family must remember that through them I am in prison, through them a bankrupt, and that they can hardly allow people whom they ruined so completely to go to the workhouse.

I was touched and helped immeasurably by your telling me that some friends of mine have arranged that for eighteen months I am to have enough to live on: that gives me breathing space. But of course I cannot trespass for a lifetime on those on whom I have no more claim than any other of the poor and wretched and homeless people of whom God's world is so full. I couldn't do it. And I may live longer than eighteen months. A heart may be broken and yet fulfil its natural functions. The soul may sit in the shadow of death, and yet the body walk in the ways of life, and breathe and eat and know the sun and rain. I have no organic disease of any kind. I am troubled with insomnia, but I get my four or five hours of sleep every night. Supposing I live on? I should not be at all surprised if I did. I come of a long-lived race. The Queensberry family had better consider the point, the Douglases we will call them, as the other name is loathsome. There are debts of dishonour in a family as well as debts of honour. If the Douglas estates have to be burdened with a prospective claim of some paltry life-interest, let them be so burdened. A family cannot ruin a man like me, and look on the whole thing merely as a subject for sentiment or reminiscence over the walnuts and the wine. People, as somebody in one of Ibsen's plays says, don't do these things.[84] It is dreadful that it should fall on me to remind them. They should consult their family solicitor, and let him communicate the result to my solicitor. That is all that is necessary.

You say in your letter that Bosie is so anxious to make 'some little return' to me for all I 'spent on him'. Unfortunately, I spent on him my life, my genius, my position, my name in history; for these no little, or big return is possible. But as regards the mere wretched pounds, shillings, and pence side of my ruin – the workhouse aspect – he must seriously consider the whole point. It is his duty to do so. His duty to himself as much, far more indeed, than to me. When people play a tragedy they should play it in the 'grand style'. All smallness, pettiness, meagreness of mood or gesture is out of place. If the Douglases don't recognise this, let me be informed. But I don't doubt that they will. It is a perfectly obvious matter. And as for me, my life will of course necessarily be one of great retirement, simplicity and economy of living, and many modes of self-denial, imposed and accepted. But a certain small permanence is requisite even for the practice of the virtues of thrift and economy. Bosie must consider the matter. I will be much obliged if you will copy out all that I have written, from the bottom of page one,[85] and send it off to him. It will relieve my own letter to him of a very unpleasing duty, one that a little thought on his part would have spared me.

As regards my children, I sincerely hope I may be recognised by the Court as having some little, I won't say right, but claim to be allowed to see Cyril from time to time: it would be to me a sorrow beyond words if I were not. I do hope the Court will see in me something more than a man with a tragic vice in his life. There is so much more in me, and I always was a good father to both my children. I love them dearly and was dearly loved by them, and Cyril was my friend. And it would be better for them not to be forced to think of me as an outcast, but to know me as a man who has suffered. Pray let everything be done on my behalf that is possible. A little recognition by the Court would help me so much. And it is a terrible responsibility for the Law to say to a father that he is unfit to see his own children: the consciousness of it often makes me unhappy all day long.

As regards my life-interest, should Mr Hargrove make any proposal about it, it of course will be communicated to me by you *at once*. It will require grave consideration. The advances cannot come from me, can they? Should my own solicitor come to see me, pray let it be the last week in this month. I am quite distressed at the idea of his only charging £1.1s and expenses. I think he should have at least £3.3s. Let the money be got from Leverson, and whatever Mr Stoker[86] is owed be paid to him from the same fund in Leverson's hands.

I fear you see traces of bitterness in my business letters. Yes, that is so. It is very terrible. In the prison in which my body is I am shown much kindness, but in the prison in which my soul is I can show myself none. I hope that neither in your heart nor in Robbie's, nor in the heart of any that have been good to me, will bitterness of any kind ever find a place. It makes one suffer very deeply. Your affectionate friend

Oscar Wilde

I quite see that I must accept, gratefully indeed, my discharge as a bankrupt, when I get it, and then set to work to try and pay off some of the debts. I suppose it won't be done till I go out of prison? I would like things held over, on account of the sale of copyrights etc. At present I receive no communication at all from the Receiver. That is, I suppose, right.

For the list of books, so many thanks. I am going to ask for a Bible in French: *la Sainte Bible*.[87]

De Profundis

To Lord Alfred Douglas[1]

[*January–March* 1897]   *HM Prison, Reading*

Dear Bosie,

After long and fruitless waiting I have determined to write to you myself, as much for your sake as for mine, as I would not like to think that I had passed through two long years of imprisonment without ever having received a single line from you, or any news or message even, except such as gave me pain.[2]

Our ill-fated and most lamentable friendship has ended in ruin and public infamy for me, yet the memory of our ancient affection is often with me, and the thought that loathing, bitterness and contempt should for ever take that place in my heart once held by love is very sad to me: and you yourself will, I think, feel in your heart that to write to me as I lie in the loneliness of prison-life is better than to publish my letters without my permission or to dedicate poems to me unasked, though the world will know nothing of whatever words of grief or passion, of remorse or indifference you may choose to send as your answer or your appeal.

I have no doubt that in this letter in which I have to write of your life and of mine, of the past and of the future, of sweet things changed to bitterness and of bitter things that may be turned into joy, there will be much that will wound your vanity to the quick. If it prove so, read the letter over and over again till it kills your vanity. If you find in it something of which you

feel that you are unjustly accused, remember that one should
be thankful that there is any fault of which one can be unjustly
accused. If there be in it one single passage that brings tears to
your eyes, weep as we weep in prison where the day no less
than the night is set apart for tears. It is the only thing that can
save you. If you go complaining to your mother, as you did
with reference to the scorn of you I displayed in my letter to
Robbie,[3] so that she may flatter and soothe you back into self-
complacency or conceit, you will be completely lost. If you find
one false excuse for yourself, you will soon find a hundred, and
be just what you were before. Do you still say, as you said to
Robbie in your answer, that I *'attribute unworthy motives'* to
you? Ah! you had no motives in life. You had appetites merely.
A motive is an intellectual aim. That you were *'very young'*
when our friendship began? Your defect was not that you knew
so little about life, but that you knew so much. The morning
dawn of boyhood with its delicate bloom, its clear pure light, its
joy of innocence and expectation you had left far behind. With
very swift and running feet you had passed from Romance to
Realism. The gutter and the things that live in it had begun to
fascinate you. That was the origin of the trouble in which you
sought my aid, and I, so unwisely according to the wisdom of
this world, out of pity and kindness gave it to you. You must
read this letter right through, though each word may become
to you as the fire or knife of the surgeon that makes the delicate
flesh burn or bleed. Remember that the fool in the eyes of the
gods and the fool in the eyes of man are very different. One
who is entirely ignorant of the modes of Art in its revolution or
the moods of thought in its progress, of the pomp of the Latin
line or the richer music of the vowelled Greek, of Tuscan sculp-
ture or Elizabethan song may yet be full of the very sweetest
wisdom. The real fool, such as the gods mock or mar, is he who
does not know himself. I was such a one too long. You have
been such a one too long. Be so no more. Do not be afraid.
The supreme vice is shallowness. Everything that is realised is
right. Remember also that whatever is misery to you to read,
is still greater misery to me to set down. To you the Unseen
Powers have been very good. They have permitted you to see

the strange and tragic shapes of Life as one sees shadows in a crystal. The head of Medusa that turns living men to stone, you have been allowed to look at in a mirror merely. You yourself have walked free among the flowers. From me the beautiful world of colour and motion has been taken away.

I will begin by telling you that I blame myself terribly. As I sit here in this dark cell in convict clothes, a disgraced and ruined man, I blame myself. In the perturbed and fitful nights of anguish, in the long monotonous days of pain, it is myself I blame. I blame myself for allowing an unintellectual friendship, a friendship whose primary aim was not the creation and contemplation of beautiful things, to entirely dominate my life. From the very first there was too wide a gap between us. You had been idle at your school, worse than idle at your university. You did not realise that an artist, and especially such an artist as I am,[4] one, that is to say, the quality of whose work depends on the intensification of personality, requires for the development of his art the companionship of ideas, an intellectual atmosphere, quiet, peace, and solitude. You admired my work when it was finished: you enjoyed the brilliant successes of my first nights, and the brilliant banquets that followed them: you were proud, and quite naturally so, of being the intimate friend of an artist so distinguished: but you could not understand the conditions requisite for the production of artistic work. I am not speaking in phrases of rhetorical exaggeration but in terms of absolute truth to actual fact when I remind you that during the whole time we were together I never wrote one single line. Whether at Torquay, Goring, London, Florence or elsewhere, my life, as long as you were by my side, was entirely sterile and uncreative. And with but few intervals you were, I regret to say, by my side always.

I remember, for instance, in September '93, to select merely one instance out of many, taking a set of chambers, purely in order to work undisturbed, as I had broken my contract with John Hare[5] for whom I had promised to write a play, and who was pressing me on the subject. During the first week you kept away. We had, not unnaturally indeed, differed on the question of the artistic value of your translation of *Salomé*, so you contented yourself with sending me foolish letters on the subject. In that week I wrote and completed in every detail, as it was ultimately performed, the first act of *An Ideal Husband*. The second week you returned and my work practically had to be given up. I arrived at St James's Place every morning at 11.30, in order to have the opportunity of thinking and writing without the interruptions inseparable from my own household, quiet and peaceful as that household was. But the attempt was vain. At twelve o'clock you drove up, and stayed smoking cigarettes and chattering till 1.30, when I had to take you out to luncheon at the Café Royal or the Berkeley. Luncheon with its *liqueurs* lasted usually till 3.30. For an hour you retired to White's. At tea-time you appeared again, and stayed till it was time to dress for dinner. You dined with me either at the Savoy or at Tite Street. We did not separate as a rule till after midnight, as supper at Willis's had to wind up the entrancing day. That was my life for those three months, every single day, except during the four days when you went abroad. I then, of course, had to go over to Calais to fetch you back. For one of my nature and temperament it was a position at once grotesque and tragic.

You surely must realise that now? You must see now that your incapacity of being alone: your nature so exigent in its persistent claim on the attention and time of others: your lack of any power of sustained intellectual concentration: the unfortunate accident – for I like to think it was no more – that you had not yet been able to acquire the 'Oxford temper' in intellectual matters, never, I mean, been one who could play gracefully with ideas but had arrived at violence of opinion merely – that all these things, combined with the fact that your desires and interests were in Life not in Art, were as destructive to your own progress in culture as they were to my work as an artist? When I compare my friendship with you to my friendship with such still younger men as John Gray[6] and Pierre Louÿs I feel ashamed. My real life, my higher life was with them and such as they.

Of the appalling results of my friendship with you I don't speak at present. I am thinking merely of its quality while it lasted. It was intellectually degrading to me. You had the rudiments of an artistic temperament in its germ. But I met you either too late or too soon, I don't know which. When you were away I was all right. The moment, in the early December of the year to which I have been alluding, I had succeeded in inducing your mother to send you out of England,[7] I collected again the torn and ravelled web of my imagination, got my life back into my own hands, and not merely finished the three remaining acts of *An Ideal Husband*, but conceived and had almost completed two other plays of a completely different type, the *Florentine Tragedy* and *La Sainte Courtisane*,[8] when suddenly, unbidden, unwelcome, and under circumstances fatal to my happiness you returned. The two works left then imperfect I was unable to take up again. The mood that created them I could never recover. You now, having yourself published a volume of verse, will be able to recognise the truth of everything I have said here. Whether you can or not it remains as a hideous truth in the very heart of our friendship. While you were with me you were the absolute ruin of my Art, and in allowing you to stand persistently between Art and myself I give to myself shame and blame in the fullest degree. You couldn't know, you couldn't understand, you couldn't appreciate. I had no right to expect it of you at all. Your interests were merely in your meals and moods. Your desires were simply for amusements, for ordinary or less ordinary pleasures. They were what your temperament needed, or thought it needed for the moment. I should have forbidden you my house and my chambers except when I specially invited you. I blame myself without reserve for my weakness. It was merely weakness. One half-hour with Art was always more to me than a cycle with you. Nothing really at any period of my life was ever of the smallest importance to me compared with Art. But in the case of an artist, weakness is nothing less than a crime, when it is a weakness that paralyses the imagination.

I blame myself again for having allowed you to bring me to utter and discreditable financial ruin. I remember one morning in the early October of '92 sitting in the yellowing woods at Bracknell with your mother. At that time I knew very little of your real nature. I had stayed from a Saturday to Monday with you at Oxford. You had stayed with me at Cromer for ten days and played golf. The conversation turned on you, and your mother began to speak to me about your character. She told me of your two chief faults, your vanity, and your being, as she termed it, 'all wrong about money'. I have a distinct recollection of how I laughed. I had no idea that the first would bring me to prison, and the second to bankruptcy. I thought vanity a sort of graceful flower for a young man to wear; as for extravagance – for I thought she meant no more than extravagance – the virtues of prudence and thrift were not in my own nature or my own race. But before our friendship was one month older I began to see what your mother really meant. Your insistence on a life of reckless profusion: your incessant demands for money: your claim that all your pleasures should be paid for by me whether I was with you or not: brought me after some time into serious monetary difficulties, and what made the extravagances to me at any rate so monotonously uninteresting, as your persistent grasp on my life grew stronger and stronger, was that the money was really spent on little more than the pleasures of eating, drinking, and the like. Now and then it is a joy to have one's table red with wine and roses, but you outstripped all taste and temperance. You demanded without grace and received without thanks. You grew to think that you had a sort of right to live at my expense and in a profuse luxury to which you had never been accustomed, and which for that reason made your appetites all the more keen, and at the end if you lost money gambling in some Algiers Casino you simply telegraphed next morning to me in London to lodge the amount of your losses to your account at your bank, and gave the matter no further thought of any kind.

When I tell you that between the autumn of 1892 and the date of my imprisonment I spent with you and on you more than £5000 in actual money, irrespective of the bills I incurred, you will have some idea of the sort of life on which you insisted. Do you think I exaggerate? My ordinary expenses with you for an ordinary day in London – for luncheon, dinner, supper, amusements, hansoms and the rest of it – ranged from £12 to £20, and the week's expenses were naturally in proportion and ranged from £80 to £130. For our three months at Goring my expenses (rent of course included) were £1340. Step by step with the Bankruptcy Receiver I had to go over every item of my life. It was horrible. '*Plain living and high thinking*'[9] was, of course, an ideal you could not at that time have appreciated, but such extravagance was a disgrace to both of us. One of the most delightful dinners I remember ever having had is one Robbie and I had together in a little Soho café, which cost about as many shillings as my dinners to you used to cost pounds. Out of my dinner with Robbie came the first and best of all my dialogues.[10] Idea, title, treatment, mode, everything was struck out at a 3 franc 50 c. *table-d'hôte*. Out of the reckless dinners with you nothing remains but the memory that too much was eaten and too much was drunk. And my yielding to your demands was bad for you. You know that now. It made you grasping often: at times not a little unscrupulous: ungracious always. There was on far too many occasions too little joy or privilege in being your host. You forgot – I will not say the formal courtesy of thanks, for formal courtesies will strain a close friendship – but simply the grace of sweet companionship, the charm of pleasant conversation, that τερπνὸν κακόν[11] as the Greeks called it, and all those gentle humanities that make life lovely, and are an accompaniment to life as music might be, keeping things in tune and filling with melody the harsh or silent places. And though it may seem strange to you that one in the terrible position in which I am situated should find a difference between one disgrace and another, still I frankly admit that the folly of throwing away all this money on you, and letting you squander my fortune to your own hurt as well as to mine, gives to me and in my eyes a note of common profligacy to my Bankruptcy that makes me doubly ashamed of it. I was made for other things.

But most of all I blame myself for the entire ethical degradation I allowed you to bring on me. The basis of character is will-power, and my will-power became absolutely subject to yours. It sounds a grotesque thing to say, but it is none the less true. Those incessant scenes that seemed to be almost physically necessary to you, and in which your mind and body grew distorted and you became a thing as terrible to look at as to listen to: that dreadful mania you inherit from your father, the mania for writing revolting and loathsome letters: your entire lack of any control over your emotions as displayed in your long resentful moods of sullen silence, no less than in the sudden fits of almost epileptic rage: all these things in reference to which one of my letters to you, left by you lying about at the Savoy or some other hotel and so produced in Court by your father's Counsel, contained an entreaty not devoid of pathos, had you at that time been able to recognise pathos either in its elements or its expression:[12] – these, I say, were the origin and causes of my fatal yielding to you in your daily increasing demands. You wore one out. It was the triumph of the smaller over the bigger nature. It was the case of that tyranny of the weak over the strong which somewhere in one of my plays I describe as being 'the only tyranny that lasts'.[13]

And it was inevitable. In every relation of life with others one has to find some *moyen de vivre*. In your case, one had either to give up to you or to give you up. There was no other alternative. Through deep if misplaced affection for you: through great pity for your defects of temper and temperament: through my own proverbial good-nature and Celtic laziness: through an artistic aversion to coarse scenes and ugly words: through that incapacity to bear resentment of any kind which at that time characterised me: through my dislike of seeing life made bitter and uncomely by what to me, with my eyes really fixed on other things, seemed to be mere trifles too petty for more than a moment's thought or interest – through these reasons, simple as they may sound, I gave up to you always. As a natural result, your claims, your efforts at domination, your exactions grew more and more unreasonable. Your meanest motive, your lowest appetite, your most common passion, became to you laws by which the lives of others were to be guided always, and to which, if necessary, they were to be without scruple sacrificed. Knowing that by making a scene you could always have your way, it was but natural that you should proceed, almost unconsciously I have no doubt, to every excess of vulgar violence. At the end you did not know to what goal you were hurrying, or with what aim in view. Having made your own of my

genius, my will-power, and my fortune, you required, in the
blindness of an inexhaustible greed, my entire existence. You
took it. At the one supremely and tragically critical moment
of all my life, just before my lamentable step of beginning my
absurd action, on the one side there was your father attacking
me with hideous cards left at my club, on the other side there
was you attacking me with no less loathsome letters. The letter
I received from you on the morning of the day I let you take me
down to the Police Court to apply for the ridiculous warrant
for your father's arrest was one of the worst you ever wrote,
and for the most shameful reason. Between you both I lost my
head. My judgment forsook me. Terror took its place. I saw no
possible escape, I may say frankly, from either of you. Blindly
I staggered as an ox into the shambles. I had made a gigantic
psychological error. I had always thought that my giving up to
you in small things meant nothing: that when a great moment
arrived I could reassert my will-power in its natural superiority.
It was not so. At the great moment my will-power completely
failed me. In life there is really no small or great thing. All
things are of equal value and of equal size. My habit – due to
indifference chiefly at first – of giving up to you in everything
had become insensibly a real part of my nature. Without my
knowing it, it had stereotyped my temperament to one per-
manent and fatal mood. That is why, in the subtle epilogue to
the first edition of his essays, Pater says that 'Failure is to form
habits'.[14] When he said it the dull Oxford people thought the
phrase a mere wilful inversion of the somewhat wearisome text
of Aristotelian *Ethics*, but there is a wonderful, a terrible truth
hidden in it. I had allowed you to sap my strength of charac-
ter, and to me the formation of a habit had proved to be not
Failure merely but Ruin. Ethically you had been even still more
destructive to me than you had been artistically.

The warrant once granted, your will of course directed every-
thing. At a time when I should have been in London taking
wise counsel, and calmly considering the hideous trap in which
I had allowed myself to be caught – the booby-trap as your
father calls it to the present day – you insisted on my taking
you to Monte Carlo, of all revolting places on God's earth,

that all day, and all night as well, you might gamble as long
as the Casino remained open. As for me – baccarat having no
charms for me – I was left alone outside to myself. You refused
to discuss even for five minutes the position to which you and
your father had brought me. My business was merely to pay
your hotel expenses and your losses. The slightest allusion to
the ordeal awaiting me was regarded as a bore. A new brand
of champagne that was recommended to us had more interest
for you.

On our return to London those of my friends who really
desired my welfare implored me to retire abroad, and not to
face an impossible trial. You imputed mean motives to them
for giving such advice, and cowardice to me for listening to it.
You forced me to stay to brazen it out, if possible, in the box by
absurd and silly perjuries. At the end, I was of course arrested
and your father became the hero of the hour: more indeed than
the hero of the hour merely: your family now ranks, strangely
enough, with the Immortals: for with that grotesqueness of
effect that is as it were a Gothic element in history, and makes
Clio the least serious of all the Muses, your father will always
live among the kind pure-minded parents of Sunday-school lit-
erature, your place is with the Infant Samuel, and in the lowest
mire of Malebolge I sit between Gilles de Retz and the Marquis
de Sade.[15]

Of course I should have got rid of you. I should have shaken
you out of my life as a man shakes from his raiment a thing that
has stung him. In the most wonderful of all his plays Aeschylus
tells us of the great Lord who brings up in his house the lion-
cub, the λέοντος ἴνιν, and loves it because it comes bright-eyed
to his call and fawns on him for its food: φαιδρωπὸς ποτὶ χεῖρα,
σαίνων τε γαστρὸς ἀνάγκαις. And the thing grows up and shows
the nature of its race, ἦθος τὸ πρόσθε τοκήων, and destroys the
lord and his house and all that he possesses.[16] I feel that I was
such a one as he. But my fault was, not that I did not part
from you, but that I parted from you far too often. As far as
I can make out I ended my friendship with you every three
months regularly, and each time that I did so you managed
by means of entreaties, telegrams, letters, the interposition of

your friends, the interposition of mine, and the like to induce me to allow you back. When at the end of March '93 you left my house at Torquay I had determined never to speak to you again, or to allow you under any circumstances to be with me, so revolting had been the scene you had made the night before your departure. You wrote and telegraphed from Bristol to beg me to forgive you and meet you. Your tutor, who had stayed behind, told me that he thought that at times you were quite irresponsible for what you said and did, and that most, if not all, of the men at Magdalen were of the same opinion. I consented to meet you, and of course I forgave you. On the way up to town you begged me to take you to the Savoy. That was indeed a visit fatal to me.

Three months later, in June, we are at Goring. Some of your Oxford friends come to stay from a Saturday to Monday. The morning of the day they went away you made a scene so dreadful, so distressing that I told you that we must part. I remember quite well, as we stood on the level croquet-ground with the pretty lawn all round us, pointing out to you that we were spoiling each other's lives, that you were absolutely ruining mine and that I evidently was not making you really happy, and that an irrevocable parting, a complete separation was the one wise philosophic thing to do. You went sullenly after luncheon, leaving one of your most offensive letters behind with the butler to be handed to me after your departure. Before three days had elapsed you were telegraphing from London to beg to be forgiven and allowed to return. I had taken the place to please you. I had engaged your own servants at your request. I was always terribly sorry for the hideous temper to which you were really a prey. I was fond of you. So I let you come back and forgave you. Three months later still, in September, new scenes occurred, the occasion of them being my pointing out the schoolboy faults of your attempted translation of *Salomé*.[17] You must by this time be a fair enough French scholar to know that the translation was as unworthy of you, as an ordinary Oxonian, as it was of the work it sought to render. You did not of course know it then, and in one of the violent letters you wrote to me on the point you said that you were under

'no intellectual obligation of any kind' to me. I remember that
when I read that statement, I felt that it was the one really true
thing you had written to me in the whole course of our friend-
ship. I saw that a less cultivated nature would really have suited
you much better. I am not saying this in bitterness at all, but
simply as a fact of companionship. Ultimately the bond of all
companionship, whether in marriage or in friendship, is con-
versation, and conversation must have a common basis, and
between two people of widely different culture the only com-
mon basis possible is the lowest level. The trivial in thought
and action is charming. I had made it the keystone of a very
brilliant philosophy expressed in plays and paradoxes. But the
froth and folly of our life grew often very wearisome to me: it
was only in the mire that we met: and fascinating, terribly fas-
cinating though the one topic round which your talk invariably
centred was, still at the end it became quite monotonous to me.
I was often bored to death by it, and accepted it as I accepted
your passion for going to music-halls, or your mania for absurd
extravagances in eating and drinking, or any other of your to
me less attractive characteristics, as a thing, that is to say, that
one simply had to put up with, a part of the high price one paid
for knowing you. When after leaving Goring I went to Dinard
for a fortnight you were extremely angry with me for not taking
you with me, and, before my departure there, made some very
unpleasant scenes on the subject at the Albemarle Hotel, and
sent me some equally unpleasant telegrams to a country house
I was staying at for a few days. I told you, I remember, that I
thought it was your duty to be with your own people for a little,
as you had passed the whole season away from them. But in
reality, to be perfectly frank with you, I could not under any
circumstances have let you be with me. We had been together
for nearly twelve weeks. I required rest and freedom from the
terrible strain of your companionship. It was necessary for
me to be a little by myself. It was intellectually necessary. And
so I confess I saw in your letter, from which I have quoted, a
very good opportunity for ending the fatal friendship that had
sprung up between us, and ending it without bitterness, as I
had indeed tried to do on that bright June morning at Goring,

three months before. It was however represented to me – I am
bound to say candidly by one of my own friends[18] to whom
you had gone in your difficulty – that you would be much hurt,
perhaps almost humiliated at having your work sent back to
you like a schoolboy's exercise; that I was expecting far too
much intellectually from you; and that, no matter what you
wrote or did, you were absolutely and entirely devoted to me. I
did not want to be the first to check or discourage you in your
beginnings in literature: I knew quite well that no translation,
unless one done by a poet, could render the colour and cadence
of my work in any adequate measure: devotion seemed to me,
seems to me still, a wonderful thing, not to be lightly thrown
away: so I took the translation and you back. Exactly three
months later, after a series of scenes culminating in one more
than usually revolting, when you came one Monday evening to
my rooms accompanied by two of your friends, I found myself
actually flying abroad next morning to escape from you, giving
my family[19] some absurd reason for my sudden departure, and
leaving a false address with my servant for fear you might fol-
low me by the next train. And I remember that afternoon, as I
was in the railway-carriage whirling up to Paris, thinking what
an impossible, terrible, utterly wrong state my life had got into,
when I, a man of world-wide reputation, was actually forced
to run away from England, in order to try and get rid of a
friendship that was entirely destructive of everything fine in me
either from the intellectual or ethical point of view: the person
from whom I was flying being no terrible creature sprung from
sewer or mire into modern life with whom I had entangled my
days, but you yourself, a young man of my own social rank and
position, who had been at my own college at Oxford, and was
an incessant guest at my house. The usual telegrams of entreaty
and remorse followed: I disregarded them. Finally you threat-
ened that unless I consented to meet you, you would under no
circumstances consent to proceed to Egypt. I had myself, with
your knowledge and concurrence, begged your mother to send
you to Egypt away from England, as you were wrecking your
life in London. I knew that if you did not go it would be a ter-
rible disappointment to her, and for her sake I did meet you,

and under the influence of great emotion, which even you can-
not have forgotten, I forgave the past; though I said nothing at
all about the future.

On my return to London next day I remember sitting in
my room and sadly and seriously trying to make up my mind
whether or not you really were what you seemed to me to be,
so full of terrible defects, so utterly ruinous both to yourself
and to others, so fatal a one to know even or to be with. For a
whole week I thought about it, and wondered if after all I was
not unjust and mistaken in my estimate of you. At the end of
the week a letter from your mother is handed in. It expressed
to the full every feeling I myself had about you. In it she spoke
of your blind exaggerated vanity which made you despise your
home, and treat your elder brother – that *candidissima anima*[20]
– 'as a Philistine': of your temper which made her afraid to
speak to you about your life, the life she felt, she knew, you
were leading: about your conduct in money matters, so dis-
tressing to her in more ways than one: of the degeneration and
change that had taken place in you. She saw, of course, that
heredity had burdened you with a terrible legacy, and frankly
admitted it, admitted it with terror: he is 'the one of my children
who has inherited the fatal Douglas temperament', she wrote
of you. At the end she stated that she felt bound to declare
that your friendship with me, in her opinion, had so intensified
your vanity that it had become the source of all your faults,
and earnestly begged me not to meet you abroad. I wrote to
her at once, in reply, and told her that I agreed entirely with
every word she had said. I added much more. I went as far as
I could possibly go. I told her that the origin of our friendship
was you in your undergraduate days at Oxford coming to beg
me to help you in very serious trouble of a very particular char-
acter. I told her that your life had been continually in the same
manner troubled. The reason of your going to Belgium you
had placed to the fault of your companion in that journey, and
your mother had reproached me with having introduced you
to him. I replaced the fault on the right shoulders, on yours. I
assured her at the end that I had not the smallest intention of
meeting you abroad, and begged her to try to keep you there,

either as an honorary *attaché*, if that were possible, or to learn modern languages, if it were not; or for any reason she chose, at least during two or three years, and for your sake as well as for mine.

In the meantime you are writing to me by every post from Egypt. I took not the smallest notice of any of your communications. I read them, and tore them up. I had quite settled to have no more to do with you. My mind was made up, and I gladly devoted myself to the Art whose progress I had allowed you to interrupt. At the end of three months, your mother, with that unfortunate weakness of will that characterises her, and that in the tragedy of my life has been an element no less fatal than your father's violence, actually writes to me herself – I have no doubt, of course, at your instigation – tells me that you are extremely anxious to hear from me, and in order that I should have no excuse for not communicating with you, sends me your address in Athens, which, of course, I knew perfectly well. I confess I was absolutely astounded at her letter. I could not understand how, after what she had written to me in December, and what I in answer had written to her, she could in any way try to repair or to renew my unfortunate friendship with you. I acknowledged her letter, of course, and again urged her to try and get you connected with some Embassy abroad,[21] so as to prevent your returning to England, but I did not write to you, or take any more notice of your telegrams than I did before your mother had written to me. Finally you actually telegraphed to my wife begging her to use her influence with me to get me to write to you. Our friendship had always been a source of distress to her: not merely because she had never liked you personally, but because she saw how your continual companionship altered me, and not for the better: still, just as she had always been most gracious and hospitable to you, so she could not bear the idea of my being in any way unkind – for so it seemed to her – to any of my friends. She thought, knew indeed, that it was a thing alien to my character. At her request I did communicate with you. I remember the wording of my telegram quite well. I said that time healed every wound but that for many months to come I would neither write to you nor see you. You started without delay for Paris, sending me passionate telegrams on the road to beg me to see you once, at any rate. I declined. You arrived in Paris late on a Saturday night, and found a brief letter from me waiting for you at your hotel stating that I would not see you. Next morning I received in Tite Street a telegram of some ten or eleven pages in length from you. You stated in it that no matter what you had done to me you could not believe that I would absolutely decline to see you: you reminded me that for the sake of seeing me even for one hour you had travelled six days and nights across Europe without stopping once on the way: you made what I must admit was a most pathetic appeal, and ended with what seemed to me a threat of suicide, and one not thinly veiled. You had yourself often told me how many of your race there had been who had stained their hands in their own blood; your uncle certainly, your grandfather possibly; many others in the mad, bad line from which you come.[22] Pity, my old affection for you, regard for your mother to whom your death under such dreadful circumstances would have been a blow almost too great for her to bear, the horror of the idea that so young a life, and one that amidst all its ugly faults had still promise of beauty in it, should come to so revolting an end, mere humanity itself – all these, if excuses be necessary, must serve as my excuse for consenting to accord you one last interview. When I arrived in Paris, your tears, breaking out again and again all through the evening, and falling over your cheeks like rain as we sat, at dinner first at Voisin's, at supper at Paillard's afterwards: the unfeigned joy you evinced at seeing me, holding my hand whenever you could, as though you were a gentle and penitent child: your contrition, so simple and sincere, at the moment: made me consent to renew our friendship. Two days after we had returned to London, your father saw you having luncheon with me at the Café Royal, joined my table, drank of my wine, and that afternoon, through a letter addressed to you, began his first attack on me.[23]

It may be strange, but I had once again, I will not say the chance, but the duty of separating from you forced on me. I need hardly remind you that I refer to your conduct to me at

Brighton from October 10th to 13th, 1894. Three years ago is a long time for you to go back. But we who live in prison, and in whose lives there is no event but sorrow, have to measure time by throbs of pain, and the record of bitter moments. We have nothing else to think of. Suffering – curious as it may sound to you – is the means by which we exist, because it is the only means by which we become conscious of existing; and the remembrance of suffering in the past is necessary to us as the warrant, the evidence, of our continued identity. Between myself and the memory of joy lies a gulf no less deep than that between myself and joy in its actuality. Had our life together been as the world fancied it to be, one simply of pleasure, profligacy and laughter, I would not be able to recall a single passage in it. It is because it was full of moments and days tragic, bitter, sinister in their warnings, dull or dreadful in their monotonous scenes and unseemly violences, that I can see or hear each separate incident in its detail, can indeed see or hear little else. So much in this place do men live by pain that my friendship with you, in the way through which I am forced to remember it, appears to me always as a prelude consonant with those varying modes of anguish which each day I have to realise; nay more, to necessitate them even; as though my life, whatever it had seemed to myself and to others, had all the while been a real Symphony of Sorrow, passing through its rhythmically-linked movements to its certain resolution, with that inevitableness that in Art characterises the treatment of every great theme.

I spoke of your conduct to me on three successive days, three years ago, did I not? I was trying to finish my last play at Worthing by myself.[24] The two visits you had paid to me had ended. You suddenly appeared a third time bringing with you a companion whom you actually proposed should stay in my house. I (you must admit now quite properly) absolutely declined. I entertained you, of course; I had no option in the matter: but elsewhere, and not in my own home. The next day, a Monday, your companion returned to the duties of his profession, and you stayed with me. Bored with Worthing, and still more, I have no doubt, with my fruitless efforts to concentrate my attention on my play, the only thing that really interested me at the moment, you insist on being taken to the Grand Hotel at Brighton. The night we arrive you fall ill with that dreadful low fever that is foolishly called the influenza, your second, if not third attack.[25] I need not remind you how I waited on you, and tended you, not merely with every luxury of fruit, flowers, presents, books, and the like that money can procure, but with that affection, tenderness and love that, whatever you may think, is not to be procured for money. Except for an hour's walk in the morning, an hour's drive in the afternoon, I never left the hotel. I got special grapes from London for you, as you did not care for those the hotel supplied, invented things to please you, remained either with you or in the room next to yours, sat with you every evening to quiet or amuse you.

After four or five days you recover, and I take lodgings in order to try and finish my play. You, of course, accompany me. The morning after the day on which we were installed I feel extremely ill. You have to go to London on business, but promise to return in the afternoon. In London you meet a friend, and do not come back to Brighton till late the next day, by which time I am in a terrible fever, and the doctor finds I have caught the influenza from you. Nothing could have been more uncomfortable for anyone ill than the lodgings turn out to be. My sitting-room is on the first floor, my bedroom on the third. There is no manservant to wait on one, not even anyone to send out on a message, or to get what the doctor orders. But you are there. I feel no alarm. The next two days you leave me entirely alone without care, without attendance, without anything. It was not a question of grapes, flowers, and charming gifts: it was a question of mere necessaries: I could not even get the milk the doctor had ordered for me: lemonade was pronounced an impossibility: and when I begged you to procure me a book at the bookseller's, or if they had not got whatever I had fixed on to choose something else, you never even take the trouble to go there. And when I was left all day without anything to read in consequence, you calmly tell me that you bought me the book and that they promised to send it down, a statement which I found out by chance afterwards to have been entirely untrue from beginning to end. All the while you are of course living at my expense, driving about, dining at the Grand Hotel, and indeed only appearing in my room for money. On the Saturday night, you having left me completely unattended and alone since the morning, I asked you to come back after dinner, and sit with me for a little. With irritable voice and ungracious manner you promise to do so. I wait till eleven o'clock and you never appear. I then left a note for you in your room just reminding you of the promise you had made me, and how you had kept it. At three in the morning, unable to sleep, and tortured with thirst, I made my way, in the dark and cold, down to the sitting-room in the hopes of finding some water there. I found *you*. You fell on me with every hideous word an intemperate mood, an undisciplined and untutored nature could suggest. By the terrible alchemy of egotism you converted your remorse into rage. You accused me of selfishness in expecting you to be with me when I was ill; of standing between you and your amusements; of trying to deprive you of your pleasures. You told me, and I know it was quite true, that you had come back at midnight simply in order to change your dress-clothes, and go out again to where you hoped new pleasures were waiting for you, but that by leaving for you a letter in which I had reminded you that you had neglected me the whole day and the whole evening, I had really robbed you of your desire for more enjoyments, and diminished your actual capacity for fresh delights. I went back upstairs in disgust, and remained sleepless till dawn, nor till long after dawn was I able to get anything to quench the thirst of the fever that was on me. At eleven o'clock you came into my room. In the previous scene I could not help observing that by my letter I had, at any rate, checked you in a night of more than usual excess. In the morning you were quite yourself. I waited naturally to hear what excuses you had to make, and in what way you were going to ask for the forgiveness that you knew in your heart was invariably waiting for you, no matter what you did; your absolute trust that I would always forgive you being the thing in you that I always really liked the best, perhaps the best thing in you to like. So far from doing that, you began to repeat the same scene with renewed emphasis and more violent assertion. I told you at length to leave the room: you pretended to do so, but when I lifted up my head from the pillow in which I had buried it, you were still there, and with brutality of laughter and hysteria of rage you moved suddenly towards me. A sense of horror came over me, for what exact reason I could not make out; but I got out of my bed at once, and bare-footed and just as I was, made my way down the two flights of stairs to the sitting-room, which I did not leave till the owner of the lodgings – whom I had rung for – had assured me that you had left my bedroom, and promised to remain within call, in case of necessity. After an interval of an hour, during which time the doctor had come and found me, of course, in a state of absolute nervous prostration, as well as in a worse condition of fever than I had been at the outset, you returned silently, for money: took what you could find on the dressing-table and mantelpiece, and left the house with your luggage. Need I tell you what I thought of you during the two wretched lonely days of illness that followed? Is it necessary for me to state that I saw clearly that it would be a dishonour to myself to continue even an acquaintance with such a one as you had showed yourself to be? That I recognised that the ultimate moment had come, and recognised it as being really a great relief? And that I knew that for the future my Art and Life would be freer and better and more beautiful in every possible way? Ill as I was, I felt at ease. The fact that the separation was irrevocable gave me peace. By Tuesday the fever had left me, and for the first time I dined downstairs. Wednesday was my birthday.[26] Amongst the telegrams and communications on my table was a letter in your handwriting. I opened it with a sense of sadness over me. I knew that the time had gone by when a pretty phrase, an expression of affection, a word of sorrow would make me take you back. But I was entirely deceived. I had underrated you. The letter you sent to me on my birthday was an elaborate repetition of the two scenes, set cunningly and carefully down in black and white! You mocked me with common jests. Your one satisfaction in the whole affair was, you said, that you retired to the Grand Hotel, and entered your luncheon to my account before you left for town. You congratulated me on my prudence in leaving my sickbed, on my sudden flight downstairs. '*It was an ugly moment for you,*' you said, '*uglier than you imagine.*' Ah! I felt it but too well. What it had really meant I did not know: whether you had with you the pistol you had bought to try and frighten your father with, and that, thinking it to be unloaded, you had once fired off in a public restaurant [27] in my company: whether your hand was moving towards a common dinner-knife that by chance was lying on the table between us: whether, forgetting in your rage your low stature and inferior strength, you had thought of some specially personal insult, or attack even, as I lay ill there: I could not tell. I do not know to the present moment. All I know is that a feeling of utter horror had come over me, and that I had felt that unless I left the room at once, and got away, you would have done, or tried to do, something that would have been, even to you, a source of lifelong shame. Only once before in my life had I experienced such a feeling of horror at any human being. It was when in my library at Tite Street, waving his small hands in the air in epileptic fury, your father, with his bully, or his friend, between us, had stood uttering every foul word his foul mind could think of, and screaming the loathsome threats he afterwards with such cunning carried out. In the latter case he, of course, was the one who had to leave the room first. I drove him out. In your case I went. It was not the first time I had been obliged to save you from yourself.

You concluded your letter by saying: '*When you are not on your pedestal you are not interesting. The next time you are ill I will go away at once.*' Ah! what coarseness of fibre does that reveal! What an entire lack of imagination! How callous, how common had the temperament by that time become! '*When you are not on your pedestal you are not interesting. The next time you are ill I will go away at once.*' How often have those words come back to me in the wretched solitary cell of the various prisons I have been sent to. I have said them to myself over and over again, and seen in them, I hope unjustly, some of the secret of your strange silence. For you to write thus to me, when the very illness and fever from which I was suffering

I had caught from tending you, was of course revolting in its coarseness and crudity; but for any human being in the whole world to write thus to another would be a sin for which there is no pardon, were there any sin for which there is none.

I confess that when I had finished your letter I felt almost polluted, as if by associating with one of such a nature I had soiled and shamed my life irretrievably. I had, it is true, done so, but I was not to learn how fully till just six months later on in life. I settled with myself to go back to London on the Friday,[28] and see Sir George Lewis personally and request him to write to your father to state that I had determined never under any circumstances to allow you to enter my house, to sit at my board, to talk to me, walk with me, or anywhere and at any time to be my companion at all. This done I would have written to you just to inform you of the course of action I had adopted; the reasons you would inevitably have realised for yourself. I had everything arranged on Thursday night, when on Friday morning, as I was sitting at breakfast before starting, I happened to open the newspaper and saw in it a telegram stating that your elder brother, the real head of the family, the heir to the title, the pillar of the house, had been found dead in a ditch with his gun lying discharged beside him.[29] The horror of the circumstances of the tragedy, now known to have been an accident, but then stained with a darker suggestion; the pathos of the sudden death of one so loved by all who knew him, and almost on the eve, as it were, of his marriage; my idea of what your own sorrow would, or should be; my consciousness of the misery awaiting your mother at the loss of the one to whom she clung for comfort and joy in life, and who, as she told me once herself, had from the very day of his birth never caused her to shed a single tear; my consciousness of your own isolation, both your other brothers being out of Europe, and you consequently the only one to whom your mother and sister could look, not merely for companionship in their sorrow, but also for those dreary responsibilities of dreadful detail that Death always brings with it; the mere sense of the *lacrimae rerum*,[30] of the tears of which the world is made, and of the sadness of all human things – out of the confluence of these thoughts and emotions crowding into my brain came infinite pity for you and your family. My own griefs and bitternesses against you I forgot. What you had been to me in my sickness, I could not be to you in your bereavement. I telegraphed at once to you my deepest sympathy, and in the letter that followed invited you to come to my house as soon as you were able. I felt that to abandon you at that particular moment, and formally through a solicitor, would have been too terrible for you.

On your return to town from the actual scene of the tragedy to which you had been summoned, you came at once to me very sweetly and very simply, in your suit of woe, and with your eyes dim with tears. You sought consolation and help, as a child might seek it. I opened to you my house, my home, my heart. I made your sorrow mine also, that you might have help in bearing it. Never, even by one word, did I allude to your conduct towards me, to the revolting scenes, and the revolting letter. Your grief, which was real, seemed to me to bring you nearer to me than you had ever been. The flowers you took from me to put on your brother's grave were to be a symbol not merely of the beauty of his life, but of the beauty that in all lives lies dormant and may be brought to light.

The gods are strange. It is not of our vices only they make instruments to scourge us.[31] They bring us to ruin through what in us is good, gentle, humane, loving. But for my pity and affection for you and yours, I would not now be weeping in this terrible place.

Of course I discern in all our relations, not Destiny merely, but Doom: Doom that walks always swiftly, because she goes to the shedding of blood. Through your father you come of a race, marriage with whom is horrible, friendship fatal, and that lays violent hands either on its own life or on the lives of others. In every little circumstance in which the ways of our lives met; in every point of great, or seemingly trivial import in which you came to me for pleasure or for help; in the small chances, the slight accidents that look, in their relation to life, to be no more than the dust that dances in a beam, or the leaf that flutters from a tree, Ruin followed, like the echo of a bitter cry, or the shadow that hunts with the beast of prey. Our friendship really begins with your begging me in a most pathetic and charming letter to assist you in a position appalling to anyone, doubly so to a young man at Oxford: I do so, and ultimately through your using my name as your friend with Sir George Lewis, I began to lose his esteem and friendship, a friendship of fifteen years' standing. When I was deprived of his advice and help and regard I was deprived of the one great safeguard of my life.

You send me a very nice poem, of the undergraduate school of verse, for my approval: I reply by a letter of fantastic literary conceits:[32] I compare you to Hylas, or Hyacinth, Jonquil or Narcisse,[33] or someone whom the great god of Poetry favoured, and honoured with his love. The letter is like a passage from one of Shakespeare's sonnets, transposed to a minor key. It can only be understood by those who have read the *Symposium* of Plato, or caught the spirit of a certain grave mood made beautiful for us in Greek marbles. It was, let me say frankly, the sort of letter I would, in a happy if wilful moment, have written to any graceful young man of either University who had sent me a poem of his own making, certain that he would have sufficient wit or culture to interpret rightly its fantastic phrases. Look at the history of that letter! It passes from you into the hands of a loathsome companion: from him to a gang of blackmailers: copies of it are sent about London to my friends, and to the manager of the theatre where my work is being performed:[34] every construction but the right one is put on it: Society is thrilled with the absurd rumours that I have had to pay a huge sum of money for having written an infamous letter to you: this forms the basis of your father's worst attack: I produce the original letter myself in Court to show what it really is: it is denounced by your father's Counsel as a revolting and insidious attempt to corrupt Innocence: ultimately it forms part of a criminal charge: the Crown takes it up: the Judge sums up on it with little learning and much morality: I go to prison for it at last. That is the result of writing you a charming letter.

While I am staying with you at Salisbury you are terribly alarmed at a threatening communication from a former companion of yours: you beg me to see the writer and help you: I

do so: the result is Ruin to me. I am forced to take everything
you have done on my own shoulders and answer for it. When,
having failed to take your degree, you have to go down from
Oxford, you telegraph to me in London to beg me to come to
you. I do so at once: you ask me to take you to Goring, as you
did not like, under the circumstances, to go home: at Goring
you see a house that charms you: I take it for you: the result
from every point of view is Ruin to me. One day you come to
me and ask me, as a personal favour to you, to write something
for an Oxford undergraduate magazine, about to be started by
some friend of yours, whom I had never heard of in all my life,
and knew nothing at all about. To please you – what did I not
do always to please you? – I sent him a page of paradoxes des-
tined originally for the *Saturday Review*.[35] A few months later
I find myself standing in the dock of the Old Bailey on account
of the character of the magazine. It forms part of the Crown
charge against me. I am called upon to defend your friend's
prose and your own verse. The former I cannot palliate; the lat-
ter I, loyal to the bitter extreme, to your youthful literature as
to your youthful life, do very strongly defend, and will not hear
of your being a writer of indecencies. But I go to prison, all the
same, for your friend's undergraduate magazine, and 'the Love
that dares not tell its name'.[36] At Christmas I give you a 'very
pretty present', as you described it in your letter of thanks, on
which I knew you had set your heart, worth some £40 or £50
at most. When the crash of my life comes, and I am ruined,
the bailiff who seizes my library, and has it sold, does so to
pay for the 'very pretty present'. It was for that the execution
was put into my house. At the ultimate and terrible moment
when I am taunted, and spurred-on by your taunts, to take an
action against your father and have him arrested, the last straw
to which I clutch in my wretched efforts to escape is the ter-
rible expense. I tell the solicitor in your presence that I have no
funds, that I cannot possibly afford the appalling costs, that I
have no money at my disposal. What I said was, as you know,
perfectly true. On that fatal Friday[37] instead of being in Hum-
phreys's office weakly consenting to my own ruin, I would have
been happy and free in France, away from you and your father,

unconscious of his loathsome card, and indifferent to your letters, if I had been able to leave the Avondale Hotel. But the hotel people absolutely refused to allow me to go. You had been staying with me for ten days: indeed you had ultimately, to my great and, you will admit, rightful indignation, brought a companion of yours to stay with me also: my bill for the ten days was nearly £140. The proprietor said he could not allow my luggage to be removed from the hotel till I had paid the account in full. That is what kept me in London. Had it not been for the hotel bill I would have gone to Paris on Thursday morning.

When I told the solicitor I had no money to face the gigantic expense, you interposed at once. You said that your own family would be only too delighted to pay all the necessary costs: that your father had been an incubus to them all: that they had often discussed the possibility of getting him put into a lunatic asylum so as to keep him out of the way: that he was a daily source of annoyance and distress to your mother and to everyone else: that if I would only come forward to have him shut up I would be regarded by the family as their champion and their benefactor: and that your mother's rich relations themselves would look on it as a real delight to be allowed to pay all costs and expenses that might be incurred in any such effort. The solicitor closed at once, and I was hurried to the Police Court. I had no excuse left for not going. I was forced into it. Of course your family don't pay the costs, and, when I am made bankrupt, it is by your father, and *for* the costs – the meagre balance of them – some £700.[38] At the present moment my wife, estranged from me over the important question of whether I should have £3 or £3.10s a week to live on, is preparing a divorce suit, for which, of course, entirely new evidence and an entirely new trial, to be followed perhaps by more serious proceedings, will be necessary. I, naturally, know nothing of the details. I merely know the name of the witness on whose evidence my wife's solicitors rely. It is your own Oxford servant, whom at your special request I took into my service for our summer at Goring.

But, indeed, I need not go on further with more instances of the strange Doom you seem to have brought on me in all things big or little. It makes me feel sometimes as if you yourself had been merely a puppet worked by some secret and unseen hand to bring terrible events to a terrible issue. But puppets themselves have passions. They will bring a new plot into what they are presenting, and twist the ordered issue of vicissitude to suit some whim or appetite of their own. To be entirely free, and at the same time entirely dominated by law, is the eternal paradox of human life that we realise at every moment; and this, I often think, is the only explanation possible of your nature, if indeed for the profound and terrible mysteries of a human soul there is any explanation at all, except one that makes the mystery more marvellous still.

Of course you had your illusions, lived in them indeed, and through their shifting mists and coloured veils saw all things changed. You thought, I remember quite well, that your devoting yourself to me, to the entire exclusion of your family and family life, was a proof of your wonderful appreciation of me, and your great affection. No doubt to you it seemed so. But recollect that with me was luxury, high living, unlimited pleasure, money without stint. Your family life bored you. The 'cold cheap wine of Salisbury', to use a phrase of your own making, was distasteful to you. On my side, and along with my intellectual attractions, were the fleshpots of Egypt. When you could not find me to be with, the companions whom you chose as substitutes were not flattering.

You thought again that in sending a lawyer's letter to your father to say that, rather than sever your eternal friendship with me, you would give up the allowance of £250 a year which, with I believe deductions for your Oxford debts, he was then making you, you were realising the very chivalry of friendship, touching the noblest note of self-denial. But your surrender of your little allowance did not mean that you were ready to give up even one of your most superfluous luxuries, or most unnecessary extravagances. On the contrary. Your appetite for luxurious living was never so keen. My expenses for eight days in Paris for myself, you, and your Italian servant were nearly £150: Paillard alone absorbing £85. At the rate at which you wished to live, your entire income for a whole year, if you had taken your meals alone, and been especially economical in your selection of the cheaper form of pleasures, would hardly have lasted you for three weeks. The fact that in what was merely a pretence of bravado you had surrendered your allowance, such as it was, gave you at last a plausible reason for your claim to live at my expense, or what you thought a plausible reason: and on many occasions you seriously availed yourself of it, and gave the very fullest expression to it: and the continued drain, principally of course on me, but also to a certain extent, I know, on your mother, was never so distressing, because in my case at any rate, never so completely unaccompanied by the smallest word of thanks, or sense of limit.

You thought again that in attacking your own father with dreadful letters, abusive telegrams, and insulting postcards you were really fighting your mother's battles, coming forward as her champion, and avenging the no doubt terrible wrongs and sufferings of her married life. It was quite an illusion on your part; one of your worst indeed. The way for you to have avenged your mother's wrongs on your father, if you considered it part of a son's duty to do so, was by being a better son to your mother than you had been: by not making her afraid to speak to you on serious things: by not signing bills the payment of which devolved on her: by being gentler to her, and not bringing sorrow into her days. Your brother Francis made great amends to her for what she had suffered, by his sweetness and goodness to her through the brief years of his flower-like life. You should have taken him as your model. You were wrong even in fancying that it would have been an absolute delight and joy to your mother if you *had* managed through me to get your father put into prison. I feel sure you were wrong. And if you want to know what a woman really feels when her husband, and the father of her children, is in prison dress, in a prison cell, write to my wife and ask her. She will tell you.

I also had my illusions. I thought life was going to be a brilliant comedy, and that you were to be one of many graceful figures in it. I found it to be a revolting and repellent tragedy, and that the sinister occasion of the great catastrophe, sinister in its concentration of aim and intensity of narrowed will-power, was yourself, stripped of that mask of joy and pleasure by which you, no less than I, had been deceived and led astray.

You can now understand – can you not? – a little of what I am suffering. Some paper, the *Pall Mall Gazette* I think, describing the dress-rehearsal of one of my plays, spoke of you as following me about like my shadow: the memory of our friendship is the shadow that walks with me here: that seems never to leave me: that wakes me up at night to tell me the same story over and over till its wearisome iteration makes all sleep abandon me till dawn: at dawn it begins again: it follows me into the prison-yard and makes me talk to myself as I tramp round: each detail that accompanied each dreadful moment I am forced to recall: there is nothing that happened in those ill-starred years that I cannot recreate in that chamber of the brain which is set apart for grief or for despair: every strained note of your voice, every twitch and gesture of your nervous hands, every bitter word, every poisonous phrase comes back to me: I remember the street or river down which we passed, the wall or woodland that surrounded us, at what figure on the dial stood the hands of the clock, which way went the wings of the wind, the shape and colour of the moon.

There is, I know, one answer to all that I have said to you, and that is that you loved me: that all through those two and a half years during which the Fates were weaving into one scarlet pattern the threads of our divided lives you really loved me. Yes: I know you did. No matter what your conduct to me was I always felt that at heart you really did love me. Though I saw quite clearly that my position in the world of Art, the interest my personality had always excited, my money, the luxury in which I lived, the thousand and one things that went to make up a life so charmingly, so wonderfully improbable as mine was, were, each and all of them, elements that fascinated you and made you cling to me: yet besides all this there was something more, some strange attraction for you: you loved me far better than you loved anybody else. But you, like myself, have had a terrible tragedy in your life, though one of an entirely opposite character to mine. Do you want to learn what it was? It was this. In you Hate was always stronger than Love. Your hatred of your father was of such stature that it entirely outstripped, o'erthrew, and overshadowed your love of me. There was no struggle between them at all, or but little; of such dimensions was your Hatred and of such monstrous growth. You did not realise that there is no room for both passions in the same soul. They cannot live together in that fair carven house. Love is fed by the imagination, by which we become wiser than we know, better than we feel, nobler than we are: by which we can see Life as a whole: by which, and by which alone, we can understand others in their real as in their ideal relations. Only what is fine, and finely conceived, can feed Love. But anything will feed Hate. There was not a glass of champagne you drank, not a rich dish you ate of in all those years, that did not feed your Hate and make it fat. So to gratify it, you gambled with my life, as you gambled with my money, carelessly, recklessly, indifferent to the consequence. If you lost, the loss would not, you fancied, be yours. If you won, yours, you knew, would be the exultation, and the advantages of victory.

Hate blinds people. You were not aware of that. Love can read the writing on the remotest star, but Hate so blinded you that you could see no further than the narrow, walled-in, and already lust-withered garden of your common desires. Your terrible lack of imagination, the one really fatal defect of your character, was entirely the result of the Hate that lived in you. Subtly, silently, and in secret, Hate gnawed at your nature, as the lichen bites at the root of some sallow plant, till you grew to see nothing but the most meagre interests and the most petty aims. That faculty in you which Love would have fostered, Hate poisoned and paralysed. When your father first began to attack me it was as your private friend, and in a private letter to you. As soon as I had read the letter, with its obscene threats and coarse violences, I saw at once that a terrible danger was looming on the horizon of my troubled days: I told you I would not be the catspaw between you both in your ancient hatred of each other: that I in London was naturally much bigger game for him than a Secretary for Foreign Affairs at Homburg:[39] that it would be unfair to me to place me even for a moment in such a position:

and that I had something better to do with my life than to have scenes with a man drunken, *déclassé*, and half-witted as he was. You could not be made to see this. Hate blinded you. You insisted that the quarrel had really nothing to do with me: that you would not allow your father to dictate to you in your private friendships: that it would be most unfair of me to interfere. You had already, before you saw me on the subject, sent your father a foolish and vulgar telegram,[40] as your answer. That of course committed you to a foolish and vulgar course of action to follow. The fatal errors of life are not due to man's being unreasonable: an unreasonable moment may be one's finest moment. They are due to man's being logical. There is a wide difference. That telegram conditioned the whole of your subsequent relations with your father, and consequently the whole of my life. And the grotesque thing about it is that it was a telegram of which the commonest street-boy would have been ashamed. From pert telegrams to priggish lawyers' letters was a natural progress, and the result of your lawyer's letters to your father was, of course, to urge him on still further. You left him no option but to go on. You forced it on him as a point of honour, or of dishonour rather, that your appeal should have the more effect. So the next time he attacks me, no longer in a private letter and as your private friend, but in public and as a public man. I have to expel him from my house. He goes from restaurant to restaurant looking for me, in order to insult me before the whole world, and in such a manner that if I retaliated I would be ruined, and if I did not retaliate I would be ruined also. *Then* surely was the time when *you* should have come forward, and said that you would not expose me to such hideous attacks, such infamous persecution, on your account, but would, readily and at once, resign any claim you had to my friendship? You feel that now, I suppose. But it never even occurred to you then. Hate blinded you. All you could think of (besides of course writing to him insulting letters and telegrams) was to buy a ridiculous pistol that goes off in the Berkeley, under circumstances that create a worse scandal than ever came to *your* ears. Indeed the idea of your being the object of a terrible quarrel between your father and a man of my position seemed to delight you. It,

I suppose very naturally, pleased your vanity, and flattered your self-importance. That your father might have had your body, which did not interest me, and left me your soul, which did not interest him, would have been to you a distressing solution of the question. You scented the chance of a public scandal and flew to it. The prospect of a battle in which you would be safe delighted you. I never remember you in higher spirits than you were for the rest of that season. Your only disappointment seemed to be that nothing actually happened, and that no further meeting or fracas had taken place between us. You consoled yourself by sending him telegrams of such a character that at last the wretched man wrote to you and said that he had given orders to his servants that no telegram was to be brought to him under any pretence whatsoever. That did not daunt you. You saw the immense opportunities afforded by the open postcard, and availed yourself of them to the full. You hounded him on in the chase still more. I do not suppose he would ever really have given it up. Family instincts were strong in him. His hatred of you was just as persistent as your hatred of him, and I was the stalking-horse for both of you, and a mode of attack as well as a mode of shelter. His very passion for notoriety was not merely individual but racial. Still, if his interest had flagged for a moment your letters and postcards would soon have quickened it to its ancient flame. They did so. And he naturally went on further still. Having assailed me as a private gentleman and in private, as a public man and in public, he ultimately determines to make his final and great attack on me as an artist, and in the place where my Art is being represented. He secures by fraud a seat for the first night of one of my plays, and contrives a plot to interrupt the performance, to make a foul speech about me to the audience, to insult my actors, to throw offensive or indecent missiles at me when I am called before the curtain at the close, utterly in some hideous way to ruin me through my work. By the merest chance, in the brief and accidental sincerity of a more than usually intoxicated mood, he boasts of his intention before others. Information is given to the police, and he is kept out of the theatre. You had your chance then. Then was your opportunity. Don't you realise now that you should have seen it, and come forward and said that you would not have my Art, at any rate, ruined for your sake? You knew what my Art was to me, the great primal note by which I had revealed, first myself to myself, and then myself to the world; the real passion of my life; the love to which all other loves were as marsh-water to red wine, or the glow-worm of the marsh to the magic mirror of the moon. Don't you understand now that your lack of imagination was the one really fatal defect of your character? What you had to do was quite simple, and quite clear before you, but Hate had blinded you, and you could see nothing. I could not apologise to your father for his having insulted me and persecuted me in the most loathsome manner for nearly nine months. I could not get rid of you out of my life. I had tried it again and again. I had gone so far as actually leaving England and going abroad in the hope of escaping from you. It had all been of no use. You were the only person who could have done anything. The key of the situation rested entirely with yourself. It was the one great opportunity you had of making some slight return to me for all the love and affection and kindness and generosity and care I had shown you. Had you appreciated me even at a tenth of my value as an artist you would have done so. But Hate blinded you. The faculty 'by which, and by which alone, we can understand others in their real as in their ideal relations'[41] was dead in you. You thought simply of how to get your father into prison. To see him 'in the dock', as you used to say: that was your one idea. The phrase became one of the many *scies*[42] of your daily conversation. One heard it at every meal. Well, you had your desire gratified. Hate granted you every single thing you wished for. It was an indulgent Master to you. It is so, indeed, to all who serve it. For two days you sat on a high seat with the Sheriffs, and feasted your eyes with the spectacle of your father standing in the dock of the Central Criminal Court. And on the third day I took his place. What had occurred? In your hideous game of hate together, you had both thrown dice for my soul, and you happened to have lost. That was all.

You see that I have to write your life to you, and you have to realise it. We have known each other now for more than four years. Half of the time we have been together: the other half I have had to spend in prison as the result of our friendship. Where you will receive this letter, if indeed it ever reaches you, I don't know. Rome, Naples, Paris, Venice, some beautiful city on sea or river, I have no doubt, holds you. You are surrounded, if not with all the useless luxury you had with me, at any rate with everything that is pleasurable to eye, ear, and taste. Life is quite lovely to you. And yet, if you are wise, and wish to find Life much lovelier still, and in a different manner, you will let the reading of this terrible letter – for such I know it is – prove to you as important a crisis and turning-point of your life as the writing of it is to me. Your pale face used to flush easily with wine or pleasure. If, as you read what is here written, it from time to time becomes scorched, as though by a furnace-blast, with shame, it will be all the better for you. The supreme vice is shallowness. Whatever is realised is right.

I have now got as far as the House of Detention, have I not? After a night passed in the Police Cells I am sent there in the van. You were most attentive and kind. Almost every afternoon, if not actually every afternoon till you go abroad, you took the trouble to drive up to Holloway to see me. You also wrote very sweet and nice letters. But that it was not your father but you who had put me into prison, that from beginning to end you were the responsible person, that it was through you, for you, and by you that I was there, never for one instant dawned upon you. Even the spectacle of me behind the bars of a wooden cage could not quicken that dead unimaginative nature. You had the sympathy and the sentimentality of the spectator of a rather pathetic play. That you were the true author of the hideous tragedy did not occur to you. I saw that you realised nothing of what you had done. I did not desire to be the one to tell you what your own heart should have told you, what it indeed would have told you if you had not let Hate harden it and make it insensate. Everything must come to one out of one's own nature. There is no use in telling a person a thing that they don't feel and can't understand. If I write to you now as I do it is because your own silence and conduct during my long imprisonment have made it necessary. Besides, as things had turned out, the blow had fallen upon me alone. That was a source of pleasure to me. I was content for many reasons to suffer, though there was always to my eyes, as I watched you, something not a little contemptible in your complete and wilful blindness. I remember your producing with absolute pride a letter you had published in one of the halfpenny newspapers about me.[43] It was a very prudent, temperate, indeed commonplace production. You appealed to the '*English sense of fair play*', or something very dreary of that kind, on behalf of '*a man who was down*'. It was the sort of letter you might have written had a painful charge been brought against some respectable person with whom personally you had been quite unacquainted. But you thought it a wonderful letter. You looked on it as a proof of almost quixotic chivalry. I am aware that you wrote other letters to other newspapers that they did not publish.[44] But then they were simply to say that you hated your father. Nobody cared if you did or not. Hate, you have yet to learn, is, intellectually considered, the Eternal Negation. Considered from the point of view of the emotions it is a form of Atrophy, and kills everything but itself. To write to the papers to say that one hates someone else is as if one were to write to the papers to say that one had some secret and shameful malady: the fact that the man you hated was your own father, and that the feeling was thoroughly reciprocated, did not make your Hate noble or fine in any way. If it showed anything it was simply that it was an hereditary disease.

I remember again, when an execution was put into my house, and my books and furniture were seized and advertised to be sold, and Bankruptcy was impending, I naturally wrote to tell you about it. I did not mention that it was to pay for some gifts of mine to you that the bailiffs had entered the home where you had so often dined. I thought, rightly or wrongly, that such news might pain you a little. I merely told you the bare facts. I thought it proper that you should know them. You wrote back from Boulogne in a strain of almost lyrical exultation. You said that you knew your father was 'hard up for money', and had been obliged to raise £1500 for the expenses of the trial, and that my going bankrupt was really a 'splendid score'

off him, as he would not then be able to get any of his costs
out of me! Do you realise now what Hate blinding a person is?
Do you recognise now that when I described it as an Atrophy
destructive of everything but itself, I was scientifically describing
a real psychological fact? That all my charming things were
to be sold: my Burne-Jones drawings: my Whistler drawings:
my Monticelli: my Simeon Solomons:[45] my china: my Library
with its collection of presentation volumes from almost every
poet of my time, from Hugo to Whitman, from Swinburne to
Mallarmé, from Morris to Verlaine; with its beautifully bound
editions of my father's and mother's works; its wonderful array
of college and school prizes, its *éditions de luxe*, and the like;
was absolutely nothing to you. You said it was a great bore:
that was all. What you really saw in it was the possibility that
your father might ultimately lose a few hundred pounds, and
that paltry consideration filled you with ecstatic joy. As for the
costs of the trial, you may be interested to know that your father
openly said in the Orleans Club that if it had cost him £20,000
he would have considered the money thoroughly well spent,
he had extracted such enjoyment, and delight, and triumph
out of it all. The fact that he was able not merely to put me
into prison for two years, but to take me out for an afternoon
and make me a public bankrupt was an extra-refinement of
pleasure that he had not expected. It was the crowning-point
of my humiliation, and of his complete and perfect victory.
Had your father had no claim for his costs on me, you, I know
perfectly well, would, as far as words go, at any rate have been
most sympathetic about the entire loss of my library, a loss
irreparable to a man of letters, the one of all my material losses
the most distressing to me. You might even, remembering the
sums of money I had lavishly spent on you and how you had
lived on me for years, have taken the trouble to buy in some of
my books for me. The best all went for less than £150: about
as much as I would spend on you in an ordinary week. But the
mean small pleasure of thinking that your father was going to
be a few pence out of pocket made you forget all about trying
to make me a little return, so slight, so easy, so inexpensive, so
obvious, and so enormously welcome to me, had you brought

it about. Am I right in saying that Hate blinds people? Do you
see it now? If you don't, try to see it.

How clearly I saw it then, as now, I need not tell you. But
I said to myself: '*At all costs I must keep Love in my heart. If
I go into prison without Love what will become of my Soul?*'
The letters I wrote to you at that time from Holloway were my
efforts to keep Love as the dominant note of my own nature.
I could if I had chosen have torn you to pieces with bitter
reproaches. I could have rent you with maledictions. I could
have held up a mirror to you, and shown you such an image
of yourself that you would not have recognised it as your own
till you found it mimicking back your gestures of horror, and
then you would have known whose shape it was, and hated
it and yourself for ever. More than that indeed. The sins of
another were being placed to my account. Had I so chosen, I
could on either trial have saved myself at his expense, not from
shame indeed but from imprisonment. Had I cared to show
that the Crown witnesses – the three most important – had
been carefully coached by your father and his solicitors, not
in reticences merely, but in assertions, in the absolute trans-
ference, deliberate, plotted, and rehearsed, of the actions and
doings of someone else on to me, I could have had each one of
them dismissed from the box by the Judge, more summarily
than even wretched perjured Atkins was.[46] I could have walked
out of Court with my tongue in my cheek, and my hands in my
pockets, a free man. The strongest pressure was put upon me
to do so. I was earnestly advised, begged, entreated to do so by
people whose sole interest was my welfare, and the welfare of
my house. But I refused. I did not choose to do so. I have never
regretted my decision for a single moment, even in the most bit-
ter periods of my imprisonment. Such a course of action would
have been beneath me. Sins of the flesh are nothing. They are
maladies for physicians to cure, if they should be cured. Sins
of the soul alone are shameful. To have secured my acquittal
by such means would have been a life-long torture to me. But
do you really think that you were worthy of the love I was
showing you then, or that for a single moment I thought you
were? Do you really think that at any period in our friendship

you were worthy of the love I showed you, or that for a single moment I thought you were? I knew you were not. But Love does not traffic in a marketplace, nor use a huckster's scales. Its joy, like the joy of the intellect, is to feel itself alive. The aim of Love is to love: no more, and no less. You were my enemy: such an enemy as no man ever had. I had given you my life, and to gratify the lowest and most contemptible of all human passions, Hatred and Vanity and Greed, you had thrown it away. In less than three years you had entirely ruined me from every point of view. For my own sake there was nothing for me to do but to love you. I knew, if I allowed myself to hate you, that in the dry desert of existence over which I had to travel, and am travelling still, every rock would lose its shadow, every palm tree be withered, every well of water prove poisoned at its source. Are you beginning now to understand a little? Is your imagination wakening from the long lethargy in which it has lain? You know already what Hate is. Is it beginning to dawn on you what Love is, and what is the nature of Love? It is not too late for you to learn, though to teach it to you I may have had to go to a convict's cell.

After my terrible sentence, when the prison-dress was on me, and the prison-house closed, I sat amidst the ruins of my wonderful life, crushed by anguish, bewildered with terror, dazed through pain. But I would not hate you. Every day I said to myself, '*I must keep Love in my heart today, else how shall I live through the day.*' I reminded myself that you meant no evil, to me at any rate: I set myself to think that you had but drawn a bow at a venture, and that the arrow had pierced a King between the joints of the harness.[47] To have weighed you against the smallest of my sorrows, the meanest of my losses, would have been, I felt, unfair. I determined I would regard you as one suffering too. I forced myself to believe that at last the scales had fallen from your long-blinded eyes. I used to fancy, and with pain, what your horror must have been when you contemplated your terrible handiwork. There were times, even in those dark days, the darkest of all my life, when I actually longed to console you. So sure was I that at last you had realised what you had done.

It did not occur to me then that you could have the supreme vice, shallowness. Indeed, it was a real grief to me when I had to let you know that I was obliged to reserve for family business my first opportunity of receiving a letter: but my brother-in-law had written to me to say that if I would only write once to my wife she would, for my own sake and for our children's sake, take no action for divorce. I felt my duty was to do so. Setting aside other reasons, I could not bear the idea of being separated from Cyril, that beautiful, loving, loveable child of mine, my friend of all friends, my companion beyond all companions, one single hair of whose little golden head should have been dearer and of more value to me than, I will not merely say you from top to toe, but the entire chrysolite of the whole world:[48] was so indeed to me always, though I failed to understand it till too late.

Two weeks after your application, I get news of you. Robert Sherard, that bravest and most chivalrous of all brilliant beings, comes to see me, and amongst other things tells me that in that ridiculous *Mercure de France*, with its absurd affectation of being the true centre of literary corruption, you are about to publish an article on me with specimens of my letters. He asks me if it really was by my wish. I was greatly taken aback, and much annoyed, and gave orders that the thing was to be stopped at once.[49] You had left my letters lying about for blackmailing companions to steal, for hotel servants to pilfer, for housemaids to sell. That was simply your careless want of appreciation of what I had written to you. But that you should seriously propose to publish selections from the balance was almost incredible to me. And which of my letters were they? I could get no information. That was my first news of you. It displeased me.

The second piece of news followed shortly afterwards. Your father's solicitors had appeared in the prison, and served me personally with a Bankruptcy notice, for a paltry £700, the amount of their taxed costs. I was adjudged a public insolvent, and ordered to be produced in Court. I felt most strongly, and feel still, and will revert to the subject again, that these costs should have been paid by your family. You had taken personally on yourself the responsibility of stating that your family would do so. It was that which had made the solicitor take up the case in the way he did. You were absolutely responsible. Even irrespective of your engagement on your family's behalf you should have felt that as you had brought the whole ruin on me, the least that could have been done was to spare me the additional ignominy of bankruptcy for an absolutely contemptible sum of money, less than half of what I spent on you in three brief summer months at Goring. Of that, however, no more here. I did through the solicitor's clerk, I fully admit, receive a message from you on the subject, or at any rate in connection with the occasion. The day he came to receive my depositions and statements, he leant across the table – the prison warder being present – and having consulted a piece of paper which he pulled from his pocket, said to me in a low voice: 'Prince Fleur-de-Lys wishes to be remembered to you.' I stared at him. He repeated the message again. I did not know what he meant. 'The gentleman is abroad at present,' he added mysteriously. It all flashed across me, and I remember that, for the first and last time in my entire prison-life, I laughed. In that laugh was all the scorn of all the world. Prince Fleur-de-Lys! I saw – and subsequent events showed me that I rightly saw – that nothing that had happened had made you realise a single thing. You were in your own eyes still the graceful prince of a trivial comedy, not the sombre figure of a tragic show. All that had occurred was but as a feather for the cap that gilds a narrow head, a flower to pink the doublet that hides a heart that Hate, and Hate alone, can warm, that Love, and Love alone, finds cold. Prince Fleur-de-Lys! You were, no doubt, quite right to communicate with me under an assumed name. I myself, at that time, had no name at all. In the great prison where I was then incarcerated I was merely the figure and letter of a little cell in a long gallery, one of a thousand lifeless numbers, as of a thousand lifeless lives. But surely there were many real names in real history which would have suited you much better, and by which I would have had no difficulty at all in recognising you at once? I did not look for you behind the spangles of a tinsel vizard only suitable for an amusing masquerade. Ah! had your soul been, as for its own perfection even it should have been, wounded with sorrow, bowed with remorse, and humble with grief, such was not the disguise it would have chosen beneath whose shadow to seek entrance to the House of Pain! The great things of life are what they seem to be, and for that reason, strange as it may sound to you, are often difficult to interpret. But the little things of life are symbols. We receive our bitter lessons most easily through them. Your seemingly casual choice of a feigned name was, and will remain, symbolic. It reveals you.

Six weeks later a third piece of news arrives. I am called out of the Hospital Ward, where I was lying wretchedly ill, to receive a special message from you through the Governor of the Prison. He reads me out a letter you had addressed to him in which you stated that you proposed to publish an article 'on the case of Mr Oscar Wilde', in the *Mercure de France* ('a magazine', you added for some extraordinary reason, 'corresponding to our English *Fortnightly Review*') and were anxious to obtain my permission to publish extracts and selections from – what letters? The letters I had written to you from Holloway Prison! The letters that should have been to you things sacred and secret beyond anything in the whole world! These actually were the letters you proposed to publish for the jaded *décadent* to wonder at, for the greedy *feuilletoniste*[50] to chronicle, for the little lions of the *Quartier Latin* to gape and mouth at! Had there been nothing in your own heart to cry out against so vulgar a sacrilege you might at least have remembered the sonnet he wrote who saw with such sorrow and scorn the letters of John Keats sold by public auction in London and have understood at last the real meaning of my lines

> I think they love not Art
> Who break the crystal of a poet's heart
> That small and sickly eyes may glare or gloat.[51]

For what was your article to show? That I had been too fond of you? The Paris *gamin* was quite aware of the fact. They all read the newspapers, and most of them write for them. That I was a man of genius? The French understood that, and the peculiar quality of my genius, much better than you did, or could have been expected to do. That along with genius goes often a curious perversity of passion and desire? Admirable: but the subject belongs to Lombroso[52] rather than to you. Besides, the pathological phenomenon in question is also found amongst those who have not genius. That in your war of hate with your father I was at once shield and weapon to each of you? Nay more, that in that hideous hunt for my life, that took place when the war was over, he never could have reached me had not your nets been already about my feet? Quite true: but I am told that Henri Bauër had already done it extremely well.[53] Besides, to corroborate his view, had such been your intention, you did not require to publish my letters; at any rate those written from Holloway Prison.

Will you say, in answer to my questions, that in one of my Holloway letters I had myself asked you to try, as far as you were able, to set me a little right with some small portion of the world? Certainly, I did so. Remember how and why I am here, at this very moment. Do you think I am here on account of my relations with the witnesses on my trial? My relations, real or supposed, with people of that kind were matters of no interest to either the Government or Society. They knew nothing of them, and cared less. I am here for having tried to put your father into prison. My attempt failed of course. My own Counsel threw up their briefs. Your father completely turned the tables on me, and had *me* in prison, has me there still. That is why there is contempt felt for me. That is why people despise me. That is why I have to serve out every day, every hour, every minute of my dreadful imprisonment. That is why my petitions have been refused.

You were the only person who, and without in any way exposing yourself to scorn or danger or blame, could have given another colour to the whole affair: have put the matter in a different light: have shown to a certain degree how things really stood. I would not of course have expected, nor indeed wished, you to have stated how and for what purpose you had sought my assistance in your trouble at Oxford: or how, and for what purpose, if you had a purpose at all, you had practically never left my side for nearly three years. My incessant attempts to break off a friendship that was so ruinous to me as an artist, as a man of position, as a member of society even, need not have been chronicled with the accuracy with which they have been set down here. Nor would I have desired you to have described the scenes you used to make with such almost monotonous recurrence: nor to have reprinted your wonderful series of telegrams to me with their strange mixture of romance and finance; nor to have quoted from your letters the more revolting or heartless passages, as I have been forced to do. Still, I thought it would have been good, as well for you as for me, if you had made some protest against your father's version of our friendship, one no less grotesque than venomous, and as absurd in its reference to you as it was dishonouring in its reference to me. That version has now actually passed into serious history: it is quoted, believed, and chronicled: the preacher has taken it for his text, and the moralist for his barren theme: and I who appealed to all the ages have had to accept my verdict from one who is an ape and a buffoon. I have said, and with some bitterness, I admit, in this letter that such was the irony of things that your father would live to be the hero of a Sunday-school tract: that you would rank with the Infant Samuel: and that my place would be between Gilles de Retz and the Marquis de Sade.[54] I dare say it is best so. I have no desire to complain. One of the many lessons that one learns in prison is that things are what they are, and will be what they will be. Nor have I any doubt but that the leper of mediaevalism, and the author of *Justine*, will prove better company than *Sandford and Merton*.[55]

But at the time I wrote to you I felt that for both our sakes it would be a good thing, a proper thing, a right thing *not* to accept the account your father had put forward through his Counsel for the edification of a Philistine world, and that is why I asked you to think out and write something that would be nearer the truth. It would at least have been better for you than scribbling to the French papers about the domestic life of your parents. What did the French care whether or not your parents had led a happy domestic life? One cannot conceive a subject more entirely uninteresting to them. What did interest them was how

an artist of my distinction, one who by the school and move-
ment of which he was the incarnation had exercised a marked
influence on the direction of French thought, could, having led
such a life, have brought such an action. Had you proposed for
your article to publish the letters, endless I fear in number, in
which I had spoken to you of the ruin you were bringing on my
life, of the madness of moods of rage that you were allowing
to master you to your own hurt as well as to mine, and of my
desire, nay, my determination to end a friendship so fatal to me
in every way, I could have understood it, though I would not
have allowed such letters to be published: when your father's
Counsel desiring to catch me in a contradiction suddenly pro-
duced in Court a letter of mine, written to you in March '93,
in which I stated that, rather than endure a repetition of the
hideous scenes you seemed to take such a terrible pleasure in
making, I would readily consent to be 'blackmailed by every
renter in London',[56] it was a very real grief to me that that side
of my friendship with you should incidentally be revealed to
the common gaze: but that you should have been so slow to
see, so lacking in all sensitiveness, and so dull in apprehension
of what is rare, delicate and beautiful, as to propose yourself
to publish the letters in which, and through which, I was try-
ing to keep alive the very spirit and soul of Love, that it might
dwell in my body through the long years of that body's humili-
ation – this was, and still is to me, a source of the very deepest
pain, the most poignant disappointment. Why you did so, I
fear I know but too well. If Hate blinded your eyes, Vanity
sewed your eyelids together with threads of iron. The faculty
'by which, and by which alone, one can understand others in
their real as in their ideal relations',[57] your narrow egotism had
blunted, and long disuse had made of no avail. The imagin-
ation was as much in prison as I was. Vanity had barred up the
windows, and the name of the warder was Hate.

All this took place in the early part of November of the year
before last. A great river of life flows between you and a date
so distant. Hardly, if at all, can you see across so wide a waste.
But to me it seems to have occurred, I will not say yesterday,
but today. Suffering is one long moment.[58] We cannot divide it

by seasons. We can only record its moods, and chronicle their return. With us time itself does not progress. It revolves. It seems to circle round one centre of pain. The paralysing immobility of a life, every circumstance of which is regulated after an unchangeable pattern, so that we eat and drink and walk and lie down and pray, or kneel at least for prayer, according to the inflexible laws of an iron formula: this immobile quality, that makes each dreadful day in the very minutest detail like its brother, seems to communicate itself to those external forces the very essence of whose existence is ceaseless change. Of seed-time or harvest, of the reapers bending over the corn, or the grape-gatherers threading through the vines, of the grass in the orchard made white with broken blossoms, or strewn with fallen fruit, we know nothing, and can know nothing. For us there is only one season, the season of Sorrow. The very sun and moon seem taken from us. Outside, the day may be blue and gold, but the light that creeps down through the thickly-muffled glass of the small iron-barred window beneath which one sits is grey and niggard. It is always twilight in one's cell, as it is always midnight in one's heart. And in the sphere of thought, no less than in the sphere of time, motion is no more. The thing that you personally have long ago forgotten, or can easily forget, is happening to me now, and will happen to me again tomorrow. Remember this, and you will be able to understand a little of why I am writing to you, and in this manner writing.

A week later,[59] I am transferred here. Three more months go over and my mother dies. You knew, none better, how deeply I loved and honoured her. Her death was so terrible to me that I, once a lord of language,[60] have no words in which to express my anguish and my shame. Never, even in the most perfect days of my development as an artist, could I have had words fit to bear so august a burden, or to move with sufficient stateliness of music through the purple pageant of my incommunicable woe. She and my father had bequeathed me a name they had made noble and honoured not merely in Literature, Art, Archaeology and Science, but in the public history of my own country in its evolution as a nation. I had disgraced that name eternally. I had made it a low byword among low people. I had dragged it through the very mire. I had given it to brutes that they might make it brutal, and to fools that they might turn it into a synonym for folly. What I suffered then, and still suffer, is not for pen to write or paper to record. My wife, at that time kind and gentle to me, rather than that I should hear the news from indifferent or alien lips, travelled, ill as she was, all the way from Genoa to England to break to me herself the tidings of so irreparable, so irredeemable a loss. Messages of sympathy reached me from all who had still affection for me. Even people who had not known me personally, hearing what a new sorrow had come into my broken life, wrote to ask that some expression of their condolence should be conveyed to me. You alone stood aloof, sent me no message, and wrote me no letter. Of such actions, it is best to say what Virgil says to Dante of those whose lives have been barren in noble impulse and shallow of intention: '*Non ragioniam di lor, ma guarda, e passa.*'[61]

Three more months go over. The calendar of my daily conduct and labour that hangs on the outside of my cell-door, with my name and sentence written upon it, tells me that it is Maytime. My friends come to see me again. I enquire, as I always do, after you. I am told that you are in your villa at Naples, and are bringing out a volume of poems. At the close of the interview it is mentioned casually that you are dedicating them to me. The tidings seemed to give me a sort of nausea of life. I said nothing, but silently went back to my cell with contempt and scorn in my heart. How could you dream of dedicating a volume of poems to me without first asking my permission? Dream, do I say? How could you dare to do such a thing? Will you give as your answer that in the days of my greatness and fame I had consented to receive the dedication of your early work? Certainly, I did so; just as I would have accepted the homage of any other young man beginning the difficult and beautiful art of literature. All homage is delightful to an artist, and doubly sweet when youth brings it. Laurel and bay leaf wither when aged hands pluck them. Only youth has a right to crown an artist. That is the real privilege of being young, if youth only knew it. But the days of abasement and infamy are different from those of greatness and of fame. You have yet to learn that Prosperity, Pleasure and Success may be rough of grain and common in fibre, but that Sorrow is the most sensitive of all created things. There is nothing that stirs in the whole world of thought or motion to which Sorrow does not vibrate in terrible if exquisite pulsation. The thin beaten-out leaf of tremulous gold that chronicles the direction of forces that the eye cannot see[62] is in comparison coarse. It is a wound that bleeds when any hand but that of Love touches it and even then must bleed again, though not for pain.

You could write to the Governor of Wandsworth Prison to ask my permission to publish my letters in the *Mercure de France*, 'corresponding to our English *Fortnightly Review*'. Why not have written to the Governor of the Prison at Reading to ask my permission to dedicate your poems to me, whatever fantastic description you may have chosen to give of them? Was it because in the one case the magazine in question had been prohibited by me from publishing letters, the legal copyright of which, as you are of course perfectly well aware, was and is vested entirely in me, and in the other you thought that you could enjoy the wilfulness of your own way without my knowing anything about it till it was too late to interfere? The mere fact that I was a man disgraced, ruined, and in prison should have made you, if you desired to write my name on the fore-page of your work, beg it of me as a favour, an honour, a privilege. That is the way in which one should approach those who are in distress and sit in shame.

Where there is Sorrow there is holy ground. Some day you will realise what that means. You will know nothing of life till you do. Robbie, and natures like his, can realise it. When I was brought down from my prison to the Court of Bankruptcy between two policemen, Robbie waited in the long dreary corridor, that before the whole crowd, whom an action so sweet and simple hushed into silence, he might gravely raise his hat to me, as handcuffed and with bowed head I passed him by. Men have gone to heaven for smaller things than that. It was in this spirit, and with this mode of love that the saints knelt down to wash the feet of the poor, or stooped to kiss the leper on the cheek. I

have never said one single word to him about what he did. I do
not know to the present moment whether he is aware that I was
even conscious of his action. It is not a thing for which one can
render formal thanks in formal words. I store it in the treasury-
house of my heart. I keep it there as a secret debt that I am glad
to think I can never possibly repay. It is embalmed and kept
sweet by the myrrh and cassia of many tears. When Wisdom has
been profitless to me, and Philosophy barren, and the proverbs
and phrases of those who have sought to give me consolation
as dust and ashes in my mouth, the memory of that little lowly
silent act of Love has unsealed for me all the wells of pity, made
the desert blossom like a rose, and brought me out of the bitter-
ness of lonely exile into harmony with the wounded, broken and
great heart of the world. When you are able to understand, not
merely how beautiful Robbie's action was, but why it meant so
much to me, and always will mean so much, then, perhaps, you
will realise how and in what spirit you should have approached
me for permission to dedicate to me your verses.

It is only right to state that in any case I would not have
accepted the dedication. Though, possibly, it would under other
circumstances have pleased me to have been asked, I would have
refused the request for *your* sake, irrespective of any feelings of
my own. The first volume of poems that in the very springtime
of his manhood a young man sends forth to the world should
be like a blossom or flower of spring, like the white thorn in
the meadow at Magdalen, or the cowslips in the Cumnor fields.
It should not be burdened by the weight of a terrible, a revolt-
ing tragedy, a terrible, a revolting scandal. If I had allowed my
name to serve as herald to the book it would have been a grave
artistic error. It would have brought a wrong atmosphere round
the whole work, and in modern art atmosphere counts for so
much. Modern life is complex and relative. Those are its two
distinguishing notes. To render the first we require atmosphere
with its subtlety of *nuances*, of suggestion, of strange perspect-
ives: as for the second we require background. That is why
sculpture has ceased to be a representative art; and why music
is a representative art; and why Literature is, and has been, and
always will remain the supreme representative art.

Your little book should have brought with it Sicilian and Arcadian airs, not the pestilent foulness of the criminal dock or the close breath of the convict cell. Nor would such a dedication as you proposed have been merely an error of taste in Art; it would from other points of view have been entirely unseemly. It would have looked like a continuance of your conduct before and after my arrest. It would have given people the impression of being an attempt at foolish bravado: an example of that kind of courage that is sold cheap and bought cheap in the streets of shame. As far as our friendship is concerned Nemesis has crushed us both like flies. The dedication of verses to me when I was in prison would have seemed a sort of silly effort at smart repartee, an accomplishment on which in your old days of dreadful letter-writing – days never, I sincerely hope for your sake, to return – you used openly to pride yourself and about which it was your joy to boast. It would not have produced the serious, the beautiful effect which I trust – I believe indeed – you had intended. Had you consulted me, I would have advised you to delay the publication of your verses for a little; or, if that proved displeasing to you, to publish anonymously at first, and then when you had won lovers by your song – the only sort of lovers really worth the winning – you might have turned round and said to the world 'These flowers that you admire are of my sowing, and now I offer them to one whom you regard as a pariah and an outcast, as my tribute to what I love and reverence and admire in him.' But you chose the wrong method and the wrong moment. There is a tact in love, and a tact in literature: you were not sensitive to either.

I have spoken to you at length on this point in order that you should grasp its full bearings, and understand why I wrote at once to Robbie in terms of such scorn and contempt of you,[63] and absolutely prohibited the dedication, and desired that the words I had written of you should be copied out carefully and sent to you. I felt that at last the time had come when you should be made to see, to recognise, to realise a little of what you had done. Blindness may be carried so far that it becomes grotesque, and an unimaginative nature, if something be not done to rouse it, will become petrified into absolute insensibility, so that while the body may eat, and drink, and have its pleasures, the soul, whose house it is, may, like the soul of Branca d'Oria in Dante,[64] be dead absolutely. My letter seems to have arrived not a moment too soon. It fell on you, as far as I can judge, like a thunderbolt. You describe yourself, in your answer to Robbie, as being 'deprived of all power of thought and expression'. Indeed, apparently, you can think of nothing better than to write to your mother to complain. Of course, she, with that blindness to your real good that has been her ill-starred fortune and yours, gives you every comfort she can think of, and lulls you back, I suppose, into your former unhappy, unworthy condition; while as far as I am concerned, she lets my friends know that she is 'very much annoyed' at the severity of my remarks about you. Indeed it is not merely to my friends that she conveys her sentiments of annoyance, but also to those – a very much larger number, I need hardly remind you – who are not my friends: and I am informed now, and through channels very kindly-disposed to you and yours, that in consequence of this a great deal of the sympathy that, by reason of my distinguished genius and terrible sufferings, had been gradually but surely growing up for me, has been entirely taken away. People say 'Ah! he first tried to get the kind father put into prison and failed: now he turns round and blames the innocent son for his failure. How right we were to despise him! How worthy of contempt he is!' It seems to me that, when my name is mentioned in your mother's presence, if she has no word of sorrow or regret for her share – no slight one – in the ruin of my house, it would be more seemly if she remained silent. And as for you – don't you think now that, instead of writing to *her* to complain, it would have been better for you, in every way, to have written to *me* directly, and to have had the courage to say to me whatever you had or fancied you had to say? It is nearly a year ago now since I wrote that letter. You cannot have remained during that entire time 'deprived of all power of thought and expression'. Why did you not write to me? You saw by my letter how deeply wounded, how outraged I was by your whole conduct. More than that; you saw your entire friendship with me set before you, at last, in its true light, and by a mode not to be mistaken. Often in old days I had told you that you were ruining my life. You had always laughed. When Edwin Levy[65] at the very beginning of our friendship, seeing your manner of putting me forward to bear the brunt, and annoyance, and expense even of that unfortunate Oxford mishap of yours, if we must so term it, in reference to which his advice and help had been sought, warned me for the space of a whole hour against knowing you, you laughed, as at Bracknell I described to you my long and impressive interview with him. When I told you how even that unfortunate young man who ultimately stood beside me in the Dock had warned me more than once that you would prove far more fatal in bringing me to utter destruction than any even of the common lads whom I was foolish enough to know, you laughed, though not with such sense of amusement. When my more prudent or less well-disposed friends either warned me or left me, on account of my friendship with you, you laughed with scorn. You laughed immoderately when, on the occasion of your father writing his first abusive letter to you about me, I told you that I knew I would be the mere catspaw of your dreadful quarrel and come to some evil between you. But every single thing had happened as I had said it would happen, as far as the result goes. You had no excuse for not seeing how all things had come to pass. Why did you not write to me? Was it cowardice? Was it callousness? What was it? The fact that I was outraged with you, and had expressed my sense of outrage, was all the more reason for writing. If you thought my letter just, you should have written. If you thought it in the smallest point unjust, you should have written. I waited for a letter. I felt sure that at last you would see that, if old affection, much-protested love, the thousand acts of ill-requited kindness I had showered on you, the thousand unpaid debts of gratitude you owed me – that if all these were nothing to you, mere duty itself, most barren of all bonds between man and man, should have made you write. You cannot say that you seriously thought I was obliged to receive none but business communications from members of my family. You knew perfectly well that every twelve weeks Robbie was writing to me a little budget of literary news. Nothing can be more charming than his letters, in their wit, their clever concentrated criticism, their light touch: they are real letters: they are like a person talking to one: they have the quality of a French *causerie intime*:[66] and in his delicate modes of deference to me, appealing at one time to my judgment, at another to my sense of humour, at another to my instinct for beauty or to my culture, and reminding me in a hundred subtle ways that once I was to many an arbiter of style in Art, the supreme arbiter to some, he shows how he has the tact of love as well as the tact of literature. His letters have been the little messengers between me and that beautiful unreal world of Art where once I was King, and would have remained King, indeed, had I not let myself be lured into the imperfect world of coarse uncompleted passions, of appetite without distinction, desire without limit and formless greed. Yet, when all is said, surely you might have been able to understand, or conceive, at any rate, in your own mind, that, even on the ordinary grounds of mere psychological curiosity, it would have been more interesting to me to hear from you than to learn that Alfred Austin[67] was trying to bring out a volume of poems, or that Street[68] was writing dramatic criticisms for the *Daily Chronicle*, or that by one who cannot speak a panegyric without stammering Mrs Meynell had been pronounced to be the new Sibyl of Style.[69]

Ah! had *you* been in prison – I will not say through any fault of mine, for that would be a thought too terrible for me to bear – but through fault of your own, error of your own, faith in some unworthy friend, slip in sensual mire, trust misapplied, or love ill-bestowed, or none, or all of these – do you think that I would have allowed you to eat your heart away in darkness and solitude without trying in some way, however slight, to help you to bear the bitter burden of your disgrace? Do you think that I would not have let you know that if you suffered, I was suffering too: that if you wept, there were tears in my eyes also: and that if you lay in the house of bondage and were despised of men, I out of my very griefs had built a house in which to dwell until your coming, a treasury in which all that men had denied to you would be laid up for your healing, one hundredfold in increase? If bitter necessity, or prudence, to *me* more bitter still, had prevented my being near you, and robbed

me of the joy of your presence, though seen through prison-
bars and in a shape of shame, I would have written to you in
season and out of season in the hope that some mere phrase,
some single word, some broken echo even of Love might reach
you. If you had refused to receive my letters, I would have writ-
ten none the less, so that you should have known that at any
rate there were always letters waiting for you. Many have done
so to me. Every three months people write to me, or propose to
write to me. Their letters and communications are kept. They
will be handed to me when I go out of prison. I know that they
are there. I know the names of the people who have written
them. I know that they are full of sympathy, and affection, and
kindness. That is sufficient for me. I need to know no more.
Your silence has been horrible. Nor has it been a silence of
weeks and months merely, but of years; of years even as they
have to count them who, like yourself, live swiftly in happiness,
and can hardly catch the gilt feet of the days as they dance by,
and are out of breath in the chase after pleasure. It is a silence
without excuse; a silence without palliation. I knew you had
feet of clay. Who knew it better? When I wrote, among my
aphorisms, that it was simply the feet of clay that made the
gold of the image precious,[70] it was of you I was thinking. But it
is no gold image with clay feet that you have made of yourself.
Out of the very dust of the common highway that the hooves
of horned things pash into mire you have moulded your per-
fect semblance for me to look at, so that, whatever my secret
desire might have been, it would be impossible for me now to
have for you any feeling other than that of contempt and scorn,
for myself any feeling other than that of contempt and scorn
either. And setting aside all other reasons, your indifference,
your worldly wisdom, your callousness, your prudence, what-
ever you may choose to call it, has been made doubly bitter to
me by the peculiar circumstances that either accompanied or
followed my fall.

Other miserable men, when they are thrown into prison, if
they are robbed of the beauty of the world, are at least safe, in
some measure, from the world's most deadly slings, most awful
arrows. They can hide in the darkness of their cells, and of their

very disgrace make a mode of sanctuary. The world, having had its will, goes its way, and they are left to suffer undisturbed. With me it has been different. Sorrow after sorrow has come beating at the prison doors in search of me. They have opened the gates wide and let them in. Hardly, if at all, have my friends been suffered to see me. But my enemies have had full access to me always. Twice in my public appearances at the Bankruptcy Court, twice again in my public transferences from one prison to another, have I been shown under conditions of unspeakable humiliation to the gaze and mockery of men. The messenger of Death has brought me his tidings and gone his way, and in entire solitude, and isolated from all that could give me comfort, or suggest relief, I have had to bear the intolerable burden of misery and remorse that the memory of my mother placed upon me, and places on me still. Hardly has that wound been dulled, not healed, by time, when violent and bitter and harsh letters come to me from my wife through her solicitor. I am, at once, taunted and threatened with poverty. That I can bear. I can school myself to worse than that. But my two children are taken from me by legal procedure.[71] That is and always will remain to me a source of infinite distress, of infinite pain, of grief without end or limit. That the law should decide, and take upon itself to decide, that I am one unfit to be with my own children is something quite horrible to me. The disgrace of prison is as nothing compared to it. I envy the other men who tread the yard along with me. I am sure that their children wait for them, look for their coming, will be sweet to them.

The poor are wiser, more charitable, more kind, more sensitive than we are. In their eyes prison is a tragedy in a man's life, a misfortune, a casualty, something that calls for sympathy in others. They speak of one who is in prison as of one who is '*in trouble*' simply. It is the phrase they always use, and the expression has the perfect wisdom of Love in it. With people of our rank it is different. With us prison makes a man a pariah. I, and such as I am, have hardly any right to air and sun. Our presence taints the pleasures of others. We are unwelcome when we reappear. To revisit the glimpses of the moon[72] is not for us. Our very children are taken away. Those lovely links with humanity are broken. We are doomed to be solitary while our sons still lived. We are denied the one thing that might heal us and help us, might bring balm to the bruised heart, and peace to the soul in pain.

And to all this has been added the hard, small fact that by your actions and by your silence, by what you have done and by what you have left undone, you have made every day of my long imprisonment still more difficult for me to live through. The very bread and water of prison fare you have by your conduct changed. You have rendered the one bitter and the other brackish to me. The sorrow you should have shared you have doubled, the pain you should have sought to lighten you have quickened to anguish. I have no doubt that you did not mean to do so. I know that you did not mean to do so. It was simply that 'one really fatal defect of your character, your entire lack of imagination'.[73]

And the end of it all is that I have got to forgive you. I must do so. I don't write this letter to put bitterness into your heart but to pluck it out of mine. For my own sake I must forgive you. One cannot always keep an adder in one's breast to feed on one, nor rise up every night to sow thorns in the garden of one's soul. It will not be difficult at all for me to do so, if you help me a little. Whatever you did to me in old days I always readily forgave. It did you no good then. Only one whose life is without stain of any kind can forgive sins. But now when I sit in humiliation and disgrace it is different. My forgiveness should mean a great deal to you now. Some day you will realise it. Whether you do so early or late, soon or not at all, my way is clear before me. I cannot allow you to go through life bearing in your heart the burden of having ruined a man like me. The thought might make you callously indifferent, or morbidly sad. I must take the burden from you and put it on my own shoulders.

I must say to myself that neither you nor your father, multiplied a thousand times over, could possibly have ruined a man like me: that I ruined myself: and that nobody, great or small, can be ruined except by his own hand. I am quite ready to do so. I am trying to do so, though you may not think it at the present moment. If I have brought this pitiless indictment against you, think what an indictment I bring without pity against myself. Terrible as what you did to me was, what I did to myself was far more terrible still.

I was a man who stood in symbolic relations to the art and culture of my age. I had realised this for myself at the very dawn of my manhood, and had forced my age to realise it afterwards. Few men hold such a position in their own lifetime and have it so acknowledged. It is usually discerned, if discerned at all, by the historian, or the critic, long after both the man and his age have passed away. With me it was different. I felt it myself, and made others feel it. Byron was a symbolic figure, but his relations were to the passion of his age and its weariness of passion. Mine were to something more noble, more permanent, of more vital issue, of larger scope.

The gods had given me almost everything. I had genius, a distinguished name, high social position, brilliancy, intellectual daring: I made art a philosophy, and philosophy an art: I altered the minds of men and the colours of things: there was nothing I said or did that did not make people wonder: I took the drama, the most objective form known to art, and made it as personal a mode of expression as the lyric or the sonnet, at the same time that I widened its range and enriched its characterisation: drama, novel, poem in rhyme, poem in prose, subtle or fantastic dialogue, whatever I touched I made beautiful in a new mode of beauty: to truth itself I gave what is false no less than what is true as its rightful province, and showed that the false and the true are merely forms of intellectual existence. I treated Art as the supreme reality, and life as a mere mode of fiction: I awoke the imagination of my century so that it created myth and legend around me: I summed up all systems in a phrase, and all existence in an epigram.

Along with these things, I had things that were different. I let myself be lured into long spells of senseless and sensual ease. I amused myself with being a *flâneur*, a dandy, a man of fashion. I surrounded myself with the smaller natures and the meaner minds. I became the spendthrift of my own genius, and to waste an eternal youth gave me a curious joy. Tired of being on the heights I deliberately went to the depths in the search for new sensations. What the paradox was to me in the sphere of thought, perversity became to me in the sphere of passion. Desire, at the end, was a malady, or a madness, or both. I grew careless of the lives of others. I took pleasure where it pleased me and passed on. I forgot that every little action of the common day makes or unmakes character, and that therefore what one has done in the secret chamber one has some day to cry aloud on the housetops. I ceased to be Lord over myself. I was no longer the Captain of my Soul,[74] and did not know it. I allowed you to dominate me, and your father to frighten me. I ended in horrible disgrace. There is only one thing for me now, absolute Humility: just as there is only one thing for you, absolute Humility also. You had better come down into the dust and learn it beside me.

I have lain in prison for nearly two years. Out of my nature has come wild despair; an abandonment to grief that was piteous even to look at: terrible and impotent rage: bitterness and scorn: anguish that wept aloud: misery that could find no voice: sorrow that was dumb. I have passed through every possible mood of suffering. Better than Wordsworth himself I know what Wordsworth meant when he said:

> Suffering is permanent, obscure, and dark
> And has the nature of Infinity.[75]

But while there were times when I rejoiced in the idea that my sufferings were to be endless, I could not bear them to be without meaning. Now I find hidden away in my nature something that tells me that nothing in the whole world is meaningless, and suffering least of all. That something hidden away in my nature, like a treasure in a field, is Humility.

It is the last thing left in me, and the best: the ultimate discovery at which I have arrived: the starting-point for a fresh development. It has come to me right out of myself, so I know that it has come at the proper time. It could not have come before, nor later. Had anyone told me of it, I would have rejected it. Had it been brought to me, I would have refused it. As I found it, I want to keep it. I must do so. It is the one thing that has in it the elements of life, of a new life, a *Vita Nuova*[76] for me. Of all things it is the strangest. One cannot give it away, and another may not give it to one. One cannot acquire it, except by surrendering everything that one has. It is only when one has lost all things, that one knows that one possesses it.

Now that I realise that it is in me, I see quite clearly what I have got to do, what, in fact, I must do. And when I use such a phrase as that, I need not tell you that I am not alluding to any external sanction or command. I admit none. I am far more of an individualist than I ever was. Nothing seems to me of the smallest value except what one gets out of oneself. My nature is seeking a fresh mode of self-realisation. That is all I am concerned with. And the first thing that I have got to do is to free myself from any possible bitterness of feeling against you.

I am completely penniless, and absolutely homeless. Yet there are worse things in the world than that. I am quite candid when I tell you that rather than go out from this prison with bitterness in my heart against you or against the world I would gladly and readily beg my bread from door to door. If I got nothing at the house of the rich, I would get something at the house of the poor. Those who have much are often greedy. Those who have little always share. I would not a bit mind sleeping in the cool grass in summer, and when winter came on sheltering myself by the warm close-thatched rick, or under the penthouse of a great barn, provided I had love in my heart. The external things of life seem to me now of no importance at all. You can see to what intensity of individualism I have arrived, or am arriving rather, for the journey is long, and 'where I walk there are thorns'.[77]

Of course I know that to ask for alms on the highway is not to be my lot, and that if ever I lie in the cool grass at nighttime it will be to write sonnets to the Moon. When I go out of prison, Robbie will be waiting for me on the other side of the big iron-studded gate, and he is the symbol not merely of his own affection, but of the affection of many others besides. I believe I am to have enough to live on for about eighteen months at any rate, so that, if I may not write beautiful books, I may at least read beautiful books, and what joy can be greater?

After that, I hope to be able to recreate my creative faculty. But were things different: had I not a friend left in the world: were there not a single house open to me even in pity: had I to accept the wallet and ragged cloak of sheer penury: still as long as I remained free from all resentment, hardness, and scorn, I would be able to face life with much more calm and confidence than I would were my body in purple and fine linen, and the soul within it sick with hate. And I shall really have no difficulty in forgiving you. But to make it a pleasure for me you must feel that you want it. When you really want it you will find it waiting for you.

I need not say that my task does not end there. It would be comparatively easy if it did. There is much more before me. I have hills far steeper to climb, valleys much darker to pass through. And I have to get it all out of myself. Neither Religion, Morality, nor Reason can help me at all.

Morality does not help me. I am a born antinomian. I am one of those who are made for exceptions, not for laws. But while I see that there is nothing wrong in what one does, I see that there is something wrong in what one becomes. It is well to have learned that.

Religion does not help me. The faith that others give to what is unseen, I give to what one can touch, and look at. My Gods dwell in temples made with hands, and within the circle of actual experience is my creed made perfect and complete: too complete it may be, for like many or all of those who have placed their Heaven in this earth, I have found in it not merely the beauty of Heaven, but the horror of Hell also. When I think about Religion at all, I feel as if I would like to found an order for those who cannot believe: the Confraternity of the Fatherless one might call it, where on an altar, on which no taper burned, a priest, in whose heart peace had no dwelling, might celebrate with unblessed bread and a chalice empty of wine. Everything to be true must become a religion. And agnosticism should have its ritual no less than faith. It has sown its martyrs, it should reap its saints, and praise God daily for having hidden Himself from man. But whether it be faith or agnosticism, it must be nothing external to me. Its symbols must be of my own creating. Only that is spiritual which makes its own form. If I may not find its secret within myself, I shall never find it. If I have not got it already, it will never come to me.

Reason does not help me. It tells me that the laws under which I am convicted are wrong and unjust laws, and the system under which I have suffered a wrong and unjust system. But, somehow, I have got to make both of these things just and right to me. And exactly as in Art one is only concerned with what a particular thing is at a particular moment to oneself, so it is also in the ethical evolution of one's character. I have got to make everything that has happened to me good for me. The plank-bed, the loathsome food, the hard ropes shredded into oakum till one's fingertips grow dull with pain, the menial offices with which each day begins and finishes, the harsh orders that routine seems to necessitate, the dreadful dress that makes sorrow grotesque to look at, the silence, the solitude, the shame – each and all of these things I have to transform into a spiritual experience. There is not a single degradation of the body which I must not try and make into a spiritualising of the soul.

I want to get to the point when I shall be able to say, quite simply and without affectation, that the two great turning-points of my life were when my father sent me to Oxford, and when society sent me to prison. I will not say that it is the best thing that could have happened to me, for that phrase would savour of too great bitterness towards myself. I would sooner say, or hear it said of me, that I was so typical a child of my age that in my perversity, and for that perversity's sake, I turned the good things of my life to evil, and the evil things of my life to good. What is said, however, by myself or by others matters little. The important thing, the thing that lies before me, the thing that I have to do, or be for the brief remainder of my days one maimed, marred, and incomplete, is to absorb into my nature all that has been done to me, to make it part of me, to accept it without complaint, fear, or reluctance. The supreme vice is shallowness. Whatever is realised is right.

When first I was put into prison some people advised me to try and forget who I was. It was ruinous advice. It is only by realising what I am that I have found comfort of any kind. Now

I am advised by others to try on my release to forget that I have ever been in a prison at all. I know that would be equally fatal. It would mean that I would be always haunted by an intolerable sense of disgrace, and that those things that are meant as much for me as for anyone else – the beauty of the sun and the moon, the pageant of the seasons, the music of daybreak and the silence of great nights, the rain falling through the leaves, or the dew creeping over the grass and making it silver – would all be tainted for me, and lose their healing power and their power of communicating joy. To reject one's own experiences is to arrest one's own development. To deny one's own experiences is to put a lie into the lips of one's own life. It is no less than a denial of the Soul. For just as the body absorbs things of all kinds, things common and unclean no less than those that the priest or a vision has cleansed, and converts them into swiftness or strength, into the play of beautiful muscles and the moulding of fair flesh, into the curves and colours of the hair, the lips, the eye: so the Soul, in its turn, has its nutritive functions also, and can transform into noble moods of thought, and passions of high import, what in itself is base, cruel, and degrading: nay more, may find in these its most august modes of assertion, and can often reveal itself most perfectly through what was intended to desecrate or destroy.

The fact of my having been the common prisoner of a common gaol I must frankly accept, and, curious as it may seem to you, one of the things I shall have to teach myself is not to be ashamed of it. I must accept it as a punishment, and if one is ashamed of having been punished, one might just as well never have been punished at all. Of course there are many things of which I was convicted that I had not done, but then there are many things of which I was convicted that I had done, and a still greater number of things in my life for which I was never indicted at all. And as for what I have said in this letter, that the gods are strange and punish us for what is good and humane in us as much as for what is evil and perverse, I must accept the fact that one is punished for the good as well as for the evil that one does. I have no doubt that it is quite right one should be. It helps one, or should help one, to realise both, and not to be too conceited about either. And if I then am not ashamed of my punishment, as I hope not to be, I shall be able to think, and walk, and live with freedom.

Many men on their release carry their prison along with them into the air, hide it as a secret disgrace in their hearts, and at length like poor poisoned things creep into some hole and die. It is wretched that they should have to do so, and it is wrong, terribly wrong, of Society that it should force them to do so. Society takes upon itself the right to inflict appalling punishments on the individual, but it also has the supreme vice of shallowness, and fails to realise what it has done. When the man's punishment is over, it leaves him to himself: that is to say it abandons him at the very moment when its highest duty towards him begins. It is really ashamed of its own actions, and shuns those whom it has punished, as people shun a creditor whose debt they cannot pay, or one on whom they have inflicted an irreparable, an irredeemable wrong. I claim on my side that if I realise what I have suffered, Society should realise what it has inflicted on me: and there should be no bitterness or hate on either side.

Of course I know that from one point of view things will be made more difficult for me than for others; must indeed, by the very nature of the case, be made so. The poor thieves and outcasts who are imprisoned here with me are in many respects more fortunate than I am. The little way in grey city or green field that saw their sin is small: to find those who know nothing of what they have done they need go no further than a bird might fly between the twilight before dawn and dawn itself: but for me 'the world is shrivelled to a handsbreadth',[78] and everywhere I turn my name is written on the rocks in lead. For I have come, not from obscurity into the momentary notoriety of crime, but from a sort of eternity of fame to a sort of eternity of infamy, and sometimes seem to myself to have shown, if indeed it required showing, that between the famous and the infamous there is but one step, if so much as one.

Still, in the very fact that people will recognise me wherever I go, and know all about my life, as far as its follies go, I can discern something good for me. It will force on me the necessity of again asserting myself as an artist, and as soon as I possibly can. If I can produce even one more beautiful work of art I shall be able to rob malice of its venom, and cowardice of its sneer, and to pluck out the tongue of scorn by the roots. And if life be, as it surely is, a problem to me, I am no less a problem to Life. People must adopt some attitude towards me, and so pass judgment both on themselves and me. I need not say I am not talking of particular individuals. The only people I would care to be with now are artists and people who have suffered: those who know what Beauty is, and those who know what Sorrow is: nobody else interests me. Nor am I making any demands on Life. In all that I have said I am simply concerned with my own mental attitude towards life as a whole: and I feel that not to be ashamed of having been punished is one of the first points I must attain to, for the sake of my own perfection, and because I am so imperfect.

Then I must learn how to be happy. Once I knew it, or thought I knew it, by instinct. It was always springtime once in my heart. My temperament was akin to joy. I filled my life to the very brim with pleasure, as one might fill a cup to the very brim with wine. Now I am approaching life from a completely new standpoint, and even to conceive happiness is often extremely difficult for me. I remember during my first term at Oxford reading in Pater's *Renaissance* – that book which has had such a strange influence over my life – how Dante places low in the Inferno those who wilfully live in sadness,[79] and going to the College Library and turning to the passage in the *Divine Comedy* where beneath the dreary marsh lie those who were 'sullen in the sweet air', saying for ever through their sighs:

> *Tristi fummo*
> *nell' aer dolce che dal sol s'allegra.*[80]

I knew the Church condemned *accidia*,[81] but the whole idea seemed to me quite fantastic, just the sort of sin, I fancied, a priest who knew nothing about real life would invent. Nor could I understand how Dante, who says that 'sorrow remarries us to God',[82] could have been so harsh to those who were enamoured of melancholy, if any such there really were. I had no idea that some day this would become to me one of the greatest temptations of my life.

While I was in Wandsworth Prison I longed to die. It was my one desire. When after two months in the Infirmary I was transferred here, and found myself growing gradually better in physical health, I was filled with rage. I determined to commit suicide on the very day on which I left prison. After a time that evil mood passed away, and I made up my mind to live, but to wear gloom as a King wears purple: never to smile again: to turn whatever house I entered into a house of mourning: to make my friends walk slowly in sadness with me: to teach them that melancholy is the true secret of life: to maim them with an alien sorrow: to mar them with my own pain. Now I feel quite differently. I see it would be both ungrateful and unkind of me to pull so long a face that when my friends came to see me they would have to make their faces still longer in order to show their sympathy, or, if I desired to entertain them, to invite them to sit down silently to bitter herbs and funeral baked meats. I must learn how to be cheerful and happy.

The last two occasions on which I was allowed to see my friends here I tried to be as cheerful as possible, and to show my cheerfulness in order to make them some slight return for their trouble in coming all the way from town to visit me. It is only a slight return, I know, but it is the one, I feel certain, that pleases them most. I saw Robbie for an hour on Saturday week, and I tried to give the fullest possible expression to the delight I really felt at our meeting.[83] And that, in the views and ideas I am here shaping for myself, I am quite right is shown to me by the fact that now for the first time since my imprisonment I have a real desire to live.

There is before me so much to do that I would regard it as a terrible tragedy if I died before I was allowed to complete at any rate a little of it. I see new developments in Art and Life, each one of which is a fresh mode of perfection. I long to live so that I can explore what is no less than a new world to me. Do you want to know what this new world is? I think you can guess what it is. It is the world in which I have been living.

Sorrow, then, and all that it teaches one, is my new world. I used to live entirely for pleasure. I shunned sorrow and suffering of every kind. I hated both. I resolved to ignore them as far as possible, to treat them, that is to say, as modes of imperfection. They were not part of my scheme of life. They had no place in my philosophy. My mother, who knew life as a whole, used often to quote to me Goethe's lines – written by Carlyle in a book he had given her years ago – and translated, I fancy, by him also:

> Who never ate his bread in sorrow,
> Who never spent the midnight hours
> Weeping and waiting for the morrow,
> He knows you not, ye Heavenly Powers.[84]

They were the lines that noble Queen of Prussia, whom Napoleon treated with such coarse brutality, used to quote in her humiliation and exile:[85] they were lines my mother often quoted in the troubles of her later life: I absolutely declined to accept or admit the enormous truth hidden in them. I could not understand it. I remember quite well how I used to tell her that I did not want to eat my bread in sorrow, or to pass any night weeping and watching for a more bitter dawn. I had no idea that it was one of the special things that the Fates had in store for me; that for a whole year of my life, indeed, I was to do little else. But so has my portion been meted out to me; and during the last few months I have, after terrible struggles and difficulties, been able to comprehend some of the lessons hidden in the heart of pain. Clergymen, and people who use phrases without wisdom, sometimes talk of suffering as a mystery. It is really a revelation. One discerns things that one never discerned before. One approaches the whole of history from a different standpoint. What one had felt dimly through instinct, about Art, is intellectually and emotionally realised with perfect clearness of vision and absolute intensity of apprehension.

I now see that sorrow, being the supreme emotion of which man is capable, is at once the type and test of all great Art. What the artist is always looking for is that mode of existence in which soul and body are one and indivisible: in which the outward is expressive of the inward: in which Form reveals. Of such modes of existence there are not a few: youth and the arts preoccupied with youth may serve as a model for us at one moment: at another, we may like to think that, in its subtlety and sensitiveness of impression, its suggestion of a spirit dwelling in external things and making its raiment of earth and air, of mist and city alike, and in the morbid sympathy of its moods, and tones and colours, modern landscape art is realising for us pictorially what was realised in such plastic perfection by the Greeks. Music, in which all subject is absorbed in expression and cannot be separated from it, is a complex example, and a flower or a child a simple example of what I mean: but Sorrow is the ultimate type both in life and Art.

Behind Joy and Laughter there may be a temperament, coarse, hard and callous. But behind Sorrow there is always Sorrow. Pain, unlike Pleasure, wears no mask. Truth in Art is not any correspondence between the essential idea and the accidental existence; it is not the resemblance of shape to shadow, or of the form mirrored in the crystal to the form itself: it is no Echo coming from a hollow hill, any more than it is the well of silver water in the valley that shows the Moon to the Moon and Narcissus to Narcissus. Truth in Art is the unity of a thing with itself: the outward rendered expressive of the inward: the soul made incarnate: the body instinct with spirit. For this reason there is no truth comparable to Sorrow. There are times when Sorrow seems to me to be the only truth. Other things may be illusions of the eye or the appetite, made to blind the one and cloy the other, but out of Sorrow have the worlds been built, and at the birth of a child or a star there is pain.

More than this, there is about Sorrow an intense, an extraordinary reality. I have said of myself that I was one who stood in symbolic relations to the art and culture of my age. There is not a single wretched man in this wretched place along with me who does not stand in symbolic relations to the very secret of life. For the secret of life is suffering. It is what is hidden behind everything. When we begin to live, what is sweet is so sweet to us, and what is bitter so bitter, that we inevitably direct all our desires towards pleasure, and seek not merely for 'a month or twain to feed on honeycomb',[86] but for all our years to taste no other food, ignorant the while that we may be really starving the soul.

I remember talking once on this subject to one of the most beautiful personalities I have ever known:[87] a woman, whose sympathy and noble kindness to me both before and since the tragedy of my imprisonment have been beyond power of description: one who has really assisted me, though she does not know it, to bear the burden of my troubles more than anyone else in the whole world has: and all through the mere fact of her existence: through her being what she is, partly an ideal and partly an influence, a suggestion of what one might become, as well as a real help towards becoming it, a soul that renders the common air sweet, and makes what is spiritual seem as simple and natural as sunlight or the sea, one for whom Beauty and Sorrow walk hand in hand and have the same message. On the occasion of which I am thinking I recall distinctly how I said to her that there was enough suffering in one narrow London lane to show that God did not love man, and that wherever there was any sorrow, though but that of a child in some little garden weeping over a fault that it had or had not committed, the whole face of creation was completely marred. I was entirely wrong. She told me so, but I could not believe her. I was not in the sphere in which such belief was to be attained to. Now it seems to me that Love of some kind is the only possible explanation of the extraordinary amount of suffering that there is in the world. I cannot conceive any other explanation. I am convinced that there is no other, and that if the worlds have indeed, as I have said, been built out of Sorrow, it has been by the hands of Love, because in no other way could the Soul of man for whom the worlds are made reach the full stature of its perfection. Pleasure for the beautiful body, but Pain for the beautiful Soul.

When I say that I am convinced of these things I speak with too much pride. Far off, like a perfect pearl, one can see the city of God. It is so wonderful that it seems as if a child could reach it in a summer's day. And so a child could. But with me and such as I am it is different. One can realise a thing in a single moment, but one loses it in the long hours that follow with leaden feet. It is so difficult to keep 'heights that the soul is competent to gain'.[88] We think in Eternity, but we move slowly through Time: and how slowly time goes with us who lie in prison I need not speak again, nor of the weariness and despair that creep back into one's cell, and into the cell of one's heart, with such strange insistence that one has, as it were, to garnish and sweep one's house for their coming, as for an unwelcome guest, or a bitter master, or a slave whose slave it is one's chance or choice to be. And, though at present you may find it a thing hard to believe, it is true none the less that for you, living in freedom and idleness and comfort, it is more easy to learn the lessons of Humility than it is for me, who begin the day by going down on my knees and washing the floor of my cell. For prison-life, with its endless privations and restrictions, makes one rebellious. The most terrible thing about it is not that it breaks one's heart – hearts are made to be broken – but that it turns one's heart to stone. One sometimes feels that it is only with a front of brass and a lip of scorn that one can get through the day at all. And he who is in a state of rebellion cannot receive grace, to use the phrase of which the Church is so fond – so rightly fond, I dare say – for in life, as in Art, the mood of rebellion closes up the channels of the soul, and shuts out the airs of heaven. Yet I must learn these lessons here, if I am to learn them anywhere, and must be filled with joy if my feet are on the right road, and my face set towards the 'gate which is called Beautiful',[89] though I may fall many times in the mire, and often in the mist go astray.

This new life, as through my love of Dante I like sometimes to call it, is, of course, no new life at all, but simply the continuance, by means of development, and evolution, of my former life. I remember when I was at Oxford saying to one of my friends – as we were strolling round Magdalen's narrow bird-haunted walks one morning in the June before I took my degree – that I wanted to eat of the fruit of all the trees in the garden of the world, and that I was going out into the world with that passion in my soul. And so, indeed, I went out, and so I lived. My only mistake was that I confined myself so exclusively to the trees of what seemed to me the sungilt side of the garden, and shunned the other side for its shadow and its gloom. Failure, disgrace, poverty, sorrow, despair, suffering, tears even, the broken words that come from the lips of pain, remorse that makes one walk in thorns, conscience that condemns, self-abasement that punishes, the misery that puts ashes on its head, the anguish that chooses sackcloth for its raiment and into its own drink puts gall – all these were things of which I was afraid. And as I had determined to know nothing of them, I was forced to taste each one of them in turn, to feed on them, to have for a season, indeed, no other food at all. I don't regret for a single moment having lived for pleasure. I did it to the full, as one should do everything that one does to the full. There was no pleasure I did not experience. I threw the pearl of my soul into a cup of wine. I went down the primrose path to the sound of flutes. I lived on honeycomb. But to have continued the same life would have been wrong because it would have been limiting. I had to pass on. The other half of the garden had its secrets for me also.

Of course all this is foreshadowed and prefigured in my art. Some of it is in 'The Happy Prince', some of it in 'The Young King', notably in the passage where the Bishop says to the kneeling boy, 'Is not He who made misery wiser than thou art?' a phrase which when I wrote it seemed to me little more than a phrase: a great deal of it is hidden away in the note of Doom that like a purple thread runs through the gold cloth of *Dorian Gray*: in 'The Critic as Artist' it is set forth in many colours: in *The Soul of Man*[90] it is written down simply and in letters too easy to read: it is one of the refrains whose recurring *motifs* make *Salomé* so like a piece of music and bind it together as a ballad: in the prose-poem of the man who from the bronze of the image of the 'Pleasure that liveth for a Moment' has to make the image of the 'Sorrow that abideth for Ever' it is incarnate.[91] It could not have been otherwise. At every single moment of one's life one is what one is going to be no less than what one has been. Art is a symbol, because man is a symbol.

It is, if I can fully attain to it, the ultimate realisation of the artistic life. For the artistic life is simple self-development. Humility in the artist is his frank acceptance of all experiences, just as Love in the artist is simply that sense of Beauty that reveals to the world its body and its soul. In *Marius the Epicurean*[92] Pater seeks to reconcile the artistic life with the life of religion in the deep, sweet and austere sense of the word. But Marius is little more than a spectator: an ideal spectator indeed, and one to whom it is given 'to contemplate the spectacle of life with appropriate emotions', which Wordsworth defines as the poet's true aim:[93] yet a spectator merely, and perhaps a little too much occupied with the comeliness of the vessels of the Sanctuary to notice that it is the Sanctuary of Sorrow that he is gazing at.

I see a far more intimate and immediate connection between the true life of Christ and the true life of the artist, and I take a keen pleasure in the reflection that long before Sorrow had made my days her own and bound me to her wheel I had written in *The Soul of Man* that he who would lead a Christ-like life must be entirely and absolutely himself, and had taken as my types not merely the shepherd on the hillside and the prisoner in his cell but also the painter to whom the world is a pageant and the poet for whom the world is a song. I remember saying once to André Gide, as we sat together in some Paris café, that while Metaphysics had but little real interest for me, and Morality absolutely none, there was nothing that either Plato or Christ had said that could not be transferred immediately into the sphere of Art, and there find its complete fulfilment. It was a generalisation as profound as it was novel.

Nor is it merely that we can discern in Christ that close union of personality with perfection which forms the real distinction between classical and romantic Art and makes Christ the true precursor of the romantic movement in life, but the very basis of his nature was the same as that of the nature of the artist, an intense and flamelike imagination. He realised in the entire sphere of human relations that imaginative sympathy which in the sphere of Art is the sole secret of creation. He understood the leprosy of the leper, the darkness of the blind, the fierce misery of those who live for pleasure, the strange poverty of the rich. You can see now – can you not? – that when you wrote to me in my trouble, 'When you are not on your pedestal you are not interesting. The next time you are ill I will go away at

once',[94] you were as remote from the tr...
as you were from what Matthew Arnol...
Jesus'.[95] Either would have taught you that...
to another happens to oneself, and if you wa...
to read at dawn and at night-time and for pleas...
write up on the wall of your house in letters for t...
and the moon to silver '*Whatever happens to anoth...
to oneself', and should anyone ask you what such a ...scrip-
tion can possibly mean you can answer that it means 'Lord
Christ's heart and Shakespeare's brain'.

Christ's place indeed is with the poets. His whole concep-
tion of Humanity sprang right out of the imagination and can
only be realised by it. What God was to the Pantheist, man
was to him. He was the first to conceive the divided races as a
unity. Before his time there had been gods and men. He alone
saw that on the hills of life there were but God and Man, and,
feeling through the mysticism of sympathy that in himself each
had been made incarnate, he calls himself the Son of the One
or the son of the other, according to his mood. More than any-
one else in history he wakes in us that temper of wonder to
which Romance always appeals. There is still something to
me almost incredible in the idea of a young Galilean peasant
imagining that he could bear on his own shoulders the burden
of the entire world: all that had been already done and suf-
fered, and all that was yet to be done and suffered: the sins of
Nero, of Caesar Borgia, of Alexander VI,[96] and of him who
was Emperor of Rome and Priest of the Sun:[97] the sufferings of
those whose name is Legion and whose dwelling is among the
tombs,[98] oppressed nationalities, factory children, thieves, peo-
ple in prison, outcasts, those who are dumb under oppression
and whose silence is heard only of God: and not merely imagin-
ing this but actually achieving it, so that at the present moment
all who come in contact with his personality, even though they
may neither bow to his altar nor kneel before his priest, yet
somehow find that the ugliness of their sins is taken away and
the beauty of their sorrow revealed to them.

I have said of him that he ranks with the poets. That is true.
Shelley and Sophocles are of his company. But his entire life

...e most wonderful of poems. For 'pity and terror'[99] ...e is nothing in the entire cycle of Greek Tragedy to touch it. The absolute purity of the protagonist raises the entire scheme to a height of romantic art from which the sufferings of 'Thebes and Pelops' line'[100] are by their very horror excluded, and shows how wrong Aristotle was when he said in his treatise on the Drama that it would be impossible to bear the spectacle of one blameless in pain.[101] Nor in Aeschylus or Dante, those stern masters of tenderness, in Shakespeare, the most purely human of all the great artists, in the whole of Celtic myth and legend where the loveliness of the world is shown through a mist of tears, and the life of a man is no more than the life of a flower, is there anything that for sheer simplicity of pathos wedded and made one with sublimity of tragic effect can be said to equal or approach even the last act of Christ's Passion. The little supper with his companions, one of whom had already sold him for a price: the anguish in the quiet moonlit olive-garden: the false friend coming close to him so as to betray him with a kiss: the friend who still believed in him and on whom as on a rock he had hoped to build a house of Refuge for Man denying him as the bird cried to the dawn: his own utter loneliness, his submission, his acceptance of everything: and along with it all such scenes as the high priest of Orthodoxy rending his raiment in wrath, and the Magistrate of Civil Justice calling for water in the vain hope of cleansing himself of that stain of innocent blood that makes him the scarlet figure of History: the coronation-ceremony of Sorrow, one of the most wonderful things in the whole of recorded time: the crucifixion of the Innocent One before the eyes of his mother and of the disciple whom he loved: the soldiers gambling and throwing dice for his clothes: the terrible death by which he gave the world its most eternal symbol: and his final burial in the tomb of the rich man, his body swathed in Egyptian linen with costly spices and perfumes as though he had been a King's son – when one contemplates all this from the point of view of Art alone one cannot but be grateful that the supreme office of the Church should be the playing of the tragedy without the shedding of blood, the mystical presentation by means of dialogue and costume and gesture even of the Passion of her Lord, and it is always a source of pleasure and awe to me to remember that the ultimate survival of the Greek Chorus, lost elsewhere to art, is to be found in the servitor answering the priest at Mass.

Yet the whole life of Christ – so entirely may Sorrow and Beauty be made one in their meaning and manifestation – is really an idyll, though it ends with the veil of the temple being rent, and the darkness coming over the face of the earth, and the stone rolled to the door of the sepulchre. One always thinks of him as a young bridegroom with his companions, as indeed he somewhere describes himself, or as a shepherd straying through a valley with his sheep in search of green meadow or cool stream, or as a singer trying to build out of music the walls of the city of God, or as a lover for whose love the whole world was too small. His miracles seem to me as exquisite as the coming of Spring, and quite as natural. I see no difficulty at all in believing that such was the charm of his personality that his mere presence could bring peace to souls in anguish, and that those who touched his garments or his hands forgot their pain: or that as he passed by on the highway of life people who had seen nothing of life's mysteries saw them clearly, and others who had been deaf to every voice but that of Pleasure heard for the first time the voice of Love and found it as 'musical as is Apollo's lute':[102] or that evil passions fled at his approach, and men whose dull unimaginative lives had been but a mode of death rose as it were from the grave when he called them: or that when he taught on the hillside the multitude forgot their hunger and thirst and the cares of this world, and that to his friends who listened to him as he sat at meat the coarse food seemed delicate, and the water had the taste of good wine, and the whole house became full of the odour and sweetness of nard.

Renan in his *Vie de Jésus* – that gracious Fifth Gospel, the Gospel according to St Thomas one might call it – says somewhere that Christ's great achievement was that he made himself as much loved after his death as he had been during his lifetime.[103] And certainly, if his place is among the poets, he is the leader of all the lovers. He saw that love was that lost secret of the world for which the wise men had been looking, and that it was only through love that one could approach either the heart of the leper or the feet of God.

And, above all, Christ is the most supreme of Individualists. Humility, like the artistic acceptance of all experiences, is merely a mode of manifestation. It is man's soul that Christ is always looking for. He calls it 'God's Kingdom' – ἡ βασιλεία τοῦ θεοῦ – and finds it in everyone. He compares it to little things, to a tiny seed, to a handful of leaven, to a pearl. That is because one only realises one's soul by getting rid of all alien passions, all acquired culture, and all external possessions be they good or evil.

I bore up against everything with some stubbornness of will and much rebellion of nature till I had absolutely nothing left in the world but Cyril. I had lost my name, my position, my happiness, my freedom, my wealth. I was a prisoner and a pauper. But I had still one beautiful thing left, my own eldest son. Suddenly he was taken away from me by the law. It was a blow so appalling that I did not know what to do, so I flung myself on my knees, and bowed my head, and wept and said 'The body of a child is as the body of the Lord: I am not worthy of either.'[104] That moment seemed to save me. I saw then that the only thing for me was to accept everything. Since then – curious as it will no doubt sound to you – I have been happier.

It was of course my soul in its ultimate essence that I had reached. In many ways I had been its enemy, but I found it waiting for me as a friend. When one comes in contact with the soul it makes one simple as a child, as Christ said one should be. It is tragic how few people ever 'possess their souls' before they die.[105] 'Nothing is more rare in any man', says Emerson, 'than an act of his own.'[106] It is quite true. Most people are other people. Their thoughts are someone else's opinions, their life a mimicry, their passions a quotation. Christ was not merely the supreme Individualist, but he was the first in History. People have tried to make him out an ordinary Philanthropist, like the dreadful philanthropists of the nineteenth century, or ranked him as an Altruist with the unscientific and sentimental. But he was really neither one nor the other. Pity he has, of course, for the poor, for those who are shut up in prisons, for the lowly, for the wretched, but he has far more pity for the rich, for the hard Hedonists, for those who waste their freedom in becoming slaves to things, for those who wear soft raiment and live in Kings' houses. Riches and Pleasure seemed to him to be really greater tragedies than Poverty and Sorrow. And as for Altruism, who knew better than he that it is vocation not volition that determines us, and that one cannot gather grapes off thorns or figs from thistles?

To live for others as a definite self-conscious aim was not his creed. It was not the basis of his creed. When he says 'Forgive your enemies', it is not for the sake of the enemy but for one's own sake that he says so, and because Love is more beautiful than Hate. In his entreaty to the young man whom when he looked on he loved, 'Sell all that thou hast and give it to the poor',[107] it is not of the state of the poor that he is thinking but of the soul of the young man, the lovely soul that wealth was marring. In his view of life he is one with the artist who knows that by the inevitable law of self-perfection the poet must sing, and the sculptor think in bronze, and the painter make the world a mirror for his moods, as surely and as certainly as the hawthorn must blossom in Spring, and the corn burn to gold at harvest-time, and the Moon in her ordered wanderings change from shield to sickle, and from sickle to shield.

But while Christ did not say to men, 'Live for others', he pointed out that there was no difference at all between the lives of others and one's own life. By this means he gave to man an extended, a Titan personality. Since his coming the history of each separate individual is, or can be made, the history of the world. Of course Culture has intensified the personality of man. Art has made us myriad-minded. Those who have the artistic temperament go into exile with Dante and learn how salt is the bread of others and how steep their stairs:[108] they catch for a moment the serenity and calm of Goethe, and yet know but too well why Baudelaire cried to God:

> *O Seigneur, donnez-moi la force et le courage*
> *De contempler mon corps et mon cœur sans dégoût.*[109]

Out of Shakespeare's sonnets they draw, to their own hurt it may be, the secret of his love and make it their own: they look with new eyes on modern life because they have listened to one of Chopin's nocturnes, or handled Greek things, or read the story of the passion of some dead man for some dead woman whose hair was like threads of fine gold and whose mouth was as a pomegranate. But the sympathy of the artistic temperament is necessarily with what has found expression. In words or in colour, in music or in marble, behind the painted masks of an Aeschylean play or through some Sicilian shepherd's pierced and jointed reeds the man and his message must have been revealed.

To the artist, expression is the only mode under which he can conceive life at all. To him what is dumb is dead. But to Christ it was not so. With a width and wonder of imagination, that fills one almost with awe, he took the entire world of the inarticulate, the voiceless world of pain, as his kingdom, and made of himself its eternal mouthpiece. Those of whom I have spoken, who are dumb under oppression and 'whose silence is heard only of God',[110] he chose as his brothers. He sought to become eyes to the blind, ears to the deaf, and a cry on the lips of those whose tongue had been tied. His desire was to be to the myriads who had found no utterance a very trumpet through which they might call to Heaven. And feeling, with the artistic nature of one to whom Sorrow and Suffering were modes through which he could realise his conception of the Beautiful, that an idea is of no value till it becomes incarnate and is made an image, he makes of himself the image of the Man of Sorrows, and as such has fascinated and dominated Art as no Greek god ever succeeded in doing.

For the Greek gods, in spite of the white and red of their fair fleet limbs, were not really what they appeared to be. The curved brow of Apollo was like the sun's disk crescent over a hill at dawn, and his feet were as the wings of the morning, but he himself had been cruel to Marsyas and had made Niobe childless: in the steel shields of the eyes of Pallas there had been no pity for Arachne:[111] the pomp and peacocks of Hera were all that was really noble about her: and the Father of the Gods himself had been too fond of the daughters of men. The two deep suggestive figures of Greek mythology were, for religion, Demeter, an earth-goddess, not one of the Olympians, and, for art, Dionysus, the son of a mortal woman to whom the moment of his birth had proved the moment of her death also.

But Life itself from its lowliest and most humble sphere produced one far more marvellous than the mother of Proserpina or the son of Semele.[112] Out of the carpenter's shop at Nazareth had come a personality infinitely greater than any made by myth or legend, and one, strangely enough, destined to reveal to the world the mystical meaning of wine and the real beauty of the lilies of the field as none, either on Cithaeron or at Enna,[113] had ever done it.

The song of Isaiah, '*He is despised and rejected of men, a man of sorrows and acquainted with grief: and we hid as it were our faces from him*',[114] had seemed to him to be a prefiguring of himself, and in him the prophecy was fulfilled. We must not be afraid of such a phrase. Every single work of art is the fulfilment of a prophecy. For every work of art is the conversion of an idea into an image. Every single human being should be the fulfilment of a prophecy. For every human being should be the realisation of some ideal, either in the mind of God or in the mind of man. Christ found the type, and fixed it, and the dream of a Virgilian poet, either at Jerusalem or at Babylon, became in the long progress of the centuries incarnate in him for whom the world was waiting.[115] '*His visage was marred more than any man's, and his form more than the sons of men*'[116] are among the signs noted by Isaiah as distinguishing the new ideal, and as soon as Art understood what was meant it opened like a flower at the presence of one in whom truth in Art was set forth as it had never been before. For is not truth in Art, as I have said, 'that in which the outward is expressive of the inward; in which the soul is made flesh, and the body instinct with spirit: in which Form reveals'?[117]

To me one of the things in history the most to be regretted is that the Christ's own renaissance which had produced the Cathedral of Chartres, the Arthurian cycle of legends, the life of St Francis of Assisi, the art of Giotto, and Dante's *Divine*

Comedy, was not allowed to develop on its own lines but was interrupted and spoiled by the dreary classical Renaissance that gave us Petrarch, and Raphael's frescoes, and Palladian architecture, and formal French tragedy, and St Paul's Cathedral, and Pope's poetry, and everything that is made from without and by dead rules, and does not spring from within through some spirit informing it. But wherever there is a romantic movement in Art, there somehow, and under some form, is Christ, or the soul of Christ. He is in *Romeo and Juliet*, in the *Winter's Tale*, in Provençal poetry, in 'The Ancient Mariner', in 'La Belle Dame sans Merci', and in Chatterton's 'Ballad of Charity'.[118]

We owe to him the most diverse things and people. Hugo's *Les Misérables*, Baudelaire's *Fleurs du Mal*, the note of pity in Russian novels, the stained glass and tapestries and quattrocento work of Burne-Jones and Morris, Verlaine and Verlaine's poems, belong to him no less than the Tower of Giotto, Lancelot and Guinevere, Tannhäuser, the troubled romantic marbles of Michelangelo, pointed architecture, and the love of children and flowers – for both of whom, indeed, in classical art there was but little place, hardly enough for them to grow or play in, but who from the twelfth century down to our own day have been continually making their appearance in art, under various modes and at various times, coming fitfully and wilfully as children and flowers are apt to do, Spring always seeming to one as if the flowers had been hiding, and only came out into the sun because they were afraid that grown-up people would grow tired of looking for them and give up the search, and the life of a child being no more than an April day on which there is both rain and sun for the narcissus.

And it is the imaginative quality of Christ's own nature that makes him this palpitating centre of romance. The strange figures of poetic drama and ballad are made by the imagination of others, but out of his own imagination entirely did Jesus of Nazareth create himself. The cry of Isaiah had really no more to do with his coming than the song of the nightingale has to do with the rising of the moon – no more, though perhaps no less. He was the denial as well as the affirmation of prophecy. For every expectation that he fulfilled, there was another that

he destroyed. In all beauty, says Bacon, there is 'some strange-
ness of proportion',[119] and of those who are born of the spirit,
of those, that is to say, who like himself are dynamic forces,
Christ says that they are like the wind that 'bloweth where
it listeth and no man can tell whence it cometh or whither it
goeth'.[120] That is why he is so fascinating to artists. He has all
the colour-elements of life: mystery, strangeness, pathos, sug-
gestion, ecstasy, love. He appeals to the temper of wonder, and
creates that mood by which alone he can be understood.

And it is to me a joy to remember that if he is 'of imagina-
tion all compact',[121] the world itself is of the same substance. I
said in *Dorian Gray* that the great sins of the world take place
in the brain,[122] but it is in the brain that everything takes place.
We know now that we do not see with the eye or hear with the
ear. They are merely channels for the transmission, adequate
or inadequate, of sense-impressions. It is in the brain that the
poppy is red, that the apple is odorous, that the skylark sings.

Of late I have been studying the four prose-poems about
Christ with some diligence. At Christmas I managed to get hold
of a Greek Testament, and every morning, after I have cleaned
my cell and polished my tins, I read a little of the Gospels, a
dozen verses taken by chance anywhere. It is a delightful way
of opening the day. To you, in your turbulent, ill-disciplined
life, it would be a capital thing if you would do the same. It
would do you no end of good, and the Greek is quite simple.
Endless repetition, in and out of season, has spoiled for us the
naïveté, the freshness, the simple romantic charm of the Gos-
pels. We hear them read far too often, and far too badly, and
all repetition is anti-spiritual. When one returns to the Greek
it is like going into a garden of lilies out of some narrow and
dark house.

And to me the pleasure is doubled by the reflection that
it is extremely probable that we have the actual terms, the
ipsissima verba, used by Christ. It was always supposed that
Christ talked in Aramaic. Even Renan thought so. But now
we know that the Galilean peasants, like the Irish peasants of
our own day, were bilingual, and that Greek was the ordinary
language of intercourse all over Palestine, as indeed all over

the Eastern world. I never liked the idea that we only knew of Christ's own words through a translation of a translation. It is a delight to me to think that as far as his conversation was concerned, Charmides[123] might have listened to him, and Socrates reasoned with him, and Plato understood him: that he really said ἐγώ εἰμι ὁ ποιμὴν ὁ̂καλός:[124] that when he thought of the lilies of the field and how they neither toil nor spin, his absolute expression was καταμάθετε τὰ κρίνα τοῦ ἀγροῦ πῶς αὐξάνει· οὐ κοπιᾷ οὐδὲ νήθει[125] and that his last word when he cried out 'My life has been completed, has reached its fulfilment, has been perfected' was exactly as St John tells us it was: τετέλεσται:[126] no more.

And while in reading the Gospels – particularly that of St John himself, or whatever early Gnostic took his name and mantle – I see this continual assertion of the imagination as the basis of all spiritual and material life, I see also that to Christ imagination was simply a form of Love, and that to him Love was Lord in the fullest meaning of the phrase. Some six weeks ago I was allowed by the Doctor to have white bread to eat instead of the coarse black or brown bread of ordinary prison fare. It is a great delicacy. To you it will sound strange that dry bread could possibly be a delicacy to anyone. I assure you that to me it is so much so that at the close of each meal I carefully eat whatever crumbs may be left on my tin plate, or have fallen on the rough towel that one uses as a cloth so as not to soil one's table: and do so not from hunger – I get now quite sufficient food – but simply in order that nothing should be wasted of what is given to me. So one should look on love.

Christ, like all fascinating personalities, had the power not merely of saying beautiful things himself, but of making other people say beautiful things to him; and I love the story St Mark tells us about the Greek woman – the γυνὴ Ἑλληνίς – who, when as a trial of her faith he said to her that he could not give her the bread of the bread of the children of Israel, answered him that the little dogs – κυνάρια, 'little dogs' it should be rendered – who are under the table eat of the crumbs that the children let fall.[127] Most people live *for* love and admiration. But it is *by* love and admiration that we should live.[128] If any love is shown us we should recognise that we are quite unworthy of it. Nobody is worthy to be loved. The fact that God loves man shows that in the divine order of ideal things it is written that eternal love is to be given to what is eternally unworthy. Or if that phrase seems to you a bitter one to hear, let us say that everyone is worthy of love, except he who thinks that he is. Love is a sacrament that should be taken kneeling, and *Domine, non sum dignus*[129] should be on the lips and in the hearts of those who receive it. I wish you would sometimes think of that. You need it so much.

If I ever write again, in the sense of producing artistic work, there are just two subjects on which and through which I desire to express myself: one is 'Christ, as the precursor of the Romantic movement in life': the other is 'the Artistic life considered in its relation to Conduct'. The first is, of course, intensely fascinating, for I see in Christ not merely the essentials of the supreme romantic type, but all the accidents, the wilfulnesses even, of the romantic temperament also. He was the first person who ever said to people that they should live 'flower-like' lives. He fixed the phrase. He took children as the type of what people should try to become. He held them up as examples to their elders, which I myself have always thought the chief use of children, if what is perfect should have a use. Dante describes the soul of man as coming from the hand of God 'weeping and laughing like a little child', and Christ also saw that the soul of each one should be *'a guisa di fanciulla, che piangendo e ridendo pargoleggia'*.[130] He felt that life was changeful, fluid, active, and that to allow it to be stereotyped into any form was death. He said that people should not be too serious over material, common interests: that to be unpractical was a great thing: that one should not bother too much over affairs. 'The birds didn't, why should man?' He is charming when he says, 'Take no thought for the morrow. Is not the *soul* more than meat? Is not the *body* more than raiment?'[131] A Greek might have said the latter phrase. It is full of Greek feeling. But only Christ could have said both, and so summed up life perfectly for us.

His morality is all sympathy, just what morality should be. If the only thing he had ever said had been 'Her sins are forgiven her because she loved much', it would have been worth while dying to have said it. His justice is all poetical justice, exactly what justice should be. The beggar goes to heaven because he had been unhappy. I can't conceive a better reason for his being sent there. The people who work for an hour in the vineyard in the cool of the evening receive just as much reward as those who had toiled there all day long in the hot sun. Why shouldn't they? Probably no one deserved anything. Or perhaps they were a different kind of people. Christ had no patience with the dull lifeless mechanical systems that treat people as if they were things, and so treat everybody alike: as if anybody, or anything for that matter, was like aught else in the world. For him there were no laws: there were exceptions merely.

That which is the very keynote of romantic art was to him the proper basis of actual life. He saw no other basis. And when they brought him one taken in the very act of sin and showed him her sentence written in the law and asked him what was to be done, he wrote with his finger on the ground as though he did not hear them, and finally, when they pressed him again and again, looked up and said 'Let him of you who has never sinned be the first to throw the stone at her'. It was worth while living to have said that.

Like all poetical natures, he loved ignorant people. He knew that in the soul of one who is ignorant there is always room for a great idea. But he could not stand stupid people, especially those who are made stupid by education – people who are full of opinions not one of which they can understand, a peculiarly modern type, and one summed up by Christ when he describes it as the type of one who has the key of knowledge, can't use it himself, and won't allow other people to use it, though it may be made to open the gate of God's Kingdom. His chief war was against the Philistines. That is the war every child of light has to wage. Philistinism was the note of the age and community in which he lived. In their heavy inaccessibility to ideas, their dull respectability, their tedious orthodoxy, their worship of vulgar success, their entire preoccupation with the gross materialistic side of life, and their ridiculous estimate of themselves and their importance, the Jew of Jerusalem in Christ's day was the exact counterpart of the British Philistine of our own. Christ mocked at the 'whited sepulchres' of respectability, and fixed that phrase for ever. He treated worldly success as a thing to be absolutely despised. He saw nothing in it at all. He looked on wealth as an encumbrance to a man. He would not hear of life being sacrificed to any system of thought or morals. He pointed out that forms and ceremonies were made for man, not man for forms and ceremonies. He took Sabbatarianism as a type of the things that should be set at nought. The cold philanthropies, the ostentatious public charities, the tedious formalisms so dear to the middle-class mind, he exposed with utter and relentless scorn. To us, what is termed Orthodoxy is merely a facile unintelligent acquiescence, but to them, and in their hands, it was a terrible and paralysing tyranny. Christ swept it aside. He showed that the spirit alone was of value. He took a keen pleasure in pointing out to them that though they were always reading the Law and the Prophets they had not really the smallest idea of what either of them meant. In opposition to their tithing of each separate day into its fixed routine of prescribed duties, as they tithed mint and rue, he preached the enormous importance of living completely for the moment.

Those whom he saved from their sins are saved simply for beautiful moments in their lives. Mary Magdalen, when she sees Christ, breaks the rich vase of alabaster that one of her seven lovers had given her and spills the odorous spices over his tired, dusty feet, and for that one moment's sake sits for ever with Ruth and Beatrice in the tresses of the snow-white Rose of Paradise.[132] All that Christ says to us by way of a little warning is that *every* moment should be beautiful, that the soul should *always* be ready for the coming of the Bridegroom, *always* waiting for the voice of the Lover. Philistinism being simply that side of man's nature that is not illumined by the imagination, he sees all the lovely influences of life as modes of Light: the imagination itself is the world-light, τὸ φῶς τοῦ κοσμοῦ: the world is made by it, and yet the world cannot understand it: that is because the imagination is simply a manifestation of

Love, and it is love, and the capacity for it, that distinguishes one human being from another.

But it is when he deals with the Sinner that he is most romantic, in the sense of most real. The world had always loved the Saint as being the nearest possible approach to the perfection of God. Christ, through some divine instinct in him, seems to have always loved the sinner as being the nearest possible approach to the perfection of man. His primary desire was not to reform people, any more than his primary desire was to relieve suffering. To turn an interesting thief into a tedious honest man was not his aim. He would have thought little of the Prisoners' Aid Society and other modern movements of the kind. The conversion of a Publican into a Pharisee would not have seemed to him a great achievement by any means. But in a manner not yet understood of the world he regarded sin and suffering as being in themselves beautiful, holy things, and modes of perfection. It *sounds* a very dangerous idea. It is so. All great ideas *are* dangerous. That it was Christ's creed admits of no doubt. That it is the true creed I don't doubt myself.

Of course the sinner must repent. But why? Simply because otherwise he would be unable to realise what he had done. The moment of repentance is the moment of initiation. More than that. It is the means by which one alters one's past. The Greeks thought that impossible. They often say in their gnomic aphorisms 'Even the Gods cannot alter the past'.[133] Christ showed that the commonest sinner could do it. That it was the one thing he could do. Christ, had he been asked, would have said – I feel quite certain about it – that the moment the prodigal son fell on his knees and wept he really made his having wasted his substance with harlots, and then kept swine and hungered for the husks they ate, beautiful and holy incidents in his life. It is difficult for most people to grasp the idea. I dare say one has to go to prison to understand it. If so, it may be worth while going to prison.

There is something so unique about Christ. Of course, just as there are false dawns before the dawn itself, and winter-days so full of sudden sunlight that they will cheat the wise crocus into squandering its gold before its time, and make some foolish bird call to its mate to build on barren boughs, so there were Christians before Christ. For that we should be grateful. The unfortunate thing is that there have been none since. I make one exception, St Francis of Assisi. But then God had given him at his birth the soul of a poet, and he himself when quite young had in mystical marriage taken Poverty as his bride; and with the soul of a poet and the body of a beggar he found the way to perfection not difficult. He understood Christ, and so he became like him. We do not require the *Liber Conformitatum*[134] to teach us that the life of St Francis was the true *Imitatio Christi*: a poem compared to which the book that bears that name is merely prose. Indeed, that is the charm about Christ, when all is said. He is just like a work of art himself. He does not really teach one anything, but by being brought into his presence one becomes something. And everybody is predestined to his presence. Once at least in his life each man walks with Christ to Emmaus.

As regards the other subject, the relation of the artistic life to conduct, it will no doubt seem strange to you that I should select it. People point to Reading Gaol, and say 'There is where the artistic life leads a man.' Well, it might lead one to worse places. The more mechanical people, to whom life is a shrewd speculation dependent on a careful calculation of ways and means, always know where they are going, and go there. They start with the desire of being the Parish Beadle, and in whatever sphere they are placed, they succeed in being the Parish Beadle and no more. A man whose desire is to be something separate from himself, to be a Member of Parliament, or a successful grocer, or a prominent solicitor, or a judge, or something equally tedious, invariably succeeds in being what he wants to be. That is his punishment. Those who want a mask have to wear it.

But with the dynamic forces of life, and those in whom those dynamic forces become incarnate, it is different. People whose desire is solely for self-realisation never know where they are going. They can't know. In one sense of the word it is, of course, necessary, as the Greek oracle said, to know oneself.[135] That is the first achievement of knowledge. But to recognise that the soul of a man is unknowable is the ultimate achievement of Wisdom. The final mystery is oneself. When one has weighed the sun in a balance, and measured the steps of the moon, and mapped out the seven heavens star by star, there still remains oneself. Who can calculate the orbit of his own soul? When the son of Kish went out to look for his father's asses, he did not know that a man of God was waiting for him with the very chrism of coronation, and that his own soul was already the Soul of a King.[136]

I hope to live long enough, and to produce work of such a character, that I shall be able at the end of my days to say, 'Yes: this is just where the artistic life leads a man.' Two of the most perfect lives I have come across in my own experience are the lives of Verlaine and of Prince Kropotkin: both of them men who passed years in prison:[137] the first, the one Christian poet since Dante, the other a man with the soul of that beautiful white Christ that seems coming out of Russia. And for the last seven or eight months, in spite of a succession of great troubles reaching me from the outside world almost without intermission, I have been placed in direct contact with a new spirit working in this prison through men and things, that has helped me beyond any possibility of expression in words; so that while for the first year of my imprisonment I did nothing else, and can remember doing nothing else, but wring my hands in impotent despair, and say, 'What an ending! What an appalling ending!'; now I try to say to myself, and sometimes when I am not torturing myself do really and sincerely say, 'What a beginning! What a wonderful beginning!' It may really be so. It may become so. If it does, I shall owe much to this new personality[138] that has altered every man's life in this place.

Things in themselves are of little importance, have indeed – let us for once thank Metaphysics for something that she has taught us – no real existence. The spirit alone is of importance. Punishment may be inflicted in such a way that it will heal, not make a wound, just as alms may be given in such a manner that the bread changes to a stone in the hands of the giver. What a change there is – not in the regulations, for they are fixed by iron rule, but in the spirit that uses them as its expression – you can realise when I tell you that had I been released last May, as

I tried to be, I would have left this place loathing it and every official in it with a bitterness of hatred that would have poisoned my life. I have had a year longer of imprisonment, but Humanity has been in the prison along with us all, and now when I go out I shall always remember great kindnesses that I have received here from almost everybody, and on the day of my release will give my thanks to many people and ask to be remembered by them in turn.

The prison-system is absolutely and entirely wrong. I would give anything to be able to alter it when I go out. I intend to try. But there is nothing in the world so wrong but that the spirit of Humanity, which is the spirit of Love, the spirit of the Christ who is not in Churches, may make it, if not right, at least possible to be borne without too much bitterness of heart.

I know also that much is waiting for me outside that is very delightful, from what St Francis of Assisi calls '*my brother the wind*' and '*my sister the rain*',[139] lovely things both of them, down to the shop-windows and sunsets of great cities. If I made a list of all that still remains to me, I don't know where I should stop: for, indeed, God made the world just as much for me as for anyone else. Perhaps I may go out with something I had not got before. I need not tell you that to me Reformations in Morals are as meaningless and vulgar as Reformations in Theology. But while to propose to be a better man is a piece of unscientific cant, to have become a *deeper* man is the privilege of those who have suffered. And such I think I have become. You can judge for yourself.

If after I go out a friend of mine gave a feast, and did not invite me to it, I shouldn't mind a bit. I can be perfectly happy by myself. With freedom, books, flowers, and the moon, who could not be happy? Besides, feasts are not for me any more. I have given too many to care about them. That side of life is over for me, very fortunately I dare say. But if, after I go out, a friend of mine had a sorrow, and refused to allow me to share it, I should feel it most bitterly. If he shut the doors of the house of mourning against me I would come back again and again and beg to be admitted, so that I might share in what I was entitled to share in. If he thought me unworthy, unfit to weep with him, I should feel it as the most poignant humiliation, as the most terrible mode in which disgrace could be inflicted on me. But that could not be. I have a right to share in Sorrow, and he who can look at the loveliness of the world, and share its sorrow, and realise something of the wonder of both, is in immediate contact with divine things, and has got as near to God's secret as anyone can get.

Perhaps there may come into my art also, no less than into my life, a still deeper note, one of greater unity of passion, and directness of impulse. Not width but intensity is the true aim of modern Art. We are no longer in Art concerned with the type. It is with the exception we have to do. I cannot put my sufferings into any form they took, I need hardly say. Art only begins where Imitation ends. But something must come into my work, of fuller harmony of words perhaps, of richer cadences, of more curious colour-effects, of simpler architectural-order, of some aesthetic quality at any rate.

When Marsyas was 'torn from the scabbard of his limbs' – *dalla vagina delle membre sue*,[140] to use one of Dante's most terrible, most Tacitean phrases – he had no more song, the Greeks said. Apollo had been victor. The lyre had vanquished the reed. But perhaps the Greeks were mistaken. I hear in much modern Art the cry of Marsyas.[141] It is bitter in Baudelaire, sweet and plaintive in Lamartine, mystic in Verlaine. It is in the deferred resolutions of Chopin's music. It is in the discontent that haunts the recurrent faces of Burne-Jones's women. Even Matthew Arnold, whose song of Callicles tells of 'the triumph of the sweet persuasive lyre', and the 'famous final victory', in such a clear note of lyrical beauty – even he, in the troubled undertone of doubt and distress that haunts his verse, has not a little of it.[142] Neither Goethe nor Wordsworth could heal him, though he followed each in turn, and when he seeks to mourn for 'Thyrsis' or to sing of 'the Scholar Gipsy', it is the reed that he has to take for the rendering of his strain. But whether or not the Phrygian Faun[143] was silent, I cannot be. Expression is as necessary to me as leaf and blossom are to the black branches of the trees that show themselves above the prison wall and are so restless in the wind. Between my art and the world there is now a wide gulf, but between Art and myself there is none. I hope at least that there is none.

To each of us different fates have been meted out. Freedom, pleasure, amusements, a life of ease have been your lot, and you are not worthy of it. My lot has been one of public infamy, of long imprisonment, of misery, of ruin, of disgrace, and I am not worthy of it either – not yet, at any rate. I remember I used to say that I thought I could bear a real tragedy if it came to me with purple pall and a mask of noble sorrow,[144] but that the dreadful thing about modernity was that it put Tragedy into the raiment of Comedy, so that the great realities seemed commonplace or grotesque or lacking in style. It is quite true about modernity. It has probably always been true about actual life. It is said that all martyrdoms seemed mean to the looker-on.[145] The nineteenth century is no exception to the general rule.

Everything about my tragedy has been hideous, mean, repellent, lacking in style. Our very dress makes us grotesques. We are the zanies of sorrow. We are clowns whose hearts are broken. We are specially designed to appeal to the sense of humour. On November 13th 1895 I was brought down here from London.[146] From two o'clock till half-past two on that day I had to stand on the centre platform of Clapham Junction in convict dress and handcuffed, for the world to look at. I had been taken out of the Hospital Ward without a moment's notice being given to me. Of all possible objects I was the most grotesque. When people saw me they laughed. Each train as it came up swelled the audience. Nothing could exceed their amusement. That was of course before they knew who I was. As soon as they had been informed, they laughed still more. For half an hour I stood there in the grey November rain surrounded by a jeering mob. For a year after that was done to me I wept every day at the same hour and for the same space of time. That is not such a tragic thing as possibly it sounds to you. To those who are in prison, tears are a part of every day's experience. A day in prison on which one does not weep is a day on which one's heart is hard, not a day on which one's heart is happy.

Well, now I am really beginning to feel more regret for the people who laughed than for myself. Of course when they saw me I was not on my pedestal. I was in the pillory. But it is a very unimaginative nature that only cares for people on their pedestals. A pedestal may be a very unreal thing. A pillory is a terrific reality. They should have known also how to interpret sorrow better. I have said that behind Sorrow there is always Sorrow. It were still wiser to say that behind sorrow there is always a soul. And to mock at a soul in pain is a dreadful thing. Unbeautiful are their lives who do it. In the strangely simple economy of the world people only get what they give, and to those who have not enough imagination to penetrate the mere outward of things and feel pity, what pity can be given save that of scorn?

I have told you this account of the mode of my being conveyed here simply that you should realise how hard it has been for me to get anything out of my punishment but bitterness and despair. I have however to do it, and now and then I have moments of submission and acceptance. All the spring may be hidden in a single bud, and the low ground-nest of the lark may hold the joy that is to herald the feet of many rose-red dawns, and so perhaps whatever beauty of life still remains to me is contained in some moment of surrender, abasement and humiliation. I can, at any rate, merely proceed on the lines of my own development, and by accepting all that has happened to me make myself worthy of it.

People used to say of me that I was too individualistic. I must be far more of an individualist than I ever was. I must get far more out of myself than I ever got, and ask far less of the world than I ever asked. Indeed my ruin came, not from too great individualism of life, but from too little. The one disgraceful, unpardonable, and to all time contemptible action of my life was my allowing myself to be forced into appealing to Society for help and protection against your father. To have made such an appeal against anyone would have been from the individualist point of view bad enough, but what excuse can there ever be put forward for having made it against one of such nature and aspect?

Of course once I had put into motion the forces of Society, Society turned on me and said, 'Have you been living all this time in defiance of my laws, and do you now appeal to those laws for protection? You shall have those laws exercised to the full. You shall abide by what you have appealed to.' The result is I am in gaol. And I used to feel bitterly the irony and ignominy of my position when in the course of my three trials, beginning at the Police Court, I used to see your father bustling in and out in the hopes of attracting public attention, as if anyone could fail to note or remember the stableman's gait and dress, the bowed legs, the twitching hands, the hanging lower lip, the bestial and half-witted grin. Even when he was not there, or was out of sight, I used to feel conscious of his presence, and the blank dreary walls of the great Court-room, the very air itself, seemed to me at times to be hung with multitudinous masks of that apelike face. Certainly no man ever fell so ignobly, and by such ignoble instruments, as I did. I say, in *Dorian Gray* somewhere, that 'a man cannot be too careful in the choice of his enemies'.[147] I little thought that it was by a pariah that I was to be made a pariah myself.

This urging me, forcing me to appeal to Society for help, is one of the things that make me despise you so much, that make me despise myself so much for having yielded to you. Your not appreciating me as an artist was quite excusable. It was temperamental. You couldn't help it. But you might have appreciated me as an Individualist. For that no culture was required. But you didn't, and so you brought the element of Philistinism into a life that had been a complete protest against it, and from some points of view a complete annihilation of it. The Philistine element in life is not the failure to understand Art. Charming people such as fishermen, shepherds, ploughboys, peasants and the like know nothing about Art, and are the very salt of the earth. He is the Philistine who upholds and aids the heavy, cumbrous, blind mechanical forces of Society, and who does not recognise the dynamic force when he meets it either in a man or a movement.

People thought it dreadful of me to have entertained at dinner the evil things of life, and to have found pleasure in their company. But they, from the point of view through which I, as an artist in life, approached them, were delightfully suggestive and stimulating. It was like feasting with panthers.[148] The danger was half the excitement. I used to feel as the snake-charmer must feel when he lures the cobra to stir from the painted cloth or reed-basket that holds it, and makes it spread its hood at his bidding, and sway to and fro in the air as a plant sways restfully in a stream. They were to me the brightest of gilded snakes. Their poison was part of their perfection. I did not know that when they were to strike at me it was to be at your piping and for your father's pay. I don't feel at all ashamed of having known them. They were intensely interesting. What I do feel ashamed of is the horrible Philistine atmosphere into which you brought me. My business as an artist was with Ariel. You set me to wrestle with Caliban. Instead of making beautiful coloured, musical things such as *Salomé*, and the *Florentine Tragedy*, and *La Sainte Courtisane*, I found myself forced to send long lawyer's letters to your father and constrained to appeal to the very things against which I had always protested. Clibborn and Atkins[149] were wonderful in their infamous war against life. To entertain them was an astounding adventure. Dumas *père*, Cellini, Goya, Edgar Allan Poe, or Baudelaire, would have done just the same. What is loathsome to me is the memory of interminable visits paid by me to the solicitor Humphreys in your company, when in the ghastly glare of a bleak room you and I would sit with serious faces telling serious lies to a bald man, till I really groaned and yawned with *ennui. There* is where I found myself after two years' friendship with you, right in the centre of Philistia, away from everything that was beautiful, or brilliant, or wonderful, or daring. At the end I had to come forward, on your behalf, as the champion of Respectability in conduct, of Puritanism in life, and of Morality in Art. *Voilà où mènent les mauvais chemins!*[150]

And the curious thing to me is that you should have tried to imitate your father in his chief characteristics. I cannot under-stand why he was to you an exemplar, where he should have been a warning, except that whenever there is hatred between two people there is bond or brotherhood of some kind. I sup-pose that, by some strange law of the antipathy of similars, you loathed each other, not because in so many points you were so

different, but because in some you were so like. In June 1893
when you left Oxford, without a degree and with debts, petty in
themselves, but considerable to a man of your father's income,
your father wrote you a very vulgar, violent and abusive letter.
The letter you sent him in reply was in every way worse, and of
course far less excusable, and consequently you were extremely
proud of it. I remember quite well your saying to me with your
most conceited air that you could beat your father 'at his own
trade'. Quite true. But what a trade! What a competition![151]
You used to laugh and sneer at your father for retiring from
your cousin's house where he was living in order to write filthy
letters to him from a neighbouring hotel. You used to do just
the same to me. You constantly lunched with me at some public
restaurant, sulked or made a scene during luncheon, and then
retired to White's Club and wrote me a letter of the very foulest
character. The only difference between you and your father
was that after you had dispatched your letter to me by special
messenger, you would arrive yourself at my rooms some hours
later, not to apologise, but to know if I had ordered dinner at
the Savoy, and if not, why not. Sometimes you would actually
arrive before the offensive letter had been read. I remember
on one occasion you had asked me to invite to luncheon at
the Café Royal two of your friends, one of whom I had never
seen in my life. I did so, and at your special request ordered
beforehand a specially luxurious luncheon to be prepared. The
chef, I remember, was sent for, and particular instructions given
about the wines. Instead of coming to luncheon you sent me at
the Café an abusive letter, timed so as to reach me after we had
been waiting half an hour for you. I read the first line, and saw
what it was, and putting the letter in my pocket, explained to
your friends that you were suddenly taken ill, and that the rest
of the letter referred to your symptoms. In point of fact I did
not read the letter till I was dressing for dinner at Tite Street
that evening. As I was in the middle of its mire, wondering with
infinite sadness how you could write letters that were really like
the froth and foam on the lips of an epileptic, my servant came
in to tell me that you were in the hall and were very anxious
to see me for five minutes. I at once sent down and asked you

to come up. You arrived, looking I admit very frightened and pale, to beg my advice and assistance, as you had been told that a man from Lumley, the solicitor, had been enquiring for you at Cadogan Place, and you were afraid that your Oxford trouble or some new danger was threatening you. I consoled you, told you, what proved to be the case, that it was merely a trades- man's bill probably, and let you stay to dinner, and pass your evening with me. You never mentioned a single word about your hideous letter, nor did I. I treated it as simply an unhappy symptom of an unhappy temperament. The subject was never alluded to. To write to me a loathsome letter at 2.30, and fly to me for help and sympathy at 7.15 the same afternoon, was a perfectly ordinary occurrence in your life. You went quite beyond your father in such habits, as you did in others. When his revolting letters to you were read in open Court he natur- ally felt ashamed and pretended to weep. Had your letters to him been read by his own Counsel still more horror and repug- nance would have been felt by everyone. Nor was it merely in style that you 'beat him at his own trade', but in mode of attack you distanced him completely. You availed yourself of the pub- lic telegram, and the open postcard. I think you might have left such modes of annoyance to people like Alfred Wood[152] whose sole source of income it is. Don't you? What was a profession to him and his class was a pleasure to you, and a very evil one. Nor have you given up your horrible habit of writing offensive letters, after all that has happened to me through them and for them. You still regard it as one of your accomplishments, and you exercise it on my friends, on those who have been kind to me in prison like Robert Sherard and others. That is disgrace- ful of you. When Robert Sherard heard from me that I did not wish you to publish any article on me in the *Mercure de France*, with or without letters, you should have been grateful to him for having ascertained my wishes on the point, and for having saved you from, without intending it, inflicting more pain on me than you had done already. You must remember that a pat- ronising and Philistine letter about 'fair play' for a 'man who is down' is all right for an English newspaper. It carries on the old traditions of English journalism in regard to their attitude towards artists. But in France such a tone would have exposed me to ridicule and you to contempt. I could not have allowed any article till I had known its aim, temper, mode of approach and the like. In art good intentions are not of the smallest value. All bad art is the result of good intentions.

Nor is Robert Sherard the only one of my friends to whom you have addressed acrimonious and bitter letters because they sought that my wishes and my feelings should be consulted in matters concerning myself, the publication of articles on me, the dedication of your verses, the surrender of my letters and presents, and such like. You have annoyed or sought to annoy others also.

Does it ever occur to you what an awful position I would have been in if for the last two years, during my appalling sentence, I had been dependent on you as a friend? Do you ever think of that? Do you ever feel any gratitude to those who by kindness without stint, devotion without limit, cheerfulness and joy in giving, have lightened my black burden for me, have visited me again and again, have written to me beautiful and sympathetic letters, have managed my affairs for me, have arranged my future life for me, have stood by me in the teeth of obloquy, taunt, open sneer or insult even? I thank God every day that he gave me friends other than you. I owe everything to them. The very books in my cell are paid for by Robbie out of his pocket-money. From the same source are to come clothes for me, when I am released. I am not ashamed of taking a thing that is given by love and affection. I am proud of it. But do you ever think of what my friends such as More Adey, Robbie, Robert Sherard, Frank Harris, and Arthur Clifton, have been to me in giving me comfort, help, affection, sympathy and the like? I suppose that has never dawned on you. And yet – if you had any imagination in you – you would know that there is not a single person who has been kind to me in my prison-life, down to the warder who may give me a good-morning or a good-night that is not one of his prescribed duties – down to the common policemen who in their homely rough way strove to comfort me on my journeys to and fro from the Bankruptcy Court under conditions of terrible mental distress – down to the poor thief who, recognising me as we tramped round the yard at Wandsworth, whispered to me in the hoarse prison-voice men get from long and compulsory silence: '*I am sorry for you: it is harder for the likes of you than it is for the likes of us*' – not one of them all, I say, the very mire from whose shoes you should not be proud to be allowed to kneel down and clean.

Have you imagination enough to see what a fearful tragedy it was for me to have come across your family? What a tragedy it would have been for anyone at all, who had a great position, a great name, anything of importance to lose? There is hardly one of the elders of your family – with the exception of Percy, who is really a good fellow – who did not in some way contribute to my ruin.

I have spoken of your mother to you with some bitterness, and I strongly advise you to let her see this letter, for your own sake chiefly. If it is painful to her to read such an indictment against one of her sons, let her remember that *my* mother, who intellectually ranks with Elizabeth Barrett Browning, and historically with Madame Roland,[153] died broken-hearted because the son of whose genius and art she had been so proud, and whom she had regarded always as a worthy continuer of a distinguished name, had been condemned to the treadmill for two years. You will ask me in what way your mother contributed to my destruction. I will tell you. Just as you strove to shift on to me all your immoral responsibilities, so your mother strove to shift on to me all her moral responsibilities with regard to you. Instead of speaking directly to you about your life, as a mother should, she always wrote privately to me with earnest, frightened entreaties not to let you know that she was writing to me. You see the position in which I was placed between you and your mother. It was one as false, as absurd, and as tragic as the one in which I was placed between you and your father. In August 1892, and on the 8th of November in the same year, I had two long interviews with your mother about you. On both occasions I asked her why she did not speak directly to you herself. On both occasions she gave the same answer: '*I am afraid to: he gets so angry when he is spoken to.*' The first time, I knew you so slightly that I did not understand what she meant.

The second time, I knew you so well that I understood perfectly. (During the interval you had had an attack of jaundice and been ordered by the doctor to go for a week to Bournemouth, and had induced me to accompany you as you hated being alone.) But the first duty of a mother is not to be afraid of speaking seriously to her son. Had your mother spoken seriously to you about the trouble she saw you were in in July 1892 and made you confide in her it would have been much better, and much happier ultimately for both of you. All the underhand and secret communications with me were wrong. What was the use of your mother sending me endless little notes, marked 'Private' on the envelope, begging me not to ask you so often to dinner, and not to give you any money, each note ending with an earnest postscript '*On no account let Alfred know that I have written to you*'? What good could come of such a correspondence? Did you ever wait to be asked to dinner? Never. You took all your meals as a matter of course with me. If I remonstrated, you always had one observation: '*If I don't dine with you, where am I to dine? You don't suppose that I am going to dine at home?*' It was unanswerable. And if I absolutely refused to let you dine with me, you always threatened that you would do something foolish, and always did it. What possible result could there be from letters such as your mother used to send me, except that which did occur, a foolish and fatal shifting of the moral responsibility on to my shoulders? Of the various details in which your mother's weakness and lack of courage proved so ruinous to herself, to you, and to me, I don't want to speak any more, but surely, when she heard of your father coming down to my house to make a loathsome scene and create a public scandal, she might then have seen that a serious crisis was impending, and taken some serious steps to try and avoid it? But all she could think of doing was to send down plausible George Wyndham[154] with his pliant tongue to propose to me – what? That I should 'gradually drop you'!

As if it had been possible for me to gradually drop you! I had tried to end our friendship in every possible way, going so far as actually to leave England and give a false address abroad in the hopes of breaking at one blow a bond that had become irksome, hateful, and ruinous to me. Do you think that I *could* have 'gradually dropped' you? Do you think that would have satisfied your father? You know it would not. What your father wanted, indeed, was not the cessation of our friendship, but a public scandal. That is what he was striving for. His name had not been in the papers for years. He saw the opportunity of appearing before the British public in an entirely new character, that of the affectionate father. His sense of humour was roused. Had I severed my friendship with you it would have been a terrible disappointment to him, and the small notoriety of a second divorce suit,[155] however revolting its details and origin, would have proved but little consolation to him. For what he was aiming at was popularity, and to pose as a champion of purity, as it is termed, is, in the present condition of the British public, the surest mode of becoming for the nonce a heroic figure. Of this public I have said in one of my plays that if it is Caliban for one half of the year, it is Tartuffe for the other,[156] and your father, in whom both characters may be said to have become incarnate, was in this way marked out as the proper representative of Puritanism in its aggressive and most characteristic form. No gradual dropping of you would have been of any avail, even had it been practicable. Don't you feel now that the only thing for your mother to have done was to have asked me to come to see her, and had you and your brother present, and said definitely that the friendship must absolutely cease? She would have found in me her warmest seconder, and with Drumlanrig and myself in the room she need not have been afraid of speaking to you. She did not do so. She was afraid of her responsibilities, and tried to shift them on to me. One letter she did certainly write to me. It was a brief one, to ask me not to send the lawyer's letter to your father warning him to desist. She was quite right. It was ridiculous my consulting lawyers and seeking their protection. But she nullified any effect her letter might have produced by her usual postscript: '*On no account let Alfred know that I have written to you.*'

You were entranced at the idea of my sending lawyers' letters to your father, as well as yourself. It was your suggestion. I could not tell you that your mother was strongly against the idea, for she had bound me with the most solemn promises never to tell you about her letters to me, and I foolishly kept my promise to her. Don't you see that it was wrong of her not to speak directly to you? That all the backstairs-interviews with me, and the area-gate correspondence were wrong? Nobody can shift their responsibilities on anyone else. They always return ultimately to the proper owner. Your one idea of life, your one philosophy, if you are to be credited with a philosophy, was that whatever you did was to be paid for by someone else: I don't mean merely in the financial sense – that was simply the practical application of your philosophy to everyday life – but in the broadest, fullest sense of transferred responsibility. You made that your creed. It was very successful as far as it went. You forced me into taking the action because you knew that your father would not attack your life or yourself in any way, and that I would defend both to the utmost, and take on my own shoulders whatever would be thrust on me. You were quite right. Your father and I, each from different motives of course, did exactly as you counted on our doing. But somehow, in spite of everything, you have not really escaped. The 'Infant Samuel theory', as for brevity's sake one may term it, is all very well as far as the general world goes. It may be a good deal scorned in London, and a little sneered at in Oxford, but that is merely because there are a few people who know you in each place, and because in each place you left traces of your passage. Outside of a small set in those two cities, the world looks on you as the good young man who was very nearly tempted into wrong-doing by the wicked and immoral artist, but was rescued just in time by his kind and loving father. It sounds all right. And yet, you know you have not escaped. I am not referring to a silly question asked by a silly juryman, which was of course treated with contempt by the Crown and by the Judge.[157] No one cared about that. I am referring perhaps principally to yourself. In your own eyes, and some day you will have to think of your conduct, you are not, cannot be quite satisfied at the way in which things have turned out. Secretly you must think of yourself with a good deal of shame. A brazen face is a capital thing to show the world, but now and then when you are alone, and have no audience, you have, I suppose, to take the mask off for mere breathing purposes. Else, indeed, you would be stifled.

And in the same manner your mother must at times regret that she tried to shift her grave responsibilities on someone else, who already had enough of a burden to carry. She occupied the position of both parents to you. Did she really fulfil the duties of either? If I bore with your bad temper and your rudeness and your scenes, she might have borne with them too. When last I saw my wife – fourteen months ago now – I told her that she would have to be to Cyril a father as well as a mother. I told her everything about your mother's mode of dealing with you in every detail as I have set it down in this letter, only of course far more fully. I told her the reason of the endless notes with 'Private' on the envelope that used to come to Tite Street from your mother, so constantly that my wife used to laugh and say that we must be collaborating in a society novel or something of that kind. I implored her not to be to Cyril what your mother was to you. I told her that she should bring him up so that if he shed innocent blood he would come and tell her, that she might cleanse his hands for him first, and then teach him how by penance or expiation to cleanse his soul afterwards. I told her that if she was frightened of facing the responsibility of the life of another, though her own child, she should get a guardian to help her. That she has, I am glad to say, done. She has chosen Adrian Hope, a man of high birth and culture and fine character, her own cousin, whom you met once at Tite Street, and with him Cyril and Vyvyan have a good chance of a beautiful future.[158] Your mother, if she was afraid of talking seriously to you, should have chosen someone amongst her own relatives to whom you might have listened. But she should not have been afraid. She should have had it out with you and faced it. At any rate, look at the result. Is she satisfied and pleased?

I know she puts the blame on me. I hear of it, not from people who know you, but from people who do not know you, and do not desire to know you. I hear of it often. She talks of the influence of an elder over a younger man, for instance. It is one of her favourite attitudes towards the question, and it is always a successful appeal to popular prejudice and ignorance. I need not ask you what influence I had over you. You know I had none. It was one of your frequent boasts that I had none, and the only one indeed that was well-founded. What was there, as a mere matter of fact, in you that I could influence? Your brain? It was undeveloped. Your imagination? It was dead. Your heart? It was not yet born. Of all the people who have ever crossed my life you were the one, and the only one, I was unable in any way to influence in any direction. When I lay ill and helpless in a fever caught from tending on you, I had not sufficient influence over you to induce you to get me even a cup of milk to drink, or to see that I had the ordinary necessaries of a sickroom, or to take the trouble to drive a couple of hundred yards to a bookseller's to get me a book at my own expense. When I was actually engaged in writing, and penning comedies that were to beat Congreve for brilliancy, and Dumas *fils* for philosophy, and I suppose everybody else for every other quality, I had not sufficient influence with you to get you to leave me undisturbed as an artist should be left. Wherever my writing room was, it was to you an ordinary lounge, a place to smoke and drink hock-and-seltzer in, and chatter about absurdities. The 'influence of an elder over a younger man' is an excellent theory till it comes to my ears. Then it becomes grotesque. When it comes to your ears, I suppose you smile – to yourself. You are certainly entitled to do so. I hear also much of what she says about money. She states, and with perfect justice, that she was ceaseless in her entreaties to me not to supply you with money. I admit it. Her letters were endless, and the postscript '*Pray do not let Alfred know that I have written to you*' appears in them all. But it was no pleasure to me to have to pay every single thing for you from your morning shave to your midnight hansom. It was a horrible bore. I used to complain to you again and again about it. I used to tell you – you remember, don't you? – how I loathed your regarding me as a '*useful*' person, how no artist wishes to be so regarded or so treated; artists, like art itself, being of their very essence quite useless. You used to get very angry when I said it to you. The truth always made you angry. Truth, indeed, is a thing that is most painful to listen to and most painful to utter. But it did not make you alter your views or your mode of life. Every day I had to pay for every single thing you did all day long. Only a person of absurd good nature or of indescribable folly would have done so. I unfortunately was a complete combination of both. When I used to suggest that your mother should supply you with the money you wanted, you always had a very pretty and graceful answer. You said that the income allowed her by your father – some £1500 a year I believe – was quite inadequate to the wants of a lady of her position, and that you could not go to her for more money than you were getting already. You were quite right about her income being one absolutely unsuitable to a lady of her position and tastes, but you should not have made that an excuse for living in luxury on me: it should on the contrary have been a suggestion to you for economy in your own life. The fact is that you were, and are I suppose still, a typical sentimentalist. For a sentimentalist is simply one who desires to have the luxury of an emotion without paying for it. To propose to spare your mother's pocket was beautiful. To do so at my expense was ugly. You think that one can have one's emotions for nothing. One cannot. Even the finest and the most self-sacrificing emotions have to be paid for. Strangely enough, that is what makes them fine. The intellectual and emotional life of ordinary people is a very contemptible affair. Just as they borrow their ideas from a sort of circulating library of thought – the *Zeitgeist* of an age that has no soul – and send them back soiled at the end of each week, so they always try to get their emotions on credit, and refuse to pay the bill when it comes in. You should pass out of that conception of life. As soon as you have to pay for an emotion you will know its quality, and be the better for such knowledge. And remember that the sentimentalist is always a cynic at heart. Indeed sentimentality is merely the bank holiday of cynicism. And delightful as cynicism is from its intellectual side, now that it has left the Tub for the Club, it never can be more than the perfect philosophy for a man who has no soul.[159] It has its social value, and to an artist all modes of expression are interesting, but in itself it is a poor affair, for to the true cynic nothing is ever revealed.

I think that if you look back now to
your mother's income, and your attitud
you will not feel proud of yourself, and
day, if you don't show your mother thi
that your living on me was a matter in
not consulted for a moment. It was sim
me personally most distressing, form tha
took. To make yourself dependent on m
well as the largest sums lent you in your own eyes all the charm
of childhood, and in the insisting on my paying for every one
of your pleasures you thought that you had found the secret of
eternal youth. I confess that it pains me when I hear of your
mother's remarks about me, and I am sure that on reflection
you will agree with me that if she has no word of regret or
sorrow for the ruin your race has brought on mine it would be
better if she remained silent. Of course there is no reason she
should see any portion of this letter that refers to any mental
development I have been going through, or to any point of
departure I hope to attain to. It would not be interesting to her.
But the parts concerned purely with your life I should show her
if I were you.

If I were you, in fact, I would not care about being loved on
false pretences. There is no reason why a man should show his
life to the world. The world does not understand things. But
with people whose affection one desires to have it is different.
A great friend of mine – a friend of ten years' standing[160] –
came to see me some time ago and told me that he did not
believe a single word of what was said against me, and wished
me to know that he considered me quite innocent, and the
victim of a hideous plot concocted by your father. I burst into
tears at what he said, and told him that while there was much
amongst your father's definite charges that was quite untrue
and transferred to me by revolting malice, still that my life had
been full of perverse pleasures and strange passions, and that
unless he accepted that fact as a fact about me and realised it to
the full, I could not possibly be friends with him any more, or
ever be in his company. It was a terrible shock to him, but we
are friends, and I have not got his friendship on false pretences.

to you that to speak the truth is a painful thing. To
to tell lies is much worse.

remember as I was sitting in the dock on the occasion of
last trial listening to Lockwood's[161] appalling denunciation
of me – like a thing out of Tacitus, like a passage in Dante,
like one of Savonarola's indictments of the Popes at Rome[162]
– and being sickened with horror at what I heard. Suddenly
it occurred to me, '*How splendid it would be, if I was saying
all this about myself!*' I saw then at once that what is said of a
man is nothing. The point is, who says it. A man's very highest
moment is, I have no doubt at all, when he kneels in the dust,
and beats his breast, and tells all the sins of his life. So with
you. You would be much happier if you let your mother know
a little at any rate of your life from yourself. I told her a good
deal about it in December 1893, but of course I was forced into
reticences and generalities. It did not seem to give her any more
courage in her relations with you. On the contrary. She avoided
looking at the truth more persistently than ever. If you told
her yourself it would be different. My words may perhaps be
often too bitter to you. But the facts you cannot deny. Things
were as I have said they were, and if you have read this letter as
carefully as you should have done you have met yourself face
to face.

I have now written, and at great length, to you in order that
you should realise what you were to me before my imprison-
ment, during those three years' fatal friendship: what you have
been to me during my imprisonment, already within two moons
of its completion almost: and what I hope to be to myself and
to others when my imprisonment is over. I cannot reconstruct
my letter, or rewrite it. You must take it as it stands, blotted
in many places with tears, in some with the signs of passion
or pain, and make it out as best you can, blots, corrections
and all. As for the corrections and *errata*, I have made them
in order that my words should be an absolute expression of
my thoughts, and err neither through surplusage nor through
being inadequate. Language requires to be tuned, like a violin:
and just as too many or too few vibrations in the voice of the
singer or the trembling of the string will make the note false,

so too much or too little in words will spoil the message. As it stands, at any rate, my letter has its definite meaning behind every phrase. There is in it nothing of rhetoric. Wherever there is erasion or substitution, however slight, however elaborate, it is because I am seeking to render my real impression, to find for my mood its exact equivalent. Whatever is first in feeling comes always last in form.

I will admit that it is a severe letter. I have not spared you. Indeed you may say that, after admitting that to weigh you against the smallest of my sorrows, the meanest of my losses, would be really unfair to you, I have actually done so, and made scruple by scruple the most careful assay of your nature. That is true. But you must remember that you put yourself into the scales.

You must remember that, if when matched with one mere moment of my imprisonment the balance in which you lie kicks the beam, Vanity made you choose the balance, and Vanity made you cling to it. *There* was the one great psychological error of our friendship, its entire want of proportion. You forced your way into a life too large for you, one whose orbit transcended your power of vision no less than your power of cyclic motion, one whose thoughts, passions and actions were of intense import, of wide interest, and fraught, too heavily indeed, with wonderful or awful consequence. Your little life of little whims and moods was admirable in its own little sphere. It was admirable at Oxford, where the worst that could happen to you was a reprimand from the Dean or a lecture from the President, and where the highest excitement was Magdalen becoming head of the river, and the lighting of a bonfire in the quad as a celebration of the august event. It should have continued in its own sphere after you left Oxford. In yourself, you were all right. You were a very complete specimen of a very modern type. It was simply in reference to me that you were wrong. Your reckless extravagance was not a crime. Youth is always extravagant. It was your forcing me to pay for your extravagances that was disgraceful. Your desire to have a friend with whom you could pass your time from morning to night was charming. It was almost idyllic. But the friend you fastened on should not have been a man of letters, an artist, one to whom your continual presence was as utterly destructive of all beautiful work as it was actually paralysing to the creative faculty. There was no harm in your seriously considering that the most perfect way of passing an evening was to have a champagne dinner at the Savoy, a box at a Music-Hall to follow, and a champagne supper at Willis's as a *bonne-bouche* for the end. Heaps of delightful young men in London are of the same opinion. It is not even an eccentricity. It is the qualification for becoming a member of White's. But you had no right to require of me that I should become the purveyor of such pleasures for you. It showed your lack of any real appreciation of my genius. Your quarrel with your father, again, whatever one may think about its character, should obviously have remained a question entirely between the two of you. It should have been carried on in a backyard. Such quarrels, I believe, usually are. Your mistake was in insisting on its being played as a tragi-comedy on a high stage in History, with the whole world as the audience, and myself as the prize for the victor in the contemptible contest. The fact that your father loathed you, and that you loathed your father, was not a matter of any interest to the English public. Such feelings are very common in English domestic life, and should be confined to the place they characterise: the home. Away from the home-circle they are quite out of place. To translate them is an offence. Family-life is not to be treated as a red flag to be flaunted in the streets, or a horn to be blown hoarsely on the housetops. You took Domesticity out of its proper sphere, just as you took yourself out of your proper sphere.

And those who quit their proper sphere change their surroundings merely, not their natures. They do not acquire the thoughts or passions appropriate to the sphere they enter. It is not in their power to do so. Emotional forces, as I say somewhere in *Intentions*, are as limited in extent and duration as the forces of physical energy.[163] The little cup that is made to hold so much can hold so much and no more, though all the purple vats of Burgundy be filled with wine to the brim, and the treaders stand knee-deep in the gathered grapes of the stony vineyards of Spain. There is no error more common than that of thinking that those who are the causes or occasions of great tragedies share in the feelings suitable to the tragic mood: no error more fatal than expecting it of them. The martyr in his 'shirt of flame'[164] may be looking on the face of God, but to him who is piling the faggots or loosening the logs for the blast the whole scene is no more than the slaying of an ox is to the butcher, or the felling of a tree to the charcoal-burner in the forest, or the fall of a flower to one who is mowing down the grass with a scythe. Great passions are for the great of soul, and great events can be seen only by those who are on a level with them.

I know of nothing in all Drama more incomparable from the point of view of Art, or more suggestive in its subtlety of observation, than Shakespeare's drawing of Rosencrantz and Guildenstern. They are Hamlet's college friends. They have been his companions. They bring with them memories of pleasant days together. At the moment when they come across him in the play he is staggering under the weight of a burden intolerable to one of his temperament. The dead have come armed out of the grave to impose on him a mission at once too great and too mean for him. He is a dreamer, and he is called upon to act. He has the nature of the poet and he is asked to grapple with the common complexities of cause and effect, with life in its practical realisation, of which he knows nothing, not with life in its ideal essence, of which he knows much. He has no conception of what to do, and his folly is to feign folly. Brutus used madness as a cloak to conceal the sword of his purpose, the dagger of his will,[165] but to Hamlet madness is a mere mask for the hiding of weakness. In the making of mows and jests he sees a chance of delay. He keeps playing with action, as an artist plays with a theory. He makes himself the spy of his proper actions, and listening to his own words knows them to be but 'words, words, words'. Instead of trying to be the hero of his own history, he seeks to be the spectator of his own tragedy. He disbelieves in everything, including himself, and yet his doubt helps him not, as it comes not from scepticism but from a divided will.

Of all this, Guildenstern and Rosencrantz realise nothing. They bow and smirk and smile, and what the one says the other echoes with sicklier iteration. When at last, by means of the play within the play and the puppets in their dalliance, Hamlet 'catches the conscience' of the King, and drives the wretched man in terror from his throne, Guildenstern and Rosencrantz see no more in his conduct than a rather painful breach of court-etiquette. That is as far as they can attain to in 'the contemplation of the spectacle of life with appropriate emotions'.[166] They are close to his very secret and know nothing of it. Nor would there be any use in telling them. They are the little cups that can hold so much and no more. Towards the close it is suggested that, caught in a cunning springe set for another, they have met, or may meet, with a violent and sudden death. But a tragic ending of this kind, though touched by Hamlet's humour with something of the surprise and justice of comedy, is really not for such as they. They never die. Horatio who, in order to 'report Hamlet and his cause aright to the unsatisfied',[167]

> Absents him from felicity a while
> And in this harsh world draws his breath in pain,[168]

dies, though not before an audience, and leaves no brother. But Guildenstern and Rosencrantz are as immortal as Angelo[169] and Tartuffe, and should rank with them. They are what modern life has contributed to the antique ideal of friendship. He who writes a new *De Amicitia* must find a niche for them and praise them in Tusculan prose.[170] They are types fixed for all time. To censure them would show a lack of appreciation. They are merely out of their sphere: that is all. In sublimity of soul there is no contagion. High thoughts and high emotions are by their very existence isolated. What Ophelia herself could not understand was not to be realised by 'Guildenstern and gentle Rosencrantz', by 'Rosencrantz and gentle Guildenstern'. Of course I do not propose to compare you. There is a wide difference between you. What with them was chance, with you was choice. Deliberately and by me uninvited you thrust yourself into my sphere, usurped there a place for which you had neither right nor qualifications, and having by curious persistence, and by the rendering of your very presence a part of each separate day, succeeded in absorbing my entire life, could do no better with that life than break it in pieces. Strange as it may sound to you, it was but natural that you should do so. If one gives to a child a toy too wonderful for its little mind, or too beautiful for its but half-awakened eyes, it breaks the toy, if it is wilful; if it is listless it lets it fall and goes its way to its own companions. So it was with you. Having got hold of my life, you did not know what to do with it. You couldn't have known. It was too wonderful a thing to be in your grasp. You should have let it slip from your hands and gone back to your own companions at their play. But unfortunately you were wilful, and so you broke it. That, when everything is said, is perhaps the ultimate secret of all that has happened. For secrets are always smaller than their manifestations. By the displacement of an atom a world may be shaken. And that I may not spare myself any more than you I will add this: that dangerous to me as my meeting with you was, it was rendered fatal to me by the particular moment in which we met. For you were at that time of life when all that one does is no more than the sowing of the seed, and I was at that time of life when all that one does is no less than the reaping of the harvest.

There are some few things more about which I must write to you. The first is about my Bankruptcy. I heard some days ago, with great disappointment I admit, that it is too late now for your family to pay your father off, that it would be illegal, and that I must remain in my present painful position for some considerable time to come. It is bitter to me because I am assured on legal authority that I cannot even publish a book without the permission of the Receiver to whom all the accounts must be submitted. I cannot enter into a contract with the manager of a theatre, or produce a play without the receipts passing to your father and my few other creditors. I think that even you will admit now that the scheme of 'scoring off' your father by allowing him to make me a bankrupt has not really been the brilliant all-round success you imagined it was going to turn out. It has not been so to me at any rate, and my feelings of pain and humiliation at my pauperism should have been consulted rather than your own sense of humour, however caustic or unexpected. In point of actual fact, in permitting my Bankruptcy, as in urging me on to the original trial, you really were playing right into your father's hands, and doing just what he wanted. Alone, and unassisted, he would from the very outset have been powerless. In you – though you did not mean to hold such a horrible office – he has always found his chief ally.

I am told by More Adey in his letter that last summer you really did express on more than one occasion your desire to repay me 'a little of what I spent' on you. As I said to him in my answer, unfortunately I spent on you my art, my life, my name, my place in history, and if your family had all the marvellous things in the world at their command, or what the world holds as marvellous, genius, beauty, wealth, high position and the like, and laid them all at my feet, it would not repay me for one tithe of the smallest things that have been taken from me, or one tear of the least tears that I have shed. However, of course everything one does has to be paid for. Even to the Bankrupt it is so. You seem to be under the impression that Bankruptcy is a convenient means by which a man can avoid paying his debts, a 'score off his creditors' in fact. It is quite the other way. It is the method by which a man's creditors 'score off' him, if we are to continue your favourite phrase, and by which the Law by the confiscation of all his property forces him to pay every one of his debts, and if he fails to do so leaves him as penniless as the commonest mendicant who stands in an archway, or creeps down a road, holding out his hand for the alms for which, in England at any rate, he is afraid to ask. The Law has taken from me not merely all that I have, my books, furniture, pictures, my copyright in my published works, my copyright in my plays, everything in fact from *The Happy Prince* and *Lady Windermere's Fan* down to the staircarpets and door-scraper of my house, but also all that I am ever going to have. My interest in my marriage-settlement, for instance, was sold. Fortunately I was able to buy it in through my friends. Otherwise, in case my wife died, my two children during my lifetime would be as penniless as myself. My interest in our Irish estate, entailed on me by my own father, will I suppose have to go next. I feel very bitterly about its being sold, but I must submit.

Your father's seven hundred pence – or pounds is it? – stand in the way, and must be refunded. Even when I am stripped of all I have, and am ever to have, and am granted a discharge as a hopeless Insolvent, I have still got to pay my debts. The Savoy dinners – the clear turtle-soup, the luscious ortolans wrapped in their crinkled Sicilian vine-leaves, the heavy amber-coloured, indeed almost amber-scented champagne – Dagonet 1880, I think, was your favourite wine? – all have still to be paid for. The suppers at Willis's, the special *cuvée* of Perrier-Jouët reserved always for us,[171] the wonderful *pâtés* procured directly from Strasburg, the marvellous *fine champagne* served always at the bottom of great bell-shaped glasses that its bouquet might be the better savoured by the true epicures of what was really exquisite in life – these cannot be left unpaid, as bad debts of a dishonest *client*. Even the dainty sleeve-links – four heart-shaped moonstones of silver mist, girdled by alternate ruby and dia-mond for their setting – that I designed, and had made at Henry Lewis's as a special little present to you, to celebrate the success of my second comedy – these even – though I believe you sold them for a song a few months afterwards – have to be paid for. I cannot leave the jeweller out of pocket for the presents I gave you, no matter what you did with them. So, even if I get my discharge, you see I have still my debts to pay.

And what is true of a bankrupt is true of everyone else in life. For every single thing that is done someone has to pay. Even you yourself – with all your desire for absolute freedom from all duties, your insistence on having everything supplied to you by others, your attempts to reject any claim on your affection, or regard, or gratitude – even you will have some day to reflect seriously on what you have done, and try, how-ever unavailingly, to make some attempt at atonement. The fact that you will not be able really to do so will be part of your punishment. You can't wash your hands of all respon-sibility, and propose with a shrug or a smile to pass on to a new friend and a freshly spread feast. You can't treat all that you have brought upon me as a sentimental reminiscence to be served up occasionally with the cigarettes and *liqueurs*, a picturesque background to a modern life of pleasure like an old tapestry hung in a common inn. It may for the moment have the charm of a new sauce or a fresh vintage, but the scraps of a banquet grow stale, and the dregs of a bottle are bitter. Either today, or tomorrow, or some day you have got to realise it. Otherwise you may die without having done so, and then what a mean, starved, unimaginative life you would have had. In my letter to More I have suggested one point of view from which you had better approach the subject as soon as possible. He will tell you what it is. To understand it you will have to cultivate your imagination. Remember that imagination is the quality that enables one to see things and people in their real as in their ideal relations. If you cannot realise it by yourself, talk to others on the subject. I have had to look at my past face to face. Look at your past face to face. Sit down quietly and consider it. The supreme vice is shallowness. Whatever is realised is right. Talk to your brother about it. Indeed the proper person to talk to *is* Percy. Let him read this letter, and know all the circumstances of our friendship. When things are clearly put before him, no judgment is better. Had we told him the truth, what a lot would have been saved to me of suffering and disgrace! You remember I proposed to do so, the night you arrived in London from Algiers. You absolutely refused. So when he came in after dinner we had to play the comedy of your father being an insane man subject to absurd and unaccountable delusions. It was a capital comedy while it lasted, none the less so because Percy took it all quite seriously. Unfortunately it ended in a very revolting manner. The subject on which I write now is one of its results, and if it be a trouble to you, pray do not forget that it is the deepest of my humiliations, and one I must go through. I have no option. You have none either.

The second thing about which I have to speak to you is with regard to the conditions, circumstances, and place of our meeting when my term of imprisonment is over. From extracts from your letter to Robbie written in the early summer of last year I understand that you have sealed up in two packages my letters and my presents to you – such at least as remain of either – and are anxious to hand them personally to me. It is, of course, necessary that they should be given up. You did not understand why I wrote beautiful letters to you, any more than you understood why I gave you beautiful presents. You failed to see that the former were not meant to be published, any more than the latter were meant to be pawned. Besides, they belong to a side of life that is long over, to a friendship that somehow you were unable to appreciate at its proper value. You must look back with wonder now to the days when you had my entire life in your hands. I too look back to them with wonder, and with other, with far different, emotions.

I am to be released, if all goes well with me, towards the end of May, and hope to go at once to some little seaside village abroad with Robbie and More Adey. The sea, as Euripides says in one of his plays about Iphigenia, washes away the stains and wounds of the world. Θάλασσα κλύζει πάντα τ'ἀνθρώπων κακά.[172]

I hope to be at least a month with my friends, and to gain, in their healthful and affectionate company, peace, and balance, and a less troubled heart, and a sweeter mood. I have a strange longing for the great simple primeval things, such as the Sea, to me no less of a mother than the Earth. It seems to me that we all look at Nature too much, and live with her too little. I discern great sanity in the Greek attitude. They never chattered about sunsets, or discussed whether the shadows on the grass were really mauve or not. But they saw that the sea was for the swimmer, and the sand for the feet of the runner. They loved the trees for the shadow that they cast, and the forest for its silence at noon. The vineyard-dresser wreathed his hair with ivy that he might keep off the rays of the sun as he stooped over the young shoots, and for the artist and the athlete, the two types that Greece gave us, they plaited into garlands the leaves of the bitter laurel and of the wild parsley which else had been of no service to man.

We call ourselves a utilitarian age, and we do not know the uses of any single thing. We have forgotten that Water can cleanse, and Fire purify, and that the Earth is mother to us all. As a consequence our Art is of the Moon and plays with shadows, while Greek art is of the Sun and deals directly with things. I feel sure that in elemental forces there is purification, and I want to go back to them and live in their presence. Of course, to one so modern as I am, *enfant de mon siècle*, merely to look at the world will be always lovely. I tremble with pleasure when I think that on the very day of my leaving prison both the laburnum and the lilac will be blooming in the gardens, and that I shall see the wind stir into restless beauty the swaying gold of the one, and make the other toss the pale purple of its plumes so that all the air shall be Arabia for me. Linnaeus fell on his knees and wept for joy when he saw for the first time the long heath of some English upland made yellow with the tawny aromatic blossoms of the common furze,[173] and I know that for me, to whom flowers are part of desire, there are tears waiting in the petals of some rose. It has always been so with me from my boyhood. There is not a single colour hidden away in the chalice of a flower, or the curve of a shell, to which, by some subtle sympathy with the very soul of things, my nature does not answer. Like Gautier I have always been one of those *pour qui le monde visible existe*.[174]

Still, I am conscious now that behind all this Beauty, satisfying though it be, there is some Spirit hidden of which the painted forms and shapes are but modes of manifestation, and it is with this Spirit that I desire to become in harmony. I have grown tired of the articulate utterances of men and things. The Mystical in Art, the Mystical in Life, the Mystical in Nature – this is what I am looking for, and in the great symphonies of Music, in the initiation of Sorrow, in the depths of the Sea I may find it. It is absolutely necessary for me to find it somewhere.

All trials are trials for one's life, just as all sentences are sentences of death, and three times have I been tried. The first time I left the box to be arrested, the second time to be led back to the House of Detention, the third time to pass into a prison for two years. Society, as we have constituted it, will have no place for me, has none to offer; but Nature, whose sweet rains fall on unjust and just alike, will have clefts in the rocks where I may hide, and secret valleys in whose silence I may weep undisturbed. She will hang the night with stars so that I may walk abroad in the darkness without stumbling, and send the wind over my footprints so that none may track me to my hurt: she will cleanse me in great waters, and with bitter herbs make me whole.

At the end of a month, when the June roses are in all their wanton opulence, I will, if I feel able, arrange through Robbie to meet you in some quiet foreign town like Bruges, whose grey houses and green canals and cool still ways had a charm for me, years ago. For the moment you will have to change your name. The little title of which you were so vain – and indeed it made your name sound like the name of a flower – you will have to surrender, if you wish to see *me*; just as *my* name, once so musical in the mouth of Fame, will have to be abandoned by me, in turn. How narrow, and mean, and inadequate to its burdens is this century of ours! It can give to Success its palace of porphyry, but for Sorrow and Shame it does not keep even a wattled house in which they may dwell: all it can do for *me* is to bid me alter my name into some other name, where even mediaevalism would have given me the cowl of the monk or the face-cloth of the leper behind which I might be at peace.

I hope that our meeting will be what a meeting between you and me should be, after everything that has occurred. In old days there was always a wide chasm between us, the chasm of achieved Art and acquired culture: there is a still wider chasm between us now, the chasm of Sorrow: but to Humility there is nothing that is impossible, and to Love all things are easy.

As regards your letter to me in answer to this, it may be as long or as short as you choose. Address the envelope to 'The Governor, HM Prison, Reading'. Inside, in another, and an open envelope, place your own letter to me: if your paper is very thin do not write on both sides, as it makes it hard for others to read. I have written to you with perfect freedom. You can write to me with the same. What I must know from you is why you have never made any attempt to write to me, since the August of the year before last, more especially after, in the May of last year, eleven months ago now, you knew, and admitted to others that you knew, how you had made me suffer, and how I realised it. I waited month after month to hear from you. Even if I had not been waiting but had shut the doors against you, you should have remembered that no one can possibly shut the doors against Love for ever. The unjust judge in the Gospels rises up at length to give a just decision because Justice comes knocking daily at his door; and at night-time the friend, in whose heart there is no real friendship, yields at length to his friend 'because of his importunity'.[175] There is no prison in any world into which Love cannot force an entrance. If you did not understand that, you did not understand anything about Love at all. Then, let me know all about your article on me for the *Mercure de France*. I know something of it. You had better quote from it. It is set up in type. Also, let me know the exact terms of your Dedication of your poems. If it is in prose, quote the prose; if in verse, quote the verse. I have no doubt that there will be beauty in it. Write to me with full frankness about yourself: about your life: your friends: your occupations: your books. Tell me about your volume and its reception. Whatever you have to say for yourself, say it without fear. Don't write what you don't mean: that is all. If anything in your letter is false or counterfeit I shall detect it by the ring at once. It is not for nothing, or to no purpose, that in my lifelong cult of literature I have made myself

> Miser of sound and syllable, no less
> Than Midas of his coinage.[176]

Remember also that I have yet to know you. Perhaps we have yet to know each other.

For yourself, I have but this last thing to say. Do not be afraid of the past. If people tell you that it is irrevocable, do not believe them. The past, the present and the future are but one moment in the sight of God, in whose sight we should try to live. Time and space, succession and extension, are merely accidental conditions of Thought. The Imagination can transcend them, and move in a free sphere of ideal existences. Things, also, are in their essence what we choose to make them. A thing *is*, according to the mode in which one looks at it. 'Where others', says Blake, 'see but the Dawn coming over the hill, I see the sons of God shouting for joy.'[177] What seemed to the world and to myself my future I lost irretrievably when I let myself be taunted into taking the action against your father: had, I dare say, lost it really long before that. What lies before me is my past. I have got to make myself look on that with different eyes, to make the world look on it with different eyes, to make God look on it with different eyes. This I cannot do by ignoring it, or slighting it, or praising it, or denying it. It is only to be done by fully accepting it as an inevitable part of the evolution of my life and character: by bowing my head to everything that I have suffered. How far I am away from the true temper of soul, this letter in its changing, uncertain moods, its scorn and bitterness, its aspirations and its failure to realise those aspirations, shows you quite clearly. But do not forget in what a terrible school I am sitting at my task. And incomplete, imperfect, as I am, yet from me you may have still much to gain. You came to me to learn the Pleasure of Life and the Pleasure of Art. Perhaps I am chosen to teach you something much more wonderful, the meaning of Sorrow, and its beauty. Your affectionate friend

Oscar Wilde

Letters of
April 1897–March 1898

To Robert Ross[1]

My dear Robbie,

I send you, in a roll separate from this, my letter to Alfred
Douglas, which I hope will arrive safe. As soon as you, and of
course More Adey whom I always include with you, have read
it, I want you to have it carefully copied for me. There are many
reasons why I wish this to be done. One will suffice. I want
you to be my literary executor in case of my death, and to have
complete control over my plays, books and papers. As soon as
I find I have a legal right to make a will I will do so. My wife
does not understand my art, nor could be expected to have any
interest in it, and Cyril is only a child. So I turn naturally to you,
as indeed I do for everything, and would like you to have all my
works. The deficit that their sale will produce may be lodged to
the credit of Cyril and Vyvyan.

Well, if you are my literary executor, you must be in posses-
sion of the only document that really gives any explanation of
my extraordinary behaviour with regard to Queensberry and
Alfred Douglas. When you have read the letter you will see
the psychological explanation of a course of conduct that from
the outside seems a combination of absolute idiocy with vulgar
bravado. Some day the truth will have to be known: not neces-
sarily in my lifetime or in Douglas's: but I am not prepared to
sit in the grotesque pillory they put me into, for all time: for the

simple reason that I inherited from my father and my mother a name of high distinction in literature and art, and I cannot, for eternity, allow that name to be the shield and catspaw of the Queensberrys. I don't defend my conduct. I explain it.

Also there are in the letter certain passages which deal with my mental development in prison, and the inevitable evolution of character and intellectual attitude towards life that has taken place: and I want you, and others who still stand by me and have affection for me, to know exactly in what mood and manner I hope to face the world. Of course from one point of view I know that on the day of my release I shall be merely passing from one prison into another, and there are times when the whole world seems to me no larger than my cell, and as full of terror for me. Still I believe that at the beginning God made a world for each separate man, and in that world which is within us one should seek to live. At any rate, you will read those parts of my letter with less pain than the others. Of course I need not remind *you* how fluid a thing thought is with me – with us all – and of what an evanescent substance are our emotions made. Still, I do see a sort of possible goal towards which, through art, I may progress. It is not unlikely that you may help me.[2]

As regards the mode of copying: of course it is too long for any amanuensis to attempt: and your own handwriting, dear Robbie, in your last letter seems specially designed to remind me that the task is not to be yours. I may wrong you, and hope I do, but it really looks as if you were engaged in writing a three-volume novel on the dangerous prevalence of communistic opinions among the rich, or some dreadful subject of vital interest, or in some other way wasting a youth that I cannot help saying has always been, and will always remain, quite full of promise. I think that the only thing to do is to be thoroughly modern, and to have it type-written. Of course the manuscript should not pass out of your control, but could you not get Mrs Marshall[3] to send down one of her type-writing girls – women are the most reliable, as they have no memory for the important – to Hornton Street or Phillimore Gardens[4] to do it under your supervision? I assure you that the type-writing machine, when played with expression, is not more annoying than the piano when played by a sister or near relation. Indeed many, among those most devoted to domesticity, prefer it.

I wish the copy to be done not on tissue paper but on good paper such as is used for plays, and a wide rubricated margin should be left for corrections. The copy done and verified from the manuscript, the original should be dispatched to A. D. by More, and another copy done by the type-writer so that *you* should have a copy as well as myself. Also I would wish two type-written copies to be made from the fourth page of sheet 9 to the last page of sheet 14: from 'and the end of it . . . I must forgive you' down to 'Between art and myself there is none' (I quote from memory). Also on page 3 of sheet 18 from 'I am to be released if all goes well' to 'bitter herbs . . . whole' on page 4.[5] These welded together with anything else you may extract that is good and nice in intention, such as first page of sheet 15, I wish sent, one copy to the Lady of Wimbledon – whom I have spoken of, without mentioning her name – the other to Frankie Forbes-Robertson.[6] I know both these sweet women will be interested to know something of what is happening to my soul – not in the theological sense, but merely in the sense of the spiritual consciousness that is separate from the actual occupations of the body. It is a sort of message or letter I send them – the only one, of course, I dare send. If Frankie wishes she can show it to her brother Eric, of whom I was always fond, but of course it is a strict secret from the general world. The Lady of Wimbledon will know that too.

If the copying is done at Hornton Street the lady type-writer might be fed through a lattice in the door like the Cardinals when they elect a Pope, till she comes out on the balcony and can say to the world '*Habet Mundus Epistolam*';[7] for indeed it is an Encyclical Letter, and as the Bulls of the Holy Father are named from their opening words, it may be spoken of as the *Epistola: In Carcere et Vinculis*.[8]

There is no need to tell A. D. that a copy has been taken, unless he should write and complain of injustice in the letter or misrepresentation: then he should be told that a copy has been taken. I earnestly hope the letter will do him good. It is the first time anyone has ever told him the truth about himself. If he is

allowed to think that the letter is merely the result of the influ-
ence of a plank-bed on style, and that my views are distorted
by the privations of prison-life, no good will follow. I hope
someone will let him know that the letter is one he thoroughly
deserves, and that if it is unjust, he thoroughly deserves injus-
tice. Who indeed deserves it more than he who was always so
unjust to others?

In point of fact, Robbie, prison-life makes one see people
and things as they really are. That is why it turns one to stone.
It is the people outside who are deceived by the illusion of a
life in constant motion. They revolve with life and contrib-
ute to its unreality. We who are immobile both see and know.
Whether or not the letter does good to his narrow nature and
hectic brain, to me it has done great good. I have 'cleansed my
bosom of much perilous stuff',[9] to borrow a phrase from the
poet whom you and I once thought of rescuing from the Philis-
tine.[10] I need not remind you that mere expression is to an artist
the supreme and only mode of life. It is by utterance that we
live. Of the many, many things for which I have to thank the
Governor there is none for which I am more grateful than for
his permission to write fully to A. D. and at as great length as
I desired. For nearly two years I had within me a growing bur-
den of bitterness, much of which I have now got rid of. On the
other side of the prison-wall there are some poor black soot-
smirched trees that are just breaking out into buds of an almost
shrill green. I know quite well what they are going through.
They are finding expression.

There is another very serious thing about which I have to
write to you, and I address myself to you because I have got
to blame you, and I am far too fond of you to blame you to
anyone else. On the 20th March 1896,[11] more than a year ago
now, I wrote to you in the very strongest terms telling you that
I could not bear the idea of any discord being made between
myself and my wife on such a subject as money, after her sweet-
ness in coming here from Italy to break to me the news of my
mother's death, and that I desired my friends to withdraw their
proposal to purchase my life-interest against her wishes. You
should have seen that my wishes were carried out. You were

very wrong not to do so. I was quite helpless in prison and I relied on you. You thought that the thing to do was the clever thing, the smart thing, the ingenious thing. You were under a mistake. Life is not complex. We are complex. Life is simple, and the simple thing is the right thing. Look at the result! Are you pleased with it?

Again, a complete error was made in the estimate formed of Mr Hargrove. He was regarded as a solicitor of the Humphreys class, one who would threaten to gain an end, bluster, extort, and the like. Quite the contrary. He is a man of very high character, and extremely good social position. Whatever he said he meant. The idea of putting me – a wretched prisoner and pauper – up to fight Mr Hargrove and Sir George Lewis was grotesque. The idea of bidding against them absurd. Mr Hargrove – the family solicitor of the Lloyds for thirty years – would advance my wife £10,000 if she wanted it, and not feel it. I asked Mr Holman whether in case of a divorce a settlement was not *ipso facto* broken. I received no answer. I find that it is as I suspected.

Again, how silly the long serious letters advising me 'not to surrender my rights over my children', a phrase that occurs seven times in the correspondence. My rights! I had none. A claim that a formal appeal to a Judge in Chambers can quash in ten minutes is not a right. I am quite astounded at the position I have been placed in. How much better if you had done as I asked you, as at that time my wife was kind and ready to let me see my two children and be with them occasionally. A. D. put me into a false position with regard to his father, forced me into it, and held me there. More Adey, with the best intentions, forced me into a false position with regard to my wife. Even had I any legal rights – and I have none – how much more charming to have privileges given to me by affection than to extort them by threats. My wife was very sweet to me, and now she, very naturally, goes right against me. Of her character also a wrong estimate was made. She warned me that if I let my friends bid against her she would proceed to a certain course, and she will do so.[12]

Again, Swinburne says to Marie Stuart in one of his poems,

> But surely you were something better
> Than innocent![13]

and really my friends must face the fact that (setting aside such details in my indictment as belonged to my bosom-friend, three in number) I am not in prison as an innocent man. On the contrary, my record of perversities of passion and distorted romances would fill many scarlet volumes. I think it right to mention this – however surprising, and no doubt shocking, it will sound to many – because More Adey in his letter tells me that the opposite side will be obliged to furnish strict details of the dates and places and exact circumstances of the terrible charges to be brought against me. Does he seriously imagine that if I submitted to more cross-examination I would be believed? Does he propose I should do so, and repeat the Queensberry fiasco? It is the case that the charges are not true. But that is a mere detail. If a man gets drunk, whether he does so on white wine or red is of no importance. If a man has perverse passions, their particular mode of manifestation is of no importance either.

I said from the first that I relied entirely on my wife's condonation. I now learn that no condonation is of any value where more than one offence may be charged. My wife has simply to say that she condoned X, but knew nothing of Y, and would not hear of condoning Z. There is a little shilling book – ninepence for cash – called *Every Man his own Lawyer*. If my friends had only sent it to me, or even read it themselves, all this trouble, expense, and worry would have been saved. However, while I blame you *ab initio*, I am now in a mood of mind that makes me think that everything that happens is for the best, and that the world is not a mere chaos in which chance and cleverness clash. What I have to do is simply this. I have got to submit to my divorce. I don't think that the Government could possibly prosecute me again. Even for a British Government it would be too brutal a procedure. I have also, before that, to restore to my wife my interest in the settlement-money before it is taken from me. I have thirdly to state that I will accept nothing from her at all in the way of income or allowance. This seems to be the simple, straightforward, and gentlemanly thing to do. It is a great blow to me. I feel the legal deprivation of my children poignantly.

My friendship with A. D. brought me first to the dock of the Criminal Court, then to the dock of the Bankruptcy Court, and now to the dock of the Divorce Court. As far as I can make out (not having the shilling primer on the subject) there are no more docks into which he can bring me. If so, I can draw a breath of relief. But I want you to seriously consider my proposal, to ask More to do so, and his lawyer, and to write to me, and to get More to write to me, as soon as possible about it. I think my wife will have no objection to refunding the £75 paid for the *damnosa haereditas*[14] of my life-interest. She is quite just on money matters. But personally I hope there will be no bargaining. A grave mistake has been made. Submission has to follow. I propose that my life-interest should be restored to my wife, its rightful owner, as a parting gift from me. It will render my exit from marriage less ignominious than to wait for its being done by legal coercion. Whether I am married or not is a matter that does not concern me. For years I disregarded the tie. But I really think that it is hard on my wife to be tied to me. I always thought so. And, though it may surprise some of my friends, I am really very fond of my wife and very sorry for her. I sincerely hope she may have a happy marriage, if she marries again. She could not understand me, and I was bored to death with the married life. But she had some sweet points in her character, and was wonderfully loyal to me. On this point of my surrendering everything, pray let More and yourself write at once, after you have considered the point.

Also, I would take it as a great favour if More would write to the people who pawned or sold my fur coat since my imprisonment, and ask them from me whether they would be kind enough to state where it was sold or pawned as I am anxious to trace it, and if possible get it back. I have had it for twelve years, it was all over America with me, it was at all my first nights, it knows me perfectly, and I really want it. The letter should be quite courteous, addressed first to the man: if he doesn't answer, to the woman. As it was the wife who pressed me to leave it in her charge, it might be mentioned that I am surprised and distressed, particularly as I paid out of my own pocket *since my imprisonment* all the expenses of her confinement, to the extent of £50 conveyed through Leverson.[15] This might be stated as a reason for my being distressed. Their letters must be kept. I have a most particular reason for wishing it to be done – in fact, one vitally important. And the letter being one of civil request, with the reasons set forth, cannot involve argument or denial. I just require documentary evidence for my protection.

I hope to see Frank Harris on Saturday week, or soon. The news of the copying of my letter will be welcome, when I hear from you about my divorce. If Arthur Clifton would like to see the copy show it to him, or your brother Aleck. Ever yours

    Oscar Wilde

To Robert Ross

6 April [1897]   *HM Prison, Reading*

My dear Robbie,

I am going to delay for a short time my letter to Alfred Douglas for certain reasons, some of which, though not all, are suggested in a letter I am sending to More Adey at the same time as this.[16]

I write to you now, partly for the pleasure of writing to you and getting from you in return one of your delightful literary letters, and partly because I have to blame you, and I cannot bear the idea of doing that indirectly, or in a letter addressed to another.

It is now more than a year – a year and one month to be exact – since I wrote to you telling you that I wished my friends to withdraw completely all opposition to my wife buying my life-interest in my marriage-settlement, as I did not desire anything to be done that could make an estrangement between my wife and myself. My wife had come all the way from Genoa to break to me personally the news of my dear mother's death. She had been very sympathetic and sweet to me. Her offer of a third of the interest in case of her death was ample and right.

I wrote strongly to you, because I trusted that you would see that to make an estrangement between my wife and myself over a paltry money question would be wrong, unseemly, and unjust to both of us: you knew my wife better than any of my friends did. You were fond of her, and she was excessively fond of you. I felt sure I could rely on you to see that my wishes and hers were carried out. I was mistaken. Seven months later – on October 22nd – I found out through a violent and insulting letter from her lawyer, enraged at what seemed like double-dealing on my part, that my wishes had not been regarded.

I was at once thrust into a false position. Just as Alfred Douglas forced me into a false position with his father, and made me, with my life behind me, take action against the entire forces of Society, the Bar, and the Government, so my friends forced me, an isolated and pauper prisoner in an English gaol, to fight Sir George Lewis and Mr Hargrove. I was told again and again how important it was that I should not 'surrender' any of my 'rights' over my children. The phrase occurs in three letters now lying before me. As if I had any rights! I had none. The formal application to a Judge in Chambers by a solicitor's clerk deprived me of Cyril and Vyvyan in less than ten minutes. It was a mere matter of form.

I wrote to Mr Holman to ask him if a divorce would not break my marriage-settlement. I felt sure it would. I received no answer. But the purchase of a small shilling book – ninepence for cash – entitled *Every Man his own Lawyer* would have informed my friends that when a divorce is granted a settlement is annulled unless it is specified to the contrary.

I also let my friends know that my only chance of resisting a divorce was the fact of *condonation* by my wife. I now hear that condonation counts as nothing where more than one offence may be alleged. My solicitor told me it was a commonplace in law, the sort of thing an office-boy would know. More

Adey gravely writes to tell me that details and dates of each separate offence will have to be given, so that I may prepare my defence!

In one of his poems to Marie Stuart, Swinburne says to his heroine

> But surely you were something better
> Than innocent![17]

and so, though the particular offence required by the law did not find part amongst my perversities of passion, still perversities there were, or else why am I here? It may be a terrible shock to my friends to think that I had abnormal passions, and perverse desires, but if they read history they will find I am not the first artist so doomed, any more than I shall be the last. To talk of my defending the case against Sir George Lewis is childish. How can I expect to be believed on a mere detail? What limit is there to the amount of witnesses he can produce? None. He and Queensberry can sweep Piccadilly for them. It makes me sick with rage when I am told about the opportunities I shall have of defending the case. What common sense have my friends got to write such twaddle to me?

However, we must accept facts as they are. My wife is now going for a divorce. She has been forced to do so. The purchase of my life-interest against her wishes and interests has left her no option. From the first she was advised by Sir George Lewis to divorce me. She resisted out of affection for me. Now she has been forced to do so. And I feel that the only thing now for me to do is to make my wife a present of my life-interest, and to submit to the divorce. It is bitter to me, but I think it is the right thing for me to do, and it would I think be more seemly and generous of me to make my full submission and leave her perfectly free. I don't think that even a British Government with Labouchère, Stead,[18] and the Social Purity League to back them would re-arrest me and send me to prison again. It would be a ridiculous thing to do. I must live in England, if I am to be a dramatist again, so I must face it if they do. But it would be a bestial infamy to again send me to a prison for offences that in all civilised countries are questions of pathology and medical treatment if their cure is desired.

You see, Robbie, how wrong you were to pretend to me that you were carrying out my wishes and my wife's, when really you were doing the exact opposite. We all make the mistake of thinking life is complex. It is not. It is we who are complex, and people think that clever, smart, round-about schemes are the best. They are the worst. Life is quite simple. One should do the straightforward thing. Complex people waste half their strength in trying to conceal what they do. Is it any wonder they should always come to grief?

Consider now, dear Robbie, my proposal. I think my wife, who in money-matters is most honourable and high-minded, will refund the £75 paid for my share. I have no doubt she will. But I think it should be offered from me, and that I should not accept anything in the way of income from her. I can accept what is given in love and affection to me, but I could not accept what is doled out grudgingly, or with conditions. I would sooner let my wife be quite free. She may marry again. In any case I think that if free she would allow me to see my children from time to time. That is what I want. But I must set her free first, and had better do it as a gentleman by bowing my head and accepting everything.

You must consider the whole question, as it is through you and your ill-advised action it is due: and let me know what you and others think. Of course you acted for the best. But you were wrong in your view. I may say candidly that I am gradually getting to a state of mind when I think that everything that happens is for the best. This may be philosophy, or a broken heart, or religion, or the dull apathy of despair. But, whatever its origin, the feeling is strong with me. To tie my wife to me against her will would be wrong. She has a full right to her freedom. And not to be supported by her would be a pleasure to me. It is an ignominious position to be a pensioner on her. Talk over this with More Adey. Get him to show you the letter. I have written to him. Ask your brother Aleck to give me his advice. He has excellent wisdom on things.

Now to other points.

I have never had the chance of thanking you for the books. They were most welcome. Not being allowed the magazines was a blow, but Meredith's novel[19] charmed me. What a sane artist in temper! He is quite right in his assertion of sanity as the essential in romance. Still, up to the present only the abnormal have found expression in life and literature.

Rossetti's letters are dreadful.[20] Obviously forgeries by his brother. I was interested however to see how my grand-uncle's *Melmoth* and my mother's *Sidonia*[21] had been two of the books that fascinated his youth. As regards the conspiracy against him in later years I believe it really existed, and that the funds for it came out of Hake's bank. The conduct of a thrush in Cheyne Walk[22] seems to me most suspicious, though William Rossetti says, 'I could discern nothing in the thrush's song at all out of the common.'

Stevenson letters most disappointing also.[23] I see that romantic surroundings are the worst surroundings possible for a romantic writer. In Gower Street Stevenson could have written a new *Trois Mousquetaires*. In Samoa he wrote letters to *The Times* about Germans. I see also the traces of a terrible *strain* to lead a natural life. To chop wood with any advantage to oneself, or profit to others, one should not be able to describe the process. In point of fact the natural life is the unconscious life. Stevenson merely extended the sphere of the artificial by taking to digging. The whole dreary book has given me a lesson. If I spend my future life reading Baudelaire in a *café* I shall be leading a more natural life than if I take to hedger's work or plant cacao in mud-swamps.

En Route is most over-rated.[24] It is sheer journalism. It never makes one hear a note of the music it describes. The subject is delightful, but the style is of course worthless, slipshod, flaccid. It is worse French than Ohnet's.[25] Ohnet tries to be commonplace and succeeds. Huysmans tries not to be, and is . . .[26] Hardy's novel is pleasant, and Frederic's[27] very interesting in matter . . . Later on, there being hardly any novels in the prison library for the poor imprisoned fellows I live with, I think of presenting the library with about a dozen good novels: Stevenson's (none here but *The Black Arrow*!), some of Thackeray's (none here), Jane Austen (none here), and some good Dumas-*père*-like books, by Stanley Weyman[28] for instance, and any modern young man. You mentioned Henley had a *protégé*.[29] Also the 'Anthony Hope' man.[30] After Easter, you might make out a list of about fourteen, and apply to let me have them. They would please the few who do not care about Goncourt's journal. Don't forget. I would pay myself for them.

I have a horror myself of going out into a world without a single book of my own. I wonder would there be any of my friends who would give me a few books, such as Cosmo Lennox, Reggie Turner, Gilbert Burgess, Max,[31] and the like? You know the sort of books I want: Flaubert, Stevenson, Baudelaire, Maeterlinck, Dumas *père*, Keats, Marlowe, Chatterton, Coleridge, Anatole France, Gautier, Dante and all Dante literature; Goethe and ditto: and so on. I would feel it a great compliment to have books waiting for me, and perhaps there may be some friends who would like to be kind to me. One is really very grateful, though I fear I often seem not to be. But then remember I have had incessant worries besides prison-life.

In answer to this you can send me a long letter all about plays and books. Your handwriting, in your last, was so dreadful that it looked as if you were writing a three-volume novel on the terrible spread of communistic ideas among the rich, or in some other way wasting a youth that always has been, and always will remain, quite full of promise. If I wrong you in ascribing it to such a cause you must make allowances for the morbidity produced by long imprisonment. But do write clearly. Otherwise it looks as if you had nothing to conceal.

There is much that is horrid, I suppose, in this letter. But I had to blame you to yourself, not to others. Read my letter to More. F. Harris comes to see me on Saturday, I hope. Remember me to Arthur Clifton and his wife, who, I find, is so like Rossetti's wife – the same lovely hair – but of course a sweeter nature, though Miss Siddal is fascinating, and her poem A1.[32] Ever yours

Oscar

PS The names of the mystical books in *En Route* fascinate me. Try and get some of them for me when I go out. Also, try and get me a good life of St Francis of Assisi.

French Books[33]

Flaubert: [*La*] *Tentation* [*de Saint Antoine*].
>   *Trois Contes.*
>   *Salammbô.*

Mérimée: Novels.

Anatole France: *Thaïs* [1890] and his latest works.

Pierre Louÿs: Novel [*Aphrodite*, 1896].

La Jeunesse: Novel [*L'Imitation de Notre-Maître Napoléon*, 1897].

Maeterlinck: Complete.

Baudelaire: [*Les*] *Fleurs du Mal*.

Strindberg: Last plays.

Ibsen: Translation ([*Little*] *Eyolf*. [*John Gabriel*] *Borkman*).

Montaigne.

Gautier: *Émaux et Camées*.

French Bible (University Press).

French–English Dictionary.

Some mystical books.

[Gilbert] Murray: [*History of Ancient*] *Greek Literature* [1897].

Quarterly Review for April.

[D. G.] Hogarth on Alexander the Great (Murray) [*Philip and Alexander of Macedon*, 1897].

Quo Vadis? (Dent) (Translation of novel by Sienkiewicz) [1896].

English

Epic and Romance [by W. P. Ker, 1897].

St William of Norwich [: *Life and Miracles* by Thomas of Monmouth. Now first edited from unique MS. by Augustus Jessopp and M. R. James, 1896].

Ancient Ideals [by H. O. Taylor, 1896].

Wagner's Letters to Roeckel (Arrowsmith) [1887].

[J. A.] Symonds: *Italian By-ways* [1883].

[Franz] Hettinger on Dante. Translated by Father [H. S.] Bowden[34] (Burns & Oates) [1896].

Mrs Mark Pattison: *Renaissance [of Art] in France* [1879].

Dom [Francis Aidan] Gasquet: *Historical Essays* [*The Old English Bible and Other Essays*, 1897].

Yeats: *The Secret Rose* [1897].

A. E. W. Mason: *The Philanderers* (Macmillan) [1897]. Also his previous novel [*The Courtship of Morrice Buckler*, 1896].

A Bible.

Flinders Petrie on Egypt [*Egyptian Decorative Art*, 1895]. Any good book on Ancient Egypt.

Translation of Hafiz, and of oriental love-poetry.

Arthur Morrison: article in *Nineteenth Century* on Prisons and Sir Edmund Du Cane's reply. Also Arthur Morrison's Criminology series.[35]

Spanish–French Conversation Book.

Calderon: [*El*] *Mágico Prodigioso* (translated).

[*La*] *Devoción de la Cruz* (translated).

Spanish Grammar.

Silver brushes – my brother. Bag also.

White ties, made up.

English manuscript books. Pencils. Foolscap paper.

Despatch-box! Where is it? Very Important.

Guide-Book to the Morbihan, Finisterre district. Quimper, Vannes.

Guide-Book to Pyrenees.

See is there near Boulogne any small place to go to. Not more than an hour and a half.

Reviews of *Salomé*.

Salomé itself,

Humphreys.[36]

To More Adey

My dear More,

I am sending a letter of great importance to Robbie which he will show you. It deals primarily with my divorce-suit. I have been thrust into a very false position by my friends, and have to suffer for it. I see (for reasons stated at greater length to Robbie) nothing now but to submit, and to return beforehand my life-interest, as a sort of parting-gift, so as not to leave my exit from the marriage-tie too ignominious and unworthy.

The primary fault was Robbie's in not carrying out my own wishes and my wife's, conveyed to him in my letter of March 1896. Also, there has been a complete misapprehension of my wife's character, which is strong and simple, and of Mr Hargrove's. The latter has been regarded as a solicitor of the Humphreys type, one who would bluster, and threaten, and lie. He really is a man of the highest character and position and whatever he said he would do he will carry out. To put me up to fight him and Sir George Lewis was childish.

As for buying the life-interest, Mr Hargrove would raise £5000 tomorrow for my wife if she wanted it. He was the family solicitor of her grandfather, and owes much of his own wealth – which is very considerable – to Mr Horatio Lloyd.[37] Everything has been wrong. So wrong indeed have things been that it looks to me as if Alfred Douglas had been directing the operations, desirous to 'score off' Mr Hargrove, or my wife, or both. His sole idea seems to be to 'score off' people by sacrificing me. Please let me know, am I right in discerning some of his sinister small nature in the whole transaction?

At any rate, when you have read my letter to Robbie, will you seriously consider the position into which I have been led, and don't, I beg you, write to me again about defending the case. If a man gets drunk, whether he does so on white wine or red matters little, and if a man has perversities of passion there is no use his denying particular details in a civil court, whatever he may do in a criminal one: and just as there are several counts in my indictment for things done by someone else, so I will be divorced I have no doubt for things I have never done, and I dare say with people I have never seen. I have to submit. I see nothing else for it.

It, of course, breaks entirely every link with my children. There was indeed no link left but my wife's kindness to me. After the divorce, I suppose I shall never see them. And when I think it is all over a paltry £150 or £200 a year I really feel ashamed. My friends seem not to have realised that what I wanted was access to my children, and their affection and my wife's. I shall await your letter with interest.

With regard to your letter about Alfred Douglas, I see of course that I must clearly ascertain what he and his family are going to do. On the occasion of my bankruptcy, which it was disgraceful of them to allow, I received through you and others a promise from Percy that £500 was to be at my disposal on my release, it being considered by him and his brother that it would be better to give the money to me instead of to their father. This promise will, I suppose, I don't doubt, be carried out, and as my release takes place in a few weeks and I am anxious to arrange my life for the next couple of years, will you kindly write to Percy and ask him to let you have the money for me. It must not go into Leverson's hands, as he would probably use it for his own purposes or in his business. I wish you to have it.

I also think it right that Percy should know a little of the mere outlines of my unfortunate acquaintance with his brother. The friendship began in May 1892 by his brother appealing to me in a very pathetic letter to help him in terrible trouble with people who were blackmailing him. I hardly knew him at the time. I had known him eighteen months, but had only seen him four times in that space. I was, however, I admit, touched by his letter, and his appeal, and did at once get him out of his trouble at considerable difficulty and annoyance to myself. Alfred Douglas was very grateful, and practically never left me for three years – not till he had got me into prison. I wish Percy to know of my incessant efforts to break off a friendship so ruinous to me artistically, financially, and socially.

In December 1893 I went so far as to fly abroad and leave a false address to try and escape from him. During the whole time he was in Egypt I refused to write to him or take any notice of his incessant letters and telegrams. It was only on his rushing back to Paris and sending me a telegram that seemed to threaten suicide that I consented even to see him. To get him out of my life was one of the objects of my life. I completely failed to accomplish it. Nothing that I could do could keep him out of my house.

As regards money, let Percy know that I spent on A.D. and with him more than £5000 in two years and a half, exclusive of bills. This I did not do as a pleasure to myself. I was forced to. I never remember on any one occasion from May 1892 to April 1895, the date of my arrest, A.D. having any money at all from either his father or his mother. He came to me for everything, nor is it any exaggeration to say that from his morning shave to his midnight hansom I was obliged to pay for every single item in his day's expenditure. He refused to have his meals at home and insisted on having them with me at the most expensive restaurants. He arrived at twelve o'clock every morning, and practically he never left me till after midnight. It was ruinous to me in every way, but I could not get rid of him. Explain to Percy that I never gave his brother large sums of money. His name hardly appears in my cheque-book. Where it does it was simply because when he was away or abroad he used to draw cheques on his own bank where his account was always overdrawn and telegraph to me to implore me to cover it by lodging to his account the amount so that his cheque might be honoured. The real expense was his support, left entirely to me.

Also, pray explain to Percy that the night A.D. arrived from Algiers I implored him to let us tell him (Percy) the truth. He absolutely refused, and insisted on the comedy of his father's delusions. Also, let Percy know the exact circumstances of my entering the absurd action. A.D. had brought to my hotel a companion of his own, one whose age, appearance, public and private profession, rendered him the most unsuitable companion possible for me in the terribly serious position in which I was placed. On my remonstrating with him, and asking him to let his companion return to his home, he made a violent scene, and preferring the society of his companion to mine retired at once to another hotel, where I subsequently had to pay the bill for them both, I need hardly say.

From his new quarters he began to bombard me with revolting letters. On the Thursday I went to my club and found Queensberry's hideous card. I returned at once to the hotel where I found a no less loathsome letter from Alfred Douglas. I felt I stood between Caliban and Sporus,[38] and that I was in hideous danger from both of them, and, just as I had bolted from the son in December '93 to Paris, so I determined to bolt at once, to Paris again, from father as well as son. Unfortunately the bill for the ten days Alfred Douglas had planted himself on me, with his companion at the close of the period, was £148, and the hotel people would not allow my luggage to be removed till I had paid the bill in full, which I could not do. At that moment A.D. arrived, saw his father's card, and by taunts of cowardice and terror drove me to the fatal step. I stumbled like an ox into the shambles. My last straw for clutching to was the expense. I told Humphreys I had no money. A.D. at once interfered, said that his family would pay the whole expense, and be too delighted to do so. Humphreys, keen for a scandalous case, and scenting money, closed at once. I was brought in a four-wheeler by both of them to apply for a warrant, and here I am in prison. I think Percy should know these facts, as from Robbie's letter to me the Queensberry family seem to be talking foolishly about the case. So please write to Percy, and ask him from me to fulfil his promise.

Also, I want you to write to Leverson from me. During the time I was out on bail a sum of money was given to me by a friend to be of use to me in any way possible. I, not liking to have a large sum of money on me, asked Leverson and Reggie Turner to be trustees of this. They consented. Leverson personally took charge of the money. I gave Leverson a piece of paper on which my friend had written 'I desire this money to be employed for your own personal use and that of your children as you may direct'. These were the conditions of the trust. Leverson accepted it, but told me it would be better, more convenient, only to have one trustee, and that he had arranged with Reggie to retire. I was surprised, but made no objection.

On my way to Court to receive my sentence he began asking me in the carriage to repay him £250, the balance of £500 he had advanced to Alfred Douglas and myself for the first trial. I was astonished and wounded at his selecting such a moment to worry me over a debt, and told him that I could not discuss business then, and that the money held in trust was to be applied for my mother's wants primarily, and then, if it was necessary, for my children. He did disburse on my behalf to my mother some £280 or so: my children, my wife told me, required nothing. He now comes and proposes to deduct his debt of £250 before he hands over the balance. I cannot allow this for a single moment. He has to hand over the trust-money intact to me. He has no right to touch it for any claim of his own. He must know quite well that his proposing to pay himself in full, when my other creditors are receiving nothing, is an entire breach of the Bankruptcy Laws. This money was not given to me to pay my debts. It was given to me because I was at the time bankrupt and ruined, to be held in trust for me by a friend. Leverson first through you proposed to pay himself and to lend me an equivalent sum. I declined this entirely. When he came here, he calmly told me that 'money was tight in the City' and that he could not let me have the money that belonged to me! As if I cared whether money was tight in the City, or knew what it meant. I suppose it means that he was speculating with trust-money. That is a dangerous amusement. As a business man he should know better.

Kindly write to him and copy out what I have said and ask him to let me have the proper balance of the money entrusted to his care for my use. Of his original loan he has already had fifty per cent: the only one of my creditors who has had anything. For him to swoop down illegally and propose to collar the balance is not to be thought of. Nor will he do so. Of course, if he tried to do so I would never speak to him again or consent to see him, and would let everyone publicly and privately know of his dishonourable conduct. I would also take other measures.

There is also another matter: he bought for me at my sale my own portrait,[39] the picture of A.D. I commissioned Will Rothenstein to do, and Shannon's pastel of the Moon.[40] He may want to be paid for these, as he said they were a present to me from himself and his wife. If so, let him deduct from what is due to me his claim. The three things themselves I wish very much could be lodged somewhere for me – in a little garret in Hornton Street, or anywhere – so that I can get them when I want. Can you do this at once?

The Sphinx has (1) *The Duchess of Padua*. (2) The manuscript of *La Sainte Courtisane*. (3) A bundle of A.D.'s letters. Would you give her from me my kind regards and most affectionate wishes and ask her to let Robbie have them, as I want them all three as soon as I am released. This is a horrid letter, but how am I to write on horrid things but horridly? Ever yours

Oscar

To Thomas Martin

[*Circa April 1897*]   [*HM Prison, Reading*]

My dear friend,

What have I to write about except that if you had been an officer in Reading Prison a year ago my life would have been much happier. Everyone tells me I am looking better – and happier.

That is because I have a good friend who gives me the *Chronicle*, and *promises* me ginger biscuits![41]

O. W.

*

You must get me his address some day – he is such a good fellow.[42] Of course I would not for worlds get such a friend as you are into *any danger*. I quite understand your feelings.

The *Chronicle* is capital today. You must get A.3.2 to come out and clean on Saturday morning and I will give him my note then myself.

*

I hope to write about prison life and to try and change it for others, but it is too terrible and ugly to make a work of art of. I have suffered too much in it to write plays about it.

*

So sorry you have no key. Would like a long talk with you. Any more news?

To the Home Secretary[43]

22 *April 1897*   *HM Prison, Reading*

To the Right Honourable Her Majesty's Principal Secretary of State for the Home Department.

The Petition of the above-named prisoner humbly sheweth that the petitioner was sentenced to two years' imprisonment on the 20th May, 1895,[44] and that his term of imprisonment will expire on the 19th of next May, four weeks from the date of this petition.

That the petitioner is extremely anxious to avoid the notoriety and annoyance of newspaper interviews and descriptions on the occasion of his release, the date of which is of course well known. Many English, French and American papers have already announced their intention of attending the ceremony of his release, for the purpose of seeking and publishing interviews with him on the question of the treatment he has been subjected to in prison, the real circumstances that led to his original trial, and the like. The petitioner is anxious to avoid any intrusion of the kind threatened, as he considers that such interviews at such a moment would be from every point of view unseemly. He desires to go abroad quietly without attracting public attention, and his petition is that he may be released on the Saturday preceding the 19th May – Saturday the 15th in fact – so that he may go abroad unobserved and incognito.

The petitioner would beg to be allowed to mention that he was for three weeks confined in Holloway Prison before his first trial: that he was then released on bail, and surrendered to his bail to stand his trial a second time: the second trial resulting in his conviction. The petitioner will accordingly have had more than two years' detention should he be released on the 15th May as his prayer is.

The petitioner, however, is most anxious that he should not under any circumstances be transferred to another prison from the one in which he is at present confined. The ordeal he underwent in being brought in convict dress and handcuffed by a mid-day train from Clapham Junction to Reading was so utterly distressing, from the mental no less than the emotional point of view, that he feels quite unable to undergo any similar exhibition to public gaze, and he feels it his duty to say that he was assured by the former Governor of Reading Prison that he would not under any circumstances be again submitted to so terrible an experience.

Should the petitioner's request to be released on the 15th May be granted, Mr Frank Harris, the Editor of the *Saturday Review*, who has kindly invited the petitioner to go on a driving-tour in the Pyrenees with him, would at once proceed abroad with him, crossing the Channel either in a yacht, or by night, so as to avoid observation and annoyance.

And your petitioner will ever pray etc.

Oscar Wilde

To Thomas Martin

[*17 May 1897*]   [*HM Prison, Reading*]

Please find out for me the name of A.2.11.[45] Also: the names of the children who are in for the rabbits, and the amount of the fine. Can I pay this, and get them out? If so I will get them out tomorrow. Please, dear friend, do this for me. I must get them out. Think what a thing for me it would be to be able to help three little children. I would be delighted beyond words. If I can do this by paying the fine, tell the children that they are to be released tomorrow by a friend, and ask them to be happy, and not to tell anyone.

To Reginald Turner

[*Postmark 17 May 1897*]   *HM Prison, Reading*

My dear Reggie,

I write to you by kind permission of the Governor to tell you that I am to be transferred to Pentonville Prison tomorrow evening and shall be released from there. I am bound to say that the transference is to be executed under humane conditions as regards dress and not being handcuffed. Otherwise I confess I would have refused such an ordeal.

I want you, dear Reggie, to come to Pentonville Prison on Wednesday morning, to have a carriage waiting for me and to take me to some hotel in the vicinity, or wherever you think there is a quiet place. At the hotel I want to find all my clothes, your dressing-bag to which I look forward with joy and gratitude, a room to dress in, and a sitting-room. In fact, dear Reggie, you had better go yourself to an hotel tomorrow evening, and sleep there. I can dress in your room, and breakfast in a sitting-room adjoining. I dare say a hansom would do, but a little brougham with blinds might be best: you must decide. I would like coffee for breakfast, as I have been living on cocoa, and don't think I could taste tea.

The being in London, the place I wished to avoid, is terrible: but we learn humility in prison, and I have consented to go. I dare say it is best.

I suppose I had better go to Southampton on Wednesday, by some station, if possible not a big London one: I mean Vauxhall better than Waterloo etc. So get a carriage for the drive through London. There are of course only two ways by which I can travel: either third-class, which I need hardly say, dear Reggie, I don't mind a scrap: or first-class in a *reserved* carriage: it is unnecessary to explain why: you will see that while I can sit at ease with the poor, I could not with the rich: for me to enter a first-class carriage containing other people would be dreadful: they would not like it, and I would know they would not. That would distress me. So, if you can reserve a first-class carriage to Southampton, do so.

I hope that Leverson will surrender my money, and that I will have it. It is now 12.30, and he apparently has not done so. It is my own money, Reggie! He was to be the trustee of it! Can you conceive such cruelty and fraud as to try to steal it from me? I am learning bitter lessons. If however he can be got to disgorge this money he has apparently embezzled, engage a first-class carriage in any name you choose – *Mr Melmoth*[46] is my name: so let it be that. If the train stops at Vauxhall well and good: if not, I must drive to Waterloo and simply walk into the carriage and draw down the blinds.

I am told that there is an anxiety I should cross over by the day-boat to Havre: certainly: I prefer it. I did not know there was one. Engage by telegram a private cabin for Mr Melmoth: at Havre no doubt I can stay the night.

I am so distressed by the conduct of More Adey towards me in spending without my knowledge and consent the £150 he was given for my use in a hideous litigation that nearly ended in my being divorced and so left penniless either to live in exile or to be rearrested, that I could not travel with him: I will see him if he wishes at whatever hotel I go to. Robbie I will expect at Havre in two or three days. You are the only friend I have, Reggie, with whom I would like to go away. I will be gentle to you because I am grateful to you. With the others I know I shall be bitter. They have put an adder into my heart and an asp under my tongue.

If you will consent to come away with me you will be doing a service beyond words to a very heart-broken man. If you can do all this

(1) get my things,
(2) fix on a hotel, engage a carriage, have my rooms ready,
(3) meet me at Pentonville,
(4) come away with me to Havre, and stay a week with me,

well, you will be the best of dear boys. Nobody will ever shoot a tongue of scorn at you for having been kind to me. If they did, I know you would not care.

I have written to More Adey to acquaint him with the change of plan, and to ask him to hand over to you whatever money Leverson parts with *in toto*: even if it is only £175, that is something. Spare no expense, dear Reggie: I want to get away comfortably and quietly: and we will take with us £100. The rest keep for me.

If you consent to do this, kindly wire to the Governor here: 'Consent Reginald Turner.' If Leverson has parted with my money, please add 'money received': if he has not, well, I fear I must stay in London. I may receive £37 from my lawyer, from my wife, who has sweetly thought of its being of use to me. But I can't go abroad for three months on £37. More Adey wrote to me on Saturday: 'Do not worry yourself, dear Oscar, about money affairs. It is all right. You will have £37 on the day of your release.' Can you conceive a man being so tactless, so dull of wit, so unimaginative! It drives me frantic.

Send me a letter under cover to the Governor of Pentonville Prison: in this state what you have done. Ask him in a personal letter to hand it to me on my arrival. Try and find a hotel with a good *bathroom* close to bedroom: this most essential. Ever yours

Oscar

PS Have just seen my solicitor. I do not like the idea of going to Stewart Headlam's[47] at all. I don't know him very well, and I am afraid of strangers. Please will you consider the possibility of a hotel: some quiet place – Euston Road or anywhere like that. I would much prefer it. Thank Stewart Headlam from me, but tell him I am very nervous and ill and upset. If you really wish it I will go to his house: but I would sooner not. Any quiet hotel would be better for me. I am ready to go to Southampton with you – or Dieppe, if that is preferred. But the special carriage must be got, and special cabin. Come to Pentonville at 6.30 with a closed brougham: that will be the hour: drive in to the yard.

To the Editor of the Daily Chronicle[48]

27 May [1897]   [Dieppe]

Sir,

I learn with great regret, through the columns of your paper, that the warder Martin, of Reading Prison, has been dismissed by the Prison Commissioners for having given some sweet biscuits to a little hungry child. I saw the three children myself on the Monday preceding my release. They had just been convicted, and were standing in a row in the central hall in their prison dress, carrying their sheets under their arms previous to their being sent to the cells allotted to them. I happened to be passing along one of the galleries on my way to the reception room, where I was to have an interview with a friend. They were quite small children, the youngest – the one to whom the warder gave the biscuits – being a tiny little chap, for whom they had evidently been unable to find clothes small enough to fit. I had, of course, seen many children in prison during the two years during which I was myself confined. Wandsworth Prison especially contained always a large number of children. But the little child I saw on the afternoon of Monday the 17th, at Reading, was tinier than any one of them. I need not say how utterly distressed I was to see these children at Reading, for I knew the treatment in store for them. The cruelty that is practised by day and night on children in English prisons is incredible, except to those that have witnessed it and are aware of the brutality of the system.

People nowadays do not understand what cruelty is. They regard it as a sort of terrible mediaeval passion, and connect it with the race of men like Eccelino da Romano,[49] and others, to whom the deliberate infliction of pain gave a real madness of pleasure. But men of the stamp of Eccelino are merely abnormal types of perverted individualism. Ordinary cruelty is simply stupidity. It is the entire want of imagination. It is the result in our days of stereotyped systems of hard-and-fast rules, and of stupidity. Wherever there is centralisation there is stupidity. What is inhuman in modern life is officialism. Authority is as destructive to those who exercise it as it is to those on whom it is exercised. It is the Prison Board, and the system that it carries out, that is the primary source of the cruelty that is exercised on a child in prison. The people who uphold the system have excellent intentions. Those who carry it out are humane in intention also. Responsibility is shifted on to the disciplinary regulations. It is supposed that because a thing is the rule it is right.

The present treatment of children is terrible, primarily from people not understanding the peculiar psychology of a child's nature. A child can understand a punishment inflicted by an individual, such as a parent or guardian, and bear it with a certain amount of acquiescence. What it cannot understand is a punishment inflicted by society. It cannot realise what society is. With grown people it is, of course, the reverse. Those of us who are either in prison or have been sent there, can understand, and do understand, what that collective force called society means, and whatever we may think of its methods or claims, we can force ourselves to accept it. Punishment inflicted on us by an individual, on the other hand, is a thing that no grown person endures, or is expected to endure.

The child consequently, being taken away from its parents by people whom it has never seen, and of whom it knows nothing, and finding itself in a lonely and unfamiliar cell, waited on by strange faces, and ordered about and punished by the representatives of a system that it cannot understand, becomes an immediate prey to the first and most prominent emotion produced by modern prison life – the emotion of terror. The terror of a child in prison is quite limitless. I remember once in Reading, as I was going out to exercise, seeing in the dimly lit cell right opposite my own a small boy. Two warders – not unkindly men – were talking to him, with some sternness apparently, or perhaps giving him some useful advice about his conduct. One was in the cell with him, the other was standing outside. The child's face was like a white wedge of sheer terror. There was in his eyes the terror of a hunted animal. The next morning I heard him at breakfast-time crying, and calling to be let out.

His cry was for his parents. From time to time I could hear the deep voice of the warder on duty telling him to keep quiet. Yet he was not even convicted of whatever little offence he had been charged with. He was simply on remand. That I knew by his wearing his own clothes, which seemed neat enough. He was, however, wearing prison socks and shoes. This showed that he was a very poor boy, whose own shoes, if he had any, were in a bad state. Justices and magistrates, an entirely ignorant class as a rule, often remand children for a week, and then perhaps remit whatever sentence they are entitled to pass. They call this 'not sending a child to prison'. It is, of course, a stupid view on their part. To a little child, whether he is in prison on remand or after conviction is not a subtlety of social position he can comprehend. To him the horrible thing is to be there at all. In the eyes of humanity it should be a horrible thing for him to be there at all.

This terror that seizes and dominates the child, as it seizes the grown man also, is of course intensified beyond power of expression by the solitary cellular system of our prisons. Every child is confined to its cell for twenty-three hours out of the twenty-four. This is the appalling thing. To shut up a child in a dimly lit cell, for twenty-three hours out of the twenty-four, is an example of the cruelty of stupidity. If an individual, parent or guardian, did this to a child, he would be severely punished. The Society for the Prevention of Cruelty to Children would take the matter up at once. There would be on all hands the utmost detestation of whomsoever had been guilty of such cruelty. A heavy sentence would, undoubtedly, follow conviction. But our own actual society does worse itself, and to the child to be so treated by a strange abstract force, of whose claims it has no cognisance, is much worse than it would be to receive the same treatment from its father or mother, or someone it knew. The inhuman treatment of a child is always inhuman, by whomsoever it is inflicted. But inhuman treatment by society is to the child the more terrible because there is no appeal. A parent or guardian can be moved, and let out a child from the dark lonely room in which it is confined. But a warder cannot. Most warders are very fond of children. But the system prohibits them from rendering the child any assistance. Should they do so, as Warder Martin did, they are dismissed.

The second thing from which a child suffers in prison is hunger. The food that is given to it consists of a piece of usually badly-baked prison bread and a tin of water for breakfast at half-past seven. At twelve o'clock it gets dinner, composed of a tin of coarse Indian meal stirabout, and at half-past five it gets a piece of dry bread and a tin of water for its supper. This diet in the case of a strong grown man is always productive of illness of some kind, chiefly, of course, diarrhoea, with its attendant weakness. In fact in a big prison astringent medicines are served out regularly by the warders as a matter of course. In the case of a child, the child is, as a rule, incapable of eating the food at all. Anyone who knows anything about children knows how easily a child's digestion is upset by a fit of crying, or trouble and mental distress of any kind. A child who has been crying all day long, and perhaps half the night, in a lonely dimly-lit cell, and is preyed upon by terror, simply cannot eat food of this coarse, horrible kind. In the case of the little child to whom Warder Martin gave the biscuits, the child was crying with hunger on Tuesday morning, and utterly unable to eat the bread and water served to it for its breakfast. Martin went out after the breakfasts had been served, and bought the few sweet biscuits for the child rather than see it starving. It was a beautiful action on his part, and was so recognised by the child, who, utterly unconscious of the regulation of the Prison Board, told one of the senior warders how kind this junior warder had been to him. The result was, of course, a report and a dismissal.

I know Martin extremely well, and I was under his charge for the last seven weeks of my imprisonment. On his appointment at Reading he had charge of Gallery C, in which I was confined, so I saw him constantly. I was struck by the singular kindness and humanity of the way in which he spoke to me and to the other prisoners. Kind words are much in prison, and a pleasant 'Good-morning' or 'Good-evening' will make one as happy as one can be in prison. He was always gentle and considerate. I happen to know another case in which he showed great kindness to one of the prisoners, and I have no hesitation in mentioning it. One of the most horrible things in prison is the badness of the sanitary arrangements. No prisoner is allowed under any circumstances to leave his cell after half-past five p.m. If, consequently, he is suffering from diarrhoea, he has to use his cell as a latrine, and pass the night in a most fetid and unwholesome atmosphere. Some days before my release Martin was going the rounds at half-past seven with one of the senior warders for the purpose of collecting the oakum and tools of the prisoners. A man just convicted, and suffering from violent diarrhoea in consequence of the food, as is always the case, asked the senior warder to allow him to empty the slops in his cell on account of the horrible odour of the cell and the possibility of illness again in the night. The senior warder refused absolutely; it was against the rules. The man had to pass the night in this dreadful condition. Martin, however, rather than see this wretched man in such a loathsome predicament, said he would empty the man's slops himself, and did so. A warder emptying a prisoner's slops is, of course, against the rules, but Martin did this act of kindness to the man out of the simple humanity of his nature, and the man was naturally most grateful.

As regards the children, a great deal has been talked and written lately about the contaminating influence of prison on young children. What is said is quite true. A child is utterly contaminated by prison life. But the contaminating influence is not that of the prisoners. It is that of the whole prison system – of the governor, the chaplain, the warders, the lonely cell, the isolation, the revolting food, the rules of the Prison Commissioners, the mode of discipline, as it is termed, of the life. Every care is taken to isolate a child from the sight even of all prisoners over sixteen years of age. Children sit behind a curtain in chapel, and are sent to take exercise in small sunless yards – sometimes a stone-yard, sometimes a yard at the back of the mills – rather than that they should see the elder prisoners at exercise. But the only really humanising influence in prison is the influence of the prisoners. Their cheerfulness under terrible circumstances, their sympathy for each other, their humility, their gentleness, their pleasant smiles of greeting when they meet each other, their complete acquiescence in their punishments, are all quite wonderful, and I myself learned many sound lessons from them. I am not proposing that the children should not sit behind a curtain in chapel, or that they should take exercise in a corner of the common yard. I am merely pointing out that the bad influence on children is not, and could never be, that of the prisoners, but is, and will always remain, that of the prison system itself. There is not a single man in Reading Gaol that would not gladly have done the three children's punishment for them. When I saw them last it was on the Tuesday following their conviction. I was taking exercise at half-past eleven with about twelve other men, as the three children passed near us, in charge of a warder, from the damp, dreary stone-yard in which they had been at their exercise. I saw the greatest pity and sympathy in the eyes of my companions as they looked at them. Prisoners are, as a class, extremely kind and sympathetic to each other. Suffering and the community of suffering makes people kind, and day after day as I tramped the yard I used to feel with pleasure and comfort what Carlyle calls somewhere 'the silent rhythmic charm of human companionship'.[50] In this, as in all other things, philanthropists and people of that kind are astray. It is not the prisoners who need reformation. It is the prisons.

Of course no child under fourteen years of age should be sent to prison at all. It is an absurdity, and, like many absurdities, of absolutely tragic results. If, however, they are to be sent to prison, during the daytime they should be in a workshop or schoolroom with a warder. At night they should sleep in a dormitory, with a night-warder to look after them. They should be allowed exercise for at least three hours a day. The dark, badly ventilated, ill-smelling prison cells are dreadful for a child, dreadful indeed for anyone. One is always breathing bad air in prison. The food given to children should consist of tea and bread-and-butter and soup. Prison soup is very good and wholesome. A resolution of the House of Commons could settle the treatment of children in half an hour. I hope you will use your influence to have this done. The way that children are treated at present is really an outrage on humanity and common sense. It comes from stupidity.

Let me draw attention now to another terrible thing that goes on in English prisons, indeed in prisons all over the world where the system of silence and cellular confinement is practised. I refer to the large number of men who become insane or weak-minded in prison. In convict prisons this is, of course, quite common; but in ordinary gaols also, such as that I was confined in, it is to be found.

About three months ago I noticed amongst the prisoners who took exercise with me a young man who seemed to me to be silly or half-witted. Every prison, of course, has its half-witted clients, who return again and again, and may be said to live in the prison. But this young man struck me as being more than usually half-witted on account of his silly grin and idiotic laughter to himself, and the peculiar restlessness of his eternally twitching hands. He was noticed by all the other prisoners on account of the strangeness of his conduct. From time to time he did not appear at exercise, which showed me that he was being punished by confinement to his cell. Finally, I discovered that he was under observation, and being watched night and day by warders. When he did appear at exercise he always seemed hysterical, and used to walk round crying or laughing. At chapel he had to sit right under the observation of two warders, who carefully watched him all the time. Sometimes he would bury his head in his hands, an offence against the chapel regulations, and his head would be immediately struck by a warder so that he should keep his eyes fixed permanently in the direction of the Communion-table. Sometimes he would cry – not making any disturbance – but with tears streaming down his face and an hysterical throbbing in the throat. Sometimes he would grin idiot-like to himself and make faces. He was on more than one occasion sent out of chapel to his cell, and of course he was continually punished. As the bench on which I used to sit in chapel was directly behind the bench at the end of which this unfortunate man was placed I had full opportunity of observing him. I also saw him, of course, at exercise continually, and I saw that he was becoming insane, and was being treated as if he was shamming.

On Saturday week last I was in my cell at about one o'clock occupied in cleaning and polishing the tins I had been using for dinner. Suddenly I was startled by the prison silence being broken by the most horrible and revolting shrieks, or rather howls, for at first I thought some animal like a bull or a cow was being unskilfully slaughtered outside the prison walls. I soon realised, however, that the howls proceeded from the basement of the prison, and I knew that some wretched man was being flogged. I need not say how hideous and terrible it was for me, and I began to wonder who it was who was being punished in this revolting manner. Suddenly it dawned upon me that they might be flogging this unfortunate lunatic. My feelings on the subject need not be chronicled; they have nothing to do with the question.

The next day, Sunday 16th, I saw the poor fellow at exercise, his weak, ugly, wretched face bloated by tears and hysteria almost beyond recognition. He walked in the centre ring along with the old men, the beggars, and the lame people, so that I was able to observe him the whole time. It was my last Sunday in prison, a perfectly lovely day, the finest day we had had the whole year, and there, in the beautiful sunlight, walked this poor creature – made once in the image of God – grinning like an ape, and making with his hands the most fantastic gestures, as though he was playing in the air on some invisible stringed instrument, or arranging and dealing counters in some curious game. All the while these hysterical tears, without which none of us ever saw him, were making soiled runnels on his white swollen face. The hideous and deliberate grace of his gestures made him like an antic. He was a living grotesque. The other prisoners all watched him, and not one of them smiled. Everybody knew what had happened to him, and that he was being driven insane – was insane already. After half an hour he was ordered in by the warder, and I suppose punished. At least he was not at exercise on Monday, though I think I caught sight of him at the corner of the stone-yard, walking in charge of a warder.

On the Tuesday – my last day in prison – I saw him at exercise. He was worse than before, and again was sent in. Since then I know nothing of him, but I found out from one of the prisoners who walked with me at exercise that he had had twenty-four lashes in the cookhouse on Saturday afternoon, by order of the visiting justices on the report of the doctor. The howls that had horrified us all were his.

This man is undoubtedly becoming insane. Prison doctors have no knowledge of mental disease of any kind. They are as a class ignorant men. The pathology of the mind is unknown to them. When a man grows insane, they treat him as shamming. They have him punished again and again. Naturally the man becomes worse. When ordinary punishments are exhausted, the doctor reports the case to the justices. The result is flogging. Of course the flogging is not done with a cat-of-nine-tails. It is what is called birching. The instrument is a rod; but the result on the wretched half-witted man may be imagined.

His number is, or was, A.2.11. I also managed to find out his name. It is Prince. Something should be done at once for him. He is a soldier, and his sentence is one of court-martial. The term is six months. Three have yet to run. May I ask you to use your influence to have this case examined into, and to see that the lunatic prisoner is properly treated?[51]

No report of the Medical Commissioners is of any avail. It is not to be trusted. The medical inspectors do not seem to understand the difference between idiocy and lunacy – between the entire absence of a function or organ and the diseases of a function or organ. This man A.2.11 will, I have no doubt, be able to tell his name, the nature of his offence, the day of the month, the date of the beginning and expiration of his sentence, and answer any ordinary simple question; but that his mind is diseased admits of no doubt. At present it is a horrible duel between himself and the doctor. The doctor is fighting for a theory. The man is fighting for his life. I am anxious that the man should win. But let the whole case be examined into by experts who understand brain-disease, and by people of humane feelings who have still some common sense and some pity. There is no reason that the sentimentalist should be asked to interfere. He always does harm.

The case is a special instance of the cruelty inseparable from a stupid system, for the present Governor of Reading is a man of gentle and humane character, greatly liked and respected by all the prisoners. He was appointed in July last, and though he cannot alter the rules of the prison system he has altered the

spirit in which they used to be carried out under his predeces-
sor. He is very popular with the prisoners and with the ward-
ers. Indeed he has quite altered the whole tone of the prison
life. Upon the other hand, the system is of course beyond his
reach so far as altering its rules is concerned. I have no doubt
that he sees daily much of what he knows to be unjust, stupid,
and cruel. But his hands are tied. Of course I have no knowl-
edge of his real views of the case of A.2.11, nor, indeed, of
his views on our present system. I merely judge him by the
complete change he brought about in Reading Prison. Under
his predecessor the system was carried out with the greatest
harshness and stupidity.

I remain, sir, your obedient servant

Oscar Wilde

To an Unidentified Correspondent[52]
c/o Stoker and Hansell, 14 Gray's Inn Square

[Circa 28 May 1897]   [Berneval-sur-Mer]

My dear Friend,

I send you a line to show you that I haven't forgotten you. We
were old friends in gallery C.3, were we not? I hope you are
getting on well and in employment.

Don't, like a good little chap, get into trouble again. You
would get a terrible sentence. I send you £2 just for luck. I am
quite poor myself now, but I know you will accept it just as a
remembrance. There is also 10/– which I wish you would give
to a little dark-eyed chap who had a month in, I think, C.4.14
– he was in from February 6th to March 6th – a little chap
from Wantage, I think, and a jolly little fellow. We were great
friends. If you know him give it to him from C.3.3.

I am in France by the sea, and I suppose I am getting happy
again. I hope so. It was a bad time for me, but there were many
good fellows in Reading. Send me a line c/o my solicitors to my
own name. Your friend

C.3.3

To Major J. O. Nelson

[28 May 1897]   Hôtel de la Plage, Berneval-sur-Mer

Dear Major Nelson,

I had of course intended to write to you as soon as I had safely
reached French soil, to express, however inadequately, my real
feelings of what you must let me term, not merely sincere, but
affectionate gratitude to you for your kindness and gentleness
to me in prison, and for the real care that you took of me at the
end, when I was mentally upset and in a state of very terrible
nervous excitement. You must not mind my using the word
'gratitude'. I used to think gratitude a burden to carry. Now
I know that it is something that makes the heart lighter. The
ungrateful man is one who walks slowly with feet and heart of
lead. But when one knows the strange joy of gratitude to God
and man the earth becomes lovelier to one, and it is a pleasure
to count up, not one's wealth but one's debts, not the little that
one possesses, but the much that one owes.

I abstained from writing, however, because I was haunted by
the memory of the little children, and the wretched half-witted
lad who was flogged by the doctor's orders. I could not have
kept them out of my letter, and to have mentioned them to you
might have put *you* in a difficult position. In your reply you
might have expressed sympathy with my views – I think you
would have – and then on the appearance of my public letter
you might have felt as if I had, in some almost ungenerous
or thoughtless way, procured your private opinion on official
things, for use as corroboration.

I longed to speak to you about these things on the evening
of my departure, but I felt that in my position as a prisoner it
would have been wrong of me to do so, and that it would or
might have put you in a difficult position afterwards, as well as
at the time. I only hear of my letter being published by a tele-
gram from Mr Ross, but I hope they have printed it in full, as
I tried to express in it my appreciation and admiration of your

own humane spirit and affectionate interest in *all* the prisoners under your charge. I did not wish people to think that any exception had been specially made for me. Such exceptional treatment as I received was by order of the Commissioners. You gave me the same kindness as you gave to everyone. Of course I made more demands, but then I think I had really more needs than others, and I lacked often their cheerful acquiescence.

Of course I side with the prisoners: I was one, and I belong to their class now. I am not a scrap ashamed of having been in prison. I am horribly ashamed of the materialism of the life that brought me there. It was quite unworthy of an artist.

Of Martin, and the subjects of my letter, I of course say nothing at all, except that the man who could change the system – if any one man can do so – is yourself. At present I write to ask you to allow me to sign myself, once at any rate in life, your sincere and grateful friend

    Oscar Wilde

To Robert Ross

[29–30 May 1897]   *Hôtel de la Plage, Berneval-sur-Mer*

My dear Robbie,

Your letter is quite admirable, but, dear boy, don't you see how right *I* was to write to the *Chronicle*? All good impulses are right. Had I listened to some of my friends I would never have written.

I am sending a postscript to Massingham[53] – of some importance: if he publishes it, send it to me.

I have also asked him if he wishes my prison experiences, and if he would share in a syndicate. I think now, as the length of my letter is so great, that I could do *three* articles on Prison Life. Of course much will be psychological and introspective: and one will be on Christ as the Precursor of the Romantic Movement in Life, that lovely subject which was revealed to me when I found myself in the company of the same sort of people Christ liked, outcasts and beggars.[54]

I am terrified about Bosie. More writes to me that he has been practically interviewed about me! It is awful. More, desiring to spare me pain, I suppose, did not send me the paper, so I have had a wretched night.

Bosie can almost ruin me. I earnestly beg that some entreaty be made to him not to do so a second time. His letters to me are infamous.

I have heard from my wife. She sends me photographs of the boys – such lovely little fellows in Eton collars – but makes no promise to allow me to see them: she says *she* will see me, twice a year, but I want my boys.[55] It is a terrible punishment, dear Robbie, and oh! how well I deserve it. But it makes me feel disgraced and evil, and I don't want to feel that. Let me have the *Chronicle* regularly. Also write often. It is very good for me to be alone. I am working. Dear Robbie, ever yours

Oscar

To Michael Davitt[56]

[*Late May or early June 1897*]   *Hôtel de la Plage,*
                                                    Berneval-sur-Mer

Private and Confidential

Dear Mr Davitt,

I have been sent a cutting from a Liverpool paper which states that you intend to ask a question about the treatment of A.2.11 in Reading prison. I do not of course know if this is true, but I sincerely hope that you are *in some way* stirring in the matter. No one knows better than yourself how terrible life in an English prison is and what cruelties result from the stupidity of officialism, and the immobile ignorance of centralisation. *You* suffered for what was done by someone else.[57] I, in that respect more unfortunate, for a life of senseless pleasure and hard materialism and a mode of existence unworthy of an artist, and still more unworthy of my mother's son. But you know what prison-life is, and that there is no exaggeration in what I say. Everything that I state about the treatment of A.2.11 is absolutely true. With my own punishment I have nothing to do, except so far as it is the type of what is inflicted on much better, nicer fellows than myself. I have no bitterness at all, but I have learnt pity: and that is worth learning, if one has to tramp a yard for two years to learn it.

In any case I don't think they will flog A.2.11 again, and that is something. But of course I am quite powerless to do any more. I merely wrote as any other of the prisoners might have written, who had a pen he could use, and found a paper sufficiently large-minded to publish his letter. But with the letter I am forced to stop. It is part of my punishment – the new part that I have to face, and am facing very cheerfully and without any despair or making any complaint. I prefix to this letter *my name* for the present, and my address: but my letter requires no answer. It is simply the expression of a hope. I remain, yours faithfully

   Oscar Wilde

PS Enclosed letter has just been forwarded to me, through my solicitor. A.2.11 has apparently been flogged again – see postscript. I think it is simply revolting. After you have read the chap's letter, of course tear it up. I have his address.

To the Editor of the Daily Chronicle[58]

23 March [*1898*]   [*Paris*]

Sir,

I understand that the Home Secretary's Prison Reform Bill is to be read this week for the first or second time, and as your journal has been the one paper in England that has taken a real and vital interest in this important question, I hope that you will allow me, as one who has had long personal experience of life in an English gaol, to point out what reforms in our present stupid and barbarous system are urgently necessary.

From a leading article that appeared in your columns about a week ago, I learn that the chief reform proposed is an increase in the number of inspectors and official visitors, that are to have access to our English prisons.

Such a reform as this is entirely useless. The reason is extremely simple. The inspectors and justices of the peace that visit prisons come there for the purpose of seeing that the prison regulations are duly carried out. They come for no other purpose, nor have they any power, even if they had the desire, to alter a single clause in the regulations. No prisoner has ever had the smallest relief, or attention, or care from any of the official visitors. The visitors arrive not to help the prisoners, but to see that the rules are carried out. Their object in coming is to ensure the enforcement of a foolish and inhuman code. And, as they must have some occupation, they take very good care to do it. A prisoner who has been allowed the smallest privilege dreads the arrival of the inspectors. And on the day of any prison inspection the prison officials are more than usually brutal to the prisoners. Their object is, of course, to show the splendid discipline they maintain.

The necessary reforms are very simple. They concern the needs of the body and the needs of the mind of each unfortunate prisoner. With regard to the first, there are three permanent punishments authorised by law in English prisons:

1. Hunger.
2. Insomnia.
3. Disease.

The food supplied to prisoners is entirely inadequate. Most of it is revolting in character. All of it is insufficient. Every prisoner suffers day and night from hunger. A certain amount of food is carefully weighed out ounce by ounce for each prisoner. It is just enough to sustain, not life exactly, but existence. But one is always racked by the pain and sickness of hunger.

The result of the food – which in most cases consists of

weak gruel, badly-baked bread, suet, and water – is disease in the form of incessant diarrhoea. This malady, which ultimately with most prisoners becomes a permanent disease, is a recognised institution in every prison. At Wandsworth Prison, for instance – where I was confined for two months, till I had to be carried into hospital, where I remained for another two months – the warders go round twice or three times a day with astringent medicines, which they serve out to the prisoners as a matter of course. After about a week of such treatment it is unnecessary to say the medicine produces no effect at all. The wretched prisoner is then left a prey to the most weakening, depressing, and humiliating malady that can be conceived; and if, as often happens, he fails, from physical weakness, to complete his required revolutions at the crank or the mill he is reported for idleness, and punished with the greatest severity and brutality. Nor is this all.

Nothing can be worse than the sanitary arrangements of English prisons. In old days each cell was provided with a form of latrine. These latrines have now been suppressed. They exist no longer. A small tin vessel is supplied to each prisoner instead. Three times a day a prisoner is allowed to empty his slops. But he is not allowed to have access to the prison lavatories, except during the one hour when he is at exercise. And after five o'clock in the evening he is not allowed to leave his cell under any pretence, or for any reason. A man suffering from diarrhoea is consequently placed in a position so loathsome that it is unnecessary to dwell on it, that it would be unseemly to dwell on it. The misery and tortures that prisoners go through in consequence of the revolting sanitary arrangements are quite indescribable. And the foul air of the prison cells, increased by a system of ventilation that is utterly ineffective, is so sickening and unwholesome that it is no uncommon thing for warders, when they come in the morning out of the fresh air and open and inspect each cell, to be violently sick. I have seen this myself on more than three occasions, and several of the warders have mentioned it to me as one of the disgusting things that their office entails on them.

The food supplied to prisoners should be adequate and

wholesome. It should not be of such a character as to produce the incessant diarrhoea that, at first a malady, becomes a permanent disease.

The sanitary arrangements in English prisons should be entirely altered. Every prisoner should be allowed to have access to the lavatories when necessary, and to empty his slops when necessary. The present system of ventilation in each cell is utterly useless. The air comes through choked-up gratings, and through a small ventilator in the tiny barred window, which is far too small, and too badly constructed, to admit any adequate amount of fresh air. One is only allowed out of one's cell for one hour out of the twenty-four that compose the long day, and so for twenty-three hours one is breathing the foulest possible air.

With regard to the punishment of insomnia, it only exists in Chinese and English prisons. In China it is inflicted by placing the prisoner in a small bamboo cage; in England by means of the plank bed. The object of the plank bed is to produce insomnia. There is no other object in it, and it invariably succeeds. And even when one is subsequently allowed a hard mattress, as happens in the course of imprisonment, one still suffers from insomnia. For sleep, like all wholesome things, is a habit. Every prisoner who has been on a plank bed suffers from insomnia. It is a revolting and ignorant punishment.

With regard to the needs of the mind, I beg that you will allow me to say something.

The present prison system seems almost to have for its aim the wrecking and the destruction of the mental faculties. The production of insanity is, if not its object, certainly its result. That is a well ascertained fact. Its causes are obvious. Deprived of books, of all human intercourse, isolated from every humane and humanising influence, condemned to eternal silence, robbed of all intercourse with the external world, treated like an unintelligent animal, brutalised below the level of any of the brute-creation, the wretched man who is confined in an English prison can hardly escape becoming insane. I do not wish to dwell on these horrors; still less to excite any momentary sentimental interest in these matters. So I will merely, with your permission, point out what should be done.

Every prisoner should have an adequate supply of good books. At present, during the first three months of imprisonment, one is allowed no books at all, except a Bible, prayer-book, and hymn-book. After that, one is allowed one book a week. That is not merely inadequate, but the books that compose an ordinary prison library are perfectly useless. They consist chiefly of third-rate, badly-written, religious books, so-called, written apparently for children, and utterly unsuitable for children or for anyone else. Prisoners should be encouraged to read, and should have whatever books they want, and the books should be well chosen. At present the selection of books is made by the prison chaplain.

Under the present system a prisoner is only allowed to see his friends four times a year, for twenty minutes each time. This is quite wrong. A prisoner should be allowed to see his friends once a month, and for a reasonable time. The mode at present in vogue of exhibiting a prisoner to his friends should be altered. Under the present system the prisoner is either locked up in a large iron cage or in a large wooden box, with a small aperture, covered with wire netting, through which he is allowed to peer. His friends are placed in a similar cage, some three or four feet distant, and two warders stand between, to listen to, and, if they wish, stop or interrupt the conversation such as it may be. I propose that a prisoner should be allowed to see his relatives or friends in a room. The present regulations are inexpressibly revolting and harassing. A visit from our relatives or friends is to every prisoner an intensification of humiliation and mental distress. Many prisoners, rather than support such an ordeal, refuse to see their friends at all. And I cannot say I am surprised. When one sees one's solicitor, one sees him in a room with a glass door, on the other side of which stands the warder. When a man sees his wife and children, or his parents, or his friends, he should be allowed the same privilege. To be exhibited, like an ape in a cage, to people who are fond of one, and of whom one is fond, is a needless and horrible degradation.

Every prisoner should be allowed to write and receive a letter at least once a month. At present one is allowed to write only four times a year. This is quite inadequate. One of the tragedies of prison life is that it turns a man's heart to stone. The feelings of natural affection, like all other feelings, require to be fed. They die easily of inanition. A brief letter, four times a year, is not enough to keep alive the gentler and more humane affections by which ultimately the nature is kept sensitive to any fine or beautiful influences that may heal a wrecked and ruined life.

The habit of mutilating and expurgating prisoners' letters should be stopped. At present, if a prisoner in a letter makes any complaint of the prison system, that portion of his letter is cut out with a pair of scissors. If, upon the other hand, he makes any complaint when he speaks to his friends through the bars of the cage, or the aperture of the wooden box, he is brutalised by the warders, and reported for punishment every week till his next visit comes round, by which time he is expected to have learned, not wisdom, but cunning, and one always learns that. It is one of the few things that one does learn in prison. Fortunately, the other things are, in some instances, of higher import.

If I may trespass on your space for a little longer, may I say this? You suggested in your leading article that no prison chaplain should be allowed to have any care or employment outside the prison itself. But this is a matter of no moment. The prison chaplains are entirely useless. They are, as a class, well-meaning, but foolish, indeed silly, men. They are of no help to any prisoner. Once every six weeks or so a key turns in the lock of one's cell door, and the chaplain enters. One stands, of course, at attention. He asks one whether one has been reading the Bible. One answers 'Yes' or 'No', as the case may be. He then quotes a few texts, and goes out and locks the door. Sometimes he leaves a tract.

The officials who should not be allowed to hold any employment outside the prison, or to have any private practice, are the prison doctors. At present the prison doctors have usually, if not always, a large private practice, and hold appointments in other institutions. The consequence is that the health of the prisoners is entirely neglected, and the sanitary condition of the prison entirely overlooked. As a class I regard, and have always from my earliest youth regarded, doctors as by far the most humane profession in the community. But I must make an exception for prison doctors. They are, as far as I came across them, and from what I saw of them in hospital and elsewhere, brutal in manner, coarse in temperament, and utterly indifferent to the health of the prisoners or their comfort. If prison doctors were prohibited from private practice they would be compelled to take some interest in the health and sanitary condition of the people under their charge.

I have tried to indicate in my letter a few of the reforms necessary to our English prison system. They are simple, practical, and humane. They are, of course, only a beginning. But it is time that a beginning should be made, and it can only be started by a strong pressure of public opinion formularised in your powerful paper, and fostered by it.

But to make even these reforms effectual, much has to be done. And the first, and perhaps the most difficult, task is to humanise the governors of prisons, to civilise the warders and to Christianise the chaplains. Yours, etc.

The Author of 'The Ballad of Reading Gaol'

THE BALLAD OF
READING GAOL[1]

He did not wear his scarlet coat,[2]
  For blood and wine are red,
And blood and wine were on his hands
  When they found him with the dead,
The poor dead woman whom he loved,
  And murdered in her bed.[3]

He walked amongst the Trial Men
  In a suit of shabby grey;[4]
A cricket cap was on his head,
  And his step seemed light and gay;
But I never saw a man who looked
  So wistfully at the day.

I never saw a man who looked
  With such a wistful eye
Upon that little tent of blue
  Which prisoners call the sky,
And at every drifting cloud that went
  With sails of silver by.

I walked, with other souls in pain,
  Within another ring,[5]
And was wondering if the man had done
  A great or little thing,
When a voice behind me whispered low,
  'That fellow's got to swing.'

Dear Christ! the very prison walls
    Suddenly seemed to reel,
And the sky above my head became
    Like a casque of scorching steel;
And, though I was a soul in pain,
    My pain I could not feel.

I only knew what hunted thought
    Quickened his step, and why
He looked upon the garish day
    With such a wistful eye;
The man had killed the thing he loved,
    And so he had to die.

*

Yet each man kills the thing he loves,[6]
    By each let this be heard,
Some do it with a bitter look,
    Some with a flattering word.
The coward does it with a kiss,
    The brave man with a sword!

Some kill their love when they are young,
    And some when they are old;
Some strangle with the hands of Lust,
    Some with the hands of Gold:
The kindest use a knife, because
    The dead so soon grow cold.

Some love too little, some too long,
    Some sell, and others buy;
Some do the deed with many tears,
    And some without a sigh:
For each man kills the thing he loves,
    Yet each man does not die.

He does not die a death of shame
    On a day of dark disgrace,
Nor have a noose about his neck,
    Nor a cloth upon his face,
Nor drop feet foremost through the floor
    Into an empty space.

He does not sit with silent men
    Who watch him night and day;[7]
Who watch him when he tries to weep,
    And when he tries to pray;
Who watch him lest himself should rob
    The prison of its prey.

He does not wake at dawn to see
    Dread figures throng his room,
The shivering Chaplain robed in white,[8]
    The Sheriff stern with gloom,
And the Governor all in shiny black,[9]
    With the yellow face of Doom.

He does not rise in piteous haste
    To put on convict-clothes,
While some coarse-mouthed Doctor gloats,
      and notes
    Each new and nerve-twitched pose,
Fingering a watch whose little ticks
    Are like horrible hammer-blows.

He does not know that sickening thirst
    That sands one's throat, before
The hangman with his gardener's gloves
    Slips through the padded door,
And binds one with three leathern thongs,[10]
    That the throat may thirst no more.

He does not bend his head to hear
 The Burial Office read,
Nor, while the terror of his soul
 Tells him he is not dead,
Cross his own coffin, as he moves
 Into the hideous shed.

He does not stare upon the air
 Through a little roof of glass:
He does not pray with lips of clay
 For his agony to pass;
Nor feel upon his shuddering cheek
 The kiss of Caiaphas.[11]

2

Six weeks our guardsman walked the yard,
 In the suit of shabby grey:
His cricket cap was on his head,
 And his step seemed light and gay,
But I never saw a man who looked
 So wistfully at the day.

I never saw a man who looked
 With such a wistful eye
Upon that little tent of blue
 Which prisoners call the sky,
And at every wandering cloud that trailed
 Its ravelled fleeces by.

He did not wring his hands, as do
 Those witless men who dare
To try to rear the changeling Hope
 In the cave of black Despair:
He only looked upon the sun,
 And drank the morning air.

He did not wring his hands nor weep,
    Nor did he peek[12] or pine,
But he drank the air as though it held
    Some healthful anodyne;
With open mouth he drank the sun
    As though it had been wine!

And I and all the souls in pain,
    Who tramped the other ring,
Forgot if we ourselves had done
    A great or little thing,
And watched with gaze of dull amaze
    The man who had to swing.

And strange it was to see him pass
    With a step so light and gay,
And strange it was to see him look
    So wistfully at the day,
And strange it was to think that he
    Had such a debt to pay.

*

For oak and elm have pleasant leaves
    That in the spring-time shoot:
But grim to see is the gallows-tree,
    With its adder-bitten root,
And, green or dry,[13] a man must die
    Before it bears its fruit!

The loftiest place is that seat of grace
    For which all worldlings try:
But who would stand in hempen band
    Upon a scaffold high,
And through a murderer's collar take
    His last look at the sky?

It is sweet to dance to violins
    When Love and Life are fair:
To dance to flutes, to dance to lutes
    Is delicate and rare:
But it is not sweet with nimble feet
    To dance upon the air!

So with curious eyes and sick surmise
    We watched him day by day,
And wondered if each one of us
    Would end the self-same way,
For none can tell to what red Hell
    His sightless soul may stray.

At last the dead man walked no more
    Amongst the Trial Men,[14]
And I knew that he was standing up
    In the black dock's dreadful pen,
And that never would I see his face
    In God's sweet world again.

Like two doomed ships that pass in storm
    We had crossed each other's way:
But we made no sign, we said no word,
    We had no word to say;
For we did not meet in the holy night,
    But in the shameful day.

A prison wall was round us both,
    Two outcast men we were:
The world had thrust us from its heart,
    And God from out His care:
And the iron gin[15] that waits for Sin
    Had caught us in its snare.

3

In Debtor's Yard the stones are hard,
　　And the dripping wall is high,
So it was there he took the air
　　Beneath the leaden sky,
And by each side a Warder walked,
　　For fear the man might die.

Or else he sat with those who watched
　　His anguish night and day;
Who watched him when he rose to weep,
　　And when he crouched to pray;
Who watched him lest himself should rob
　　Their scaffold of its prey.

The Governor was strong upon
　　The Regulations Act:[16]
The Doctor[17] said that Death was but
　　A scientific fact:
And twice a day the Chaplain called,
　　And left a little tract.

And twice a day he smoked his pipe,
　　And drank his quart of beer:
His soul was resolute, and held
　　No hiding-place for fear;
He often said that he was glad
　　The hangman's hands were near.

But why he said so strange a thing
　　No warder dared to ask:
For he to whom a watcher's doom
　　Is given as his task,
Must set a lock upon his lips,
　　And make his face a mask.

Or else he might be moved, and try
　　To comfort or console:
And what should Human Pity do
　　Pent up in Murderers' Hole?
What word of grace in such a place
　　Could help a brother's soul?

With slouch and swing around the ring
　　We trod the Fools' Parade!
We did not care: we knew we were
　　The Devil's Own Brigade:
And shaven head and feet of lead
　　Make a merry masquerade.

We tore the tarry rope to shreds[18]
　　With blunt and bleeding nails;
We rubbed the doors, and scrubbed the floors,
　　And cleaned the shining rails:
And, rank by rank, we soaped the plank,[19]
　　And clattered with the pails.

We sewed the sacks, we broke the stones,
　　We turned the dusty drill:[20]
We banged the tins, and bawled the hymns,
　　And sweated on the mill:[21]
But in the heart of every man
　　Terror was lying still.

So still it lay that every day
　　Crawled like a weed-clogged wave:
And we forgot the bitter lot
　　That waits for fool and knave,
Till once, as we tramped in from work,
　　We passed an open grave.

With yawning mouth the yellow hole
    Gaped for a living thing;
The very mud cried out for blood
    To the thirsty asphalte ring:
And we knew that ere one dawn grew fair
    Some prisoner had to swing.

Right in we went, with soul intent
    On Death and Dread and Doom:
The hangman, with his little bag,
    Went shuffling through the gloom:
And each man trembled as he crept
    Into his numbered tomb.

*

That night the empty corridors
    Were full of forms of Fear,
And up and down the iron town
    Stole feet we could not hear,
And through the bars that hide the stars
    White faces seemed to peer.

He lay as one who lies and dreams
    In a pleasant meadow-land,
The watchers watched him as he slept,
    And could not understand
How one could sleep so sweet a sleep
    With a hangman close at hand.

But there is no sleep when men must weep
    Who never yet have wept:
So we – the fool, the fraud, the knave –
    That endless vigil kept,
And through each brain on hands of pain
    Another's terror crept.

Alas! it is a fearful thing
    To feel another's guilt!
For, right within, the Sword of Sin

    Pierced to its poisoned hilt,
And as molten lead were the tears we shed
    For the blood we had not spilt.

The warders with their shoes of felt
    Crept by each padlocked door,
And peeped and saw, with eyes of awe,
    Grey figures on the floor,
And wondered why men knelt to pray
    Who never prayed before.

All through the night we knelt and prayed,
    Mad mourners of a corse!
The troubled plumes of midnight were
    The plumes upon a hearse:
And bitter wine upon a sponge[22]
    Was the savour of Remorse.

               *

The grey cock crew, the red cock crew,[23]
    But never came the day:
And crooked shapes of Terror crouched,
    In the corners where we lay:
And each evil sprite that walks by night
    Before us seemed to play.

They glided past, they glided fast,
    Like travellers through a mist:
They mocked the moon in a rigadoon[24]
    Of delicate turn and twist,
And with formal pace and loathsome grace
    The phantoms kept their tryst.

With mop and mow,[25] we saw them go,
    Slim shadows hand in hand:
About, about, in ghostly rout
    They trod a saraband:
And the damned grotesques made arabesques,
    Like the wind upon the sand!

With the pirouettes of marionettes,
    They tripped on pointed tread:
But with flutes of Fear they filled the ear,
    As their grisly masque they led,
And loud they sang, and long they sang,
    For they sang to wake the dead.

'*Oho!*' they cried, '*The world is wide,*
    But fettered limbs go lame!
And once, or twice, to throw the dice
    Is a gentlemanly game,
But he does not win who plays with Sin
    In the secret House of Shame.'

No things of air these antics were,
    That frolicked with such glee:
To men whose lives were held in gyves,[26]
    And whose feet might not go free,
Ah! wounds of Christ! they were living things,
    Most terrible to see.

Around, around, they waltzed and wound;
    Some wheeled in smirking pairs;
With the mincing step of a demirep[27]
    Some sidled up the stairs:
And with subtle sneer, and fawning leer,
    Each helped us at our prayers.

The morning wind began to moan,
    But still the night went on:
Through its giant loom the web of gloom
    Crept till each thread was spun:
And, as we prayed, we grew afraid
    Of the Justice of the Sun.

The moaning wind went wandering round
    The weeping prison-wall:
Till like a wheel of turning steel
    We felt the minutes crawl:
O moaning wind! what had we done
    To have such a seneschal?[28]

At last I saw the shadowed bars,
    Like a lattice wrought in lead,
Move right across the whitewashed wall
    That faced my three-plank bed,
And I knew that somewhere in the world
    God's dreadful dawn was red.

At six o'clock we cleaned our cells,
    At seven all was still,
But the sough and swing of a mighty wing
    The prison seemed to fill,
For the Lord of Death with icy breath
    Had entered in to kill.

He did not pass in purple pomp,
    Nor ride a moon-white steed.
Three yards of cord and a sliding board
    Are all the gallows' need:
So with rope of shame the Herald came[29]
    To do the secret deed.

We were as men who through a fen
    Of filthy darkness grope:
We did not dare to breathe a prayer,
    Or to give our anguish scope:
Something was dead in each of us,
    And what was dead was Hope.

For Man's grim Justice goes its way,
    And will not swerve aside:
It slays the weak, it slays the strong,
    It has a deadly stride:
With iron heel it slays the strong,
    The monstrous parricide!

We waited for the stroke of eight:
    Each tongue was thick with thirst:
For the stroke of eight is the stroke of Fate
    That makes a man accursed,
And Fate will use a running noose [30]
    For the best man and the worst.

We had no other thing to do,
    Save to wait for the sign to come: [31]
So, like things of stone in a valley lone,
    Quiet we sat and dumb:
But each man's heart beat thick and quick,
    Like a madman on a drum!

With sudden shock the prison-clock
    Smote on the shivering air,
And from all the gaol rose up a wail
    Of impotent despair,
Like the sound that frightened marshes hear
    From some leper in his lair.

And as one sees most fearful things
        In the crystal of a dream,
We saw the greasy hempen rope
        Hooked to the blackened beam,
And heard the prayer the hangman's snare
        Strangled into a scream.[32]

And all the woe that moved him so
        That he gave that bitter cry,
And the wild regrets, and the bloody sweats,
        None knew so well as I:
For he who lives more lives than one
        More deaths than one must die.

4

There is no chapel on the day
        On which they hang a man:
The Chaplain's heart is far too sick,
        Or his face is far too wan,
Or there is that written in his eyes
        Which none should look upon.

So they kept us close till nigh on noon,
        And then they rang the bell,
And the warders with their jingling keys
        Opened each listening cell,
And down the iron stair we tramped,
        Each from his separate Hell.

Out into God's sweet air we went,
        But not in wonted way,
For this man's face was white with fear,
        And that man's face was grey,
And I never saw sad men who looked
        So wistfully at the day.

I never saw sad men who looked
        With such a wistful eye
Upon that little tent of blue
        We prisoners called the sky,
And at every careless cloud that passed
        In happy freedom by.

But there were those amongst us all
        Who walked with downcast head,
And knew that, had each got his due,
        They should have died instead:
He had but killed a thing that lived,
        Whilst they had killed the dead.

For he who sins a second time
        Wakes a dead soul to pain,
And draws it from its spotted shroud,
        And makes it bleed again,
And makes it bleed great gouts of blood,
        And makes it bleed in vain!

*

Like ape or clown, in monstrous garb
        With crooked arrows starred,[33]
Silently we went round and round
        The slippery asphalte yard;
Silently we went round and round,
        And no man spoke a word.

Silently we went round and round,
        And through each hollow mind
The Memory of dreadful things
        Rushed like a dreadful wind,
And Horror stalked before each man,
        And Terror crept behind.

*

The warders strutted up and down,
    And kept their herd of brutes,
Their uniforms were spick and span,
    And they wore their Sunday suits,
But we knew the work they had been at,
    By the quicklime on their boots.

For where a grave had opened wide,
    There was no grave at all:
Only a stretch of mud and sand
    By the hideous prison-wall,
And a little heap of burning lime,
    That the man should have his pall.
For he has a pall, this wretched man,
    Such as few men can claim:
Deep down below a prison-yard,
    Naked for greater shame,
He lies, with fetters on each foot,
    Wrapt in a sheet of flame!

And all the while the burning lime
    Eats flesh and bone away,[34]
It eats the brittle bone by night,
    And the soft flesh by day,
It eats the flesh and bone by turns,
    But it eats the heart alway.

*

For three long years they will not sow
    Or root or seedling there:
For three long years the unblessed spot
    Will sterile be and bare,
And look upon the wondering sky
    With unreproachful stare.

They think a murderer's heart would taint
    Each simple seed they sow.
It is not true! God's kindly earth
    Is kindlier than men know,
And the red rose would but blow more red,
    The white rose whiter blow.

Out of his mouth a red, red rose!
    Out of his heart a white!
For who can say by what strange way,
    Christ brings His will to light,
Since the barren staff the pilgrim bore
    Bloomed in the great Pope's sight?[35]

But neither milk-white rose nor red
    May bloom in prison-air;
The shard, the pebble, and the flint,[36]
    Are what they give us there:
For flowers have been known to heal
    A common man's despair.

So never will wine-red rose or white,
    Petal by petal, fall
On that stretch of mud and sand that lies
    By the hideous prison-wall,
To tell the men who tramp the yard
    That God's Son died for all.

Yet though the hideous prison-wall
    Still hems him round and round,
And a spirit may not walk by night
    That is with fetters bound,
And a spirit may but weep that lies
    In such unholy ground,

He is at peace – this wretched man –
    At peace, or will be soon:
There is no thing to make him mad,
    Nor does Terror walk at noon,
For the lampless Earth in which he lies
    Has neither Sun nor Moon.

They hanged him as a beast is hanged!
    They did not even toll
A requiem that might have brought
    Rest to his startled soul,
But hurriedly they took him out,
    And hid him in a hole.

They stripped him of his canvas clothes,
    And gave him to the flies:
They mocked the swollen purple throat,
    And the stark and staring eyes:
And with laughter loud they heaped the shroud
    In which their convict lies.

The Chaplain would not kneel to pray
    By his dishonoured grave:
Nor mark it with that blessed Cross
    That Christ for sinners gave,
Because the man was one of those
    Whom Christ came down to save.

Yet all is well; he has but passed
    To Life's appointed bourne:[37]
And alien tears will fill for him
    Pity's long-broken urn,
For his mourners will be outcast men,
    And outcasts always mourn.[38]

5

I know not whether Laws be right,
    Or whether Laws be wrong;
All that we know who lie in gaol
    Is that the wall is strong;
And that each day is like a year,
    A year whose days are long.

But this I know, that every Law
    That men hath made for Man,
Since first Man took his brother's life,
    And the sad world began,
But straws the wheat and saves the chaff
    With a most evil fan.[39]

This too I know – and wise it were
    If each could know the same –
That every prison that men build
    Is built with bricks of shame,
And bound with bars lest Christ should see
    How men their brothers maim.

With bars they blur the gracious moon,
    And blind the goodly sun;
And they do well to hide their Hell,
    For in it things are done
That Son of God nor son of Man
    Ever should look upon!

*

The vilest deeds like poison weeds,
    Bloom well in prison-air;
It is only what is good in Man
    That wastes and withers there:
Pale Anguish keeps the heavy gate,
    And the Warder is Despair.

For they starve the little frightened child
    Till it weeps both night and day:[40]
And they scourge the weak, and flog the fool,
    And gibe the old and grey,
And some grow mad, and all grow bad,
    And none a word may say.

Each narrow cell in which we dwell
    Is a foul and dark latrine,
And the fetid breath of living Death
    Chokes up each grated screen,
And all, but Lust, is turned to dust
    In Humanity's machine.

The brackish water that we drink
    Creeps with a loathsome slime,
And the bitter bread they weigh in scales

    Is full of chalk and lime,
And Sleep will not lie down, but walks
    Wild-eyed, and cries to Time.

*

But though lean Hunger and green Thirst
    Like asp with adder fight,
We have little care of prison fare,
    For what chills and kills outright
Is that every stone one lifts by day
    Becomes one's heart by night.

With midnight always in one's heart,
    And twilight in one's cell,
We turn the crank, or tear the rope,
    Each in his separate Hell,
And the silence is more awful far
    Than the sound of a brazen bell.

And never a human voice comes near
    To speak a gentle word:
And the eye that watches through the door
    Is pitiless and hard:
And by all forgot, we rot and rot,
    With soul and body marred.

And thus we rust Life's iron chain
    Degraded and alone:
And some men curse, and some men weep,
    And some men make no moan:
But God's eternal Laws are kind
    And break the heart of stone.

And every human heart that breaks,
    In prison-cell or yard,
Is as that broken box that gave
    Its treasure to the Lord,
And filled the unclean leper's house
    With the scent of costliest nard.[41]

Ah! happy they whose hearts can break
    And peace of pardon win!
How else may man make straight his plan
    And cleanse his soul from Sin?
How else but through a broken heart
    May Lord Christ enter in?

*

And he of the swollen purple throat,
    And the stark and staring eyes,
Waits for the holy hands that took
    The Thief to Paradise;[42]
And a broken and a contrite heart
    The Lord will not despise. [43]

The man in red who reads the Law
      Gave him three weeks of life,[44]
Three little weeks in which to heal
      His soul of his soul's strife,
And cleanse from every blot of blood
      The hand that held the knife.

And with tears of blood he cleansed the hand,
      The hand that held the steel:
For only blood can wipe out blood,
      And only tears can heal:
And the crimson stain that was of Cain
      Became Christ's snow-white seal.[45]

6

In Reading gaol by Reading town
      There is a pit of shame,
And in it lies a wretched man
      Eaten by teeth of flame,
In a burning winding-sheet he lies,
      And his grave has got no name.

And there, till Christ call forth the dead,
      In silence let him lie:
No need to waste the foolish tear,
      Or heave the windy sigh:
The man had killed the thing he loved,
      And so he had to die.

And all men kill the thing they love,
      By all let this be heard,
Some do it with a bitter look,
      Some with a flattering word,
The coward does it with a kiss,
      The brave man with a sword!

Notes

INDIVIDUALS IN THE LETTERS

Listed below are the people Oscar Wilde repeatedly mentions in his letters, including those he corresponded with. For more detail about the events leading up to his imprisonment, and the individuals involved, see the Introduction. Please note that some individuals are listed twice, i.e. once by their given name and once by their nickname.

More Adey: (1858–1942), translator, editor and gallery-owner; he attempted to petition the Home Secretary for Wilde's early release.

Bosie: Nickname of Lord Alfred Douglas.

Arthur Clifton: Arthur Bellamy Clifton (1862–1932), a solicitor who became an art dealer; he worked with Robert Ross and More Adey.

Lord Alfred Douglas: (1870–1945), third son of the Marquess of Queensberry; author, poet and translator. He met and began an affair with Wilde in 1891.

Francis Douglas, Viscount Drumlanrig: (1867–94), eldest son of the Marquess of Queensberry, brother of Lord Alfred Douglas. He served as private secretary to the Liberal politician Lord Rosebery and died in a shooting accident.

Fleur-de-Lys: One of Wilde's nicknames for Lord Alfred Douglas.

Governor: Major J. O. Nelson.

Mr Hargrove: Messrs Hargrove & Co. were the solicitors of Constance Wilde's family, the Lloyds.

Frank Harris: (1856–1931), author, editor and publisher; a friend of Wilde and other well-known figures of the day.

Mr Holman: Martin Holman of the solicitors Parker, Garrett & Holman.

Arthur Humphreys: Arthur Humphreys (1865–1946), bookseller, author and publisher.

Charles Humphreys: Solicitor who represented Wilde in his case against the Marquess of Queensberry.

Ada Leverson: (1862–1933), a journalist and novelist; she met Wilde, it seems, in 1892 and became one of his closest friends. Wilde normally addressed her as 'Sphinx'.

Ernest Leverson: (1850–1922), wealthy businessman and husband of Ada Leverson.

Sir George Lewis: (1833–1911), lawyer who advised the Marquess of Queensberry at the start of the libel action. As a close friend of Wilde, and not wishing to act against him, he then passed the brief on to Charles Russell.

Aurélien-François-Marie Lugné-Poë: (1869–1940), French actor-manager, produced Wilde's *Salomé* on 11 February 1896, with Lina Munte in the title role.

Thomas Martin: A native of Belfast, Martin came to Reading as a warder seven weeks before Wilde's release. He was kind to Wilde and constantly broke the regulations to bring him extra food as well as newspapers.

Stuart Merrill: (1863–1915), American poet living in Paris who mostly wrote in French; just as More Adey had done in Britain, he attempted to get notable figures in France to sign a petition for Wilde's release. He is buried where he wished: diagonally opposite Wilde's tomb in Père-Lachaise.

Major James Osmond Nelson: (1859–1914), was governor of Reading Gaol from July 1896. Under his governorship, conditions at the prison began to improve and Wilde was allowed to write throughout the day.

Walter Pater: (1839–94), novelist, essayist and critic whose work is frequently mentioned by Wilde.

Marquess of Queensberry: John Sholto Douglas, 9th Marquess of Queensberry (1844–1900), Scottish nobleman known for his strong atheism and love of sport. Angered by the relationship between Wilde and his son Lord Alfred Douglas, he provoked Wilde into suing him for criminal libel.

Alexander ('Aleck') Galt Ross: (1860–1927), brother of Robert, and a co-founder of the Society of Authors.

Robert ('Robbie') Ross: (1869–1918), literary journalist and art critic, Wilde's friend and literary executor. He published *De Profundis* (see note 1 on p. 242).

Adela Schuster: Daughter of a wealthy Frankfurt banker; one of Wilde's closest friends and a generous benefactress, often referred to as 'the Lady of Wimbledon' in the letters.

R. (**Robert**) **H. Sherard**: (1861–1943), journalist and friend of Wilde, later his first biographer.

Percy Sholto: Lord Douglas of Hawick (1868–1920), Lord Alfred Douglas's elder brother. He succeeded his father as 10th Marquess of Queensberry in 1900.

The Sphinx: Ada Leverson.

Reginald ('**Reggie**') **Turner**: (1869–1938), journalist, novelist and wit.

Constance Wilde (later '**Holland**'): (1858–98), born Constance Lloyd, she married Wilde in 1884. While he was in prison, she gained custody of their two sons and changed her name and theirs to Holland, a family name, to distance them from the scandal.

Cyril Wilde (later '**Holland**'): (1885–1915), Wilde's elder son.

Vyvyan Wilde (later '**Holland**'): (1886–1967), Wilde's younger son.

William ('**Willie**') **Wilde**: (1852–99), Wilde's older brother; journalist and poet.

Lady of Wimbledon: Adela Schuster.

DE PROFUNDIS AND OTHER LETTERS

Letters of March 1895–March 1897

1   A letter from Alfred Douglas to his brother Percy, dated 11 March, mentions that he and Oscar are leaving for Monte Carlo the next day. In *The Complete Letters of Oscar Wilde*, ed. Merlin Holland and Rupert Hart-Davis (London: Fourth Estate, 2000), the date is given as 'Circa 13 March 1895'.

2   *fight with panthers*: On 1 March, Wilde obtained a warrant for the arrest of the Marquess of Queensberry, who was charged with criminal libel. Wilde and Queensberry's son, Lord Alfred Douglas, arrived in Monte Carlo on 14 March.

3   *To Constance Wilde* / [? *5 April 1895*]: This letter, which is in an envelope addressed to Mrs Oscar Wilde, 16 Tite Street, was delivered by hand. It cannot be dated with confidence, but the morning of the last day of the Queensberry trial, when Wilde knew that he could not win, seems a likely time.

4   *To the Editor of the Evening News* / *5 April 1895*: On the morning of this day, the prosecution was forced to withdraw and Queensberry was acquitted. This letter, written on two envelopes from the Holborn Viaduct Hotel, is in Robert Ross's handwriting and signed by Wilde.

5   *Rather than put him in so painful a position . . . my prosecuting*

Lord Queensberry: Douglas maintained all his life that, had he been allowed to give evidence, he would have discredited his father sufficiently to allow Wilde to win. It is very unlikely that he could have done this.

6 *George Alexander, and Waller*: George Alexander (1858–1918), actor and theatre manager. His tenancy of St James's Theatre where *The Importance of Being Earnest* was produced lasted from 1891 until his death. 'Waller' is the actor-manager Lewis Waller (1860–1915).

7 *give bail*: On 6 April 1895 Wilde was charged with offences under the Criminal Law Amendment Act, 1885. Refused bail, he was imprisoned at Holloway. On 1 May the jury disagreed. He was released on bail 7 May and a new trial began on 20 May. On 25 May he was found guilty and sentenced to two years' imprisonment with hard labour. The first six months were spent in Pentonville and Wandsworth prisons, the rest at Reading.

8 *Why did the Sibyl say fair things*: A reference to Mrs Robinson, a fashionable fortune-teller.

9 *To an Unidentified Correspondent*: Perhaps Adela Schuster, who had given Wilde £1,000, or the actress Mrs Bernard Beere (1856–1915).

10 *someone whose name is Love . . . comfort him*: Lord Alfred Douglas.

11 *Sarah*: Sarah Bernhardt (1844–1923), celebrated French actress for whom Wilde wrote *Salomé* (1891). She was to appear in the title role in London in 1892 but rehearsals were cancelled by the Lord Chamberlain on the grounds that it was illegal to represent biblical characters on stage, and production of the play – in Paris, under the direction of Aurélien Lugné-Poë – did not go ahead until 1896.

12 *To Lord Alfred Douglas / Monday Evening [29 April 1895]*: In August 1895 Douglas wrote a passionate defence of Wilde for an article written in French for *Mercure de France* but, at Wilde's insistence, it was not published. Douglas included three letters from Wilde (this and two from May 1895, referred to in notes 18 and 21, on p. 237), the originals of which he destroyed but which have been translated back into English.

13 *Dear —*: Name omitted by Douglas.

14 *If I do not get bail today . . . send me some books*: He didn't. It was not until 7 May that bail was granted. The sureties were the Rev. Stewart Headlam (see note 47, p. 261), a socialist clergyman, and Alfred Douglas's elder brother, Percy. As a result, Percy

and his father came to blows publicly in Piccadilly on 21 May.

15   *Now that he*: Lord Alfred Douglas.

16   *Jonquil*: One of Wilde's nicknames for Lord Alfred Douglas – see also note 33 on p. 245.

17   *[? 146 Oakley Street]*: When Wilde was released on bail, no hotel would accept him; he stayed with his mother at 146 Oakley Street.

18   *To Lord Alfred Douglas / [May 1895]*: See note 12 on p. 236.

19   *[? 2 Courtfield Gardens]*: After a few days, the Leversons took Wilde into their house at 2 Courtfield Gardens, where he stayed until his conviction on 25 May.

20   *more sacred, more beautiful . . .* : Wilde's ellipsis.

21   *To Lord Alfred Douglas / [20 May 1895]*: See note 12 on p. 236. 'Taylor', mentioned in the second sentence of this letter, was Oscar Wilde's co-defendant, Alfred Taylor, believed to have introduced Wilde to several young men. Refusing to give evidence against him, Taylor was tried with Wilde and, like him, convicted of gross indecency and sentenced to two years' hard labour.

22   *[HM Prison, Reading]*: Wilde was moved from Pentonville to Wandsworth on 4 July 1895 and from there to Reading on 21 November. To begin with, he was allowed to write only one letter every three months. (For more detail on this, see the Introduction, p. xxv.)

23   *purchasing my life-interest*: A life interest in his marriage settlement.

24   *She was gentle . . . when she came to see me*: Lady Wilde died on 3 February 1896 and Constance travelled specially from Genoa to Reading to break the news to him. Her visit was on 19 February. It was their last meeting.

25   *his kindness was great in getting them sent*: On 12 June 1895, Richard Burton Haldane MP (1856–1928), a member of the Gladstone Committee investigating prisons, visited Wilde in Pentonville. He persuaded the Home Secretary to transfer Wilde to Wandsworth and then to Reading. He also obtained books for him. In January 1896, More Adey arranged with the Home Office to send more books, including the *Corpus Poetarum Latinorum* and *Poetae Scenici Graeci*.

26   *the lady who lives at Wimbledon*: Adela Schuster, frequently referred to in Wilde's letters as 'the Lady of Wimbledon'.

27   *Jones's play and Forbes-Robertson's management*: Henry Arthur Jones (1851–1929), English dramatist. Johnston Forbes-

Robertson (1853–1937), English actor-manager, regarded as one of the finest actors of his day.

28   *Lemaître, Bauër, and Sarcey*: Jules François Élie Lemaître (1854–1914), Henri Bauër (1851–1915) and Francisque Sarcey (1827–99) were three of the leading French dramatic critics.

29   *please write to Henri Bauër . . . his writing nicely*: On 3 June 1895, Bauër published an article in the *Echo de Paris* attacking the barbarity of Wilde's sentence.

30   *It was sweet of you to come and see me*: Ross and Ernest Leverson visited Wilde on 25 February 1896.

31   *Ask Ernest in whose name the burial-ground of my mother was taken*: Lady Wilde was buried in an unmarked grave in Kensal Green cemetery. A memorial stone was placed there on the centenary of her death in 1996.

32   *[30 May 1896]*: Sherard and Ross visited Wilde, probably on 29 May 1896.

33   *The proposal is revolting and grotesque*: When Douglas's *Poems* was published at the end of 1896, it contained no dedication.

34   *Let me know why Irving leaves Lyceum etc.*: Henry Irving (1838–1905), English actor-manager, ended his Lyceum season on 27 July 1895 and toured America for ten months. He reappeared at the Lyceum in *Cymbeline* on 22 September 1896.

35   *who did Stevenson criticise severely in his letters*: Robert Louis Stevenson died in Samoa on 3 December 1894; his *Vailima Letters*, edited by their recipient Sidney Colvin, was published on 2 November 1895.

36   *He has ruined my life – that should content him*: Douglas, devastated by this comment, replied to Ross on 4 June 1896. An extract from this letter was printed in the *Daily Telegraph* of 25 November 1921 in connection with one of Douglas's many libel actions.

37   *Carlos Blacker and Newcastle*: Carlos Blacker (1859–1928), linguist, friend of Oscar and Constance Wilde. 'The Happy Prince' (published in *The Happy Prince and Other Tales*, 1888) was dedicated to him. In 1890 he became involved in a disastrous business venture, leading him to quarrel with the Duke of Newcastle, who had acted as surety. In revenge, the duke falsely accused Blacker of cheating at cards. Wilde attempted to bring about a reconciliation between the two men, although this did not take place until 1900.

38   *To the Home Secretary*: This was written on an official form. The Home Secretary at the time was Sir Matthew White Ridley,

Bart (1842–1904). Wilde, by this stage, had begun to suffer from the painful ear infection which would kill him four years later.

39 *Lombroso and Nordau*: Cesare Lambroso (1836–1909) was an Italian criminologist; Max Simon Nordau (1849–1923) was a German author and sociologist.

40 *Sir William Dalby*: William Bartlett Dalby (1840–1918), knighted in 1886.

41 *The Petition of the above-named prisoner humbly sheweth . . . Oscar Wilde*: The petition was forwarded to the Home Office together with a short medical report from the prison doctor saying that Wilde had put on weight in prison and showed no signs of insanity. It was recommended that Wilde should have writing materials in his cell and a larger supply of books.

42 *To the Home Secretary*: See note 38 on p. 238.

43 *Solicitors' Room . . . in presence of a warder*: On 6 July the Home Office ruled that the interview might take place in the Solicitors' Room, the length of the interview being left to the governor's discretion.

44 *[26 August 1896]*: Dated by a prison official.

45 *George Ives*: George Cecil Ives (1867–1950), German-English poet, writer and penal reformer, published *A Book of Chains* anonymously in 1897, which contained poems about Wilde in prison.

46 *More Adey to Oscar Wilde*: The original of this letter is lost, but this draft of part of it in Adey's hand has survived.

47 *a beautiful play . . . rather in the style of Frou-frou*: In the fourth act of *Froufrou* (1869) by Henri Meilhac and Ludovic Halévy, the heroine's husband and lover fight a duel off stage, in which the lover is mortally wounded.

48 *I remember the Moving Sphere story . . . the Problem and the Lunatic*: Neither story was written down by Wilde. The first story and its possible sources is discussed by John Stokes in *Oscar Wilde: Myths, Miracles, and Imitations* (Cambridge: Cambridge University Press, 1996). Frank Harris adapted it and published it as 'The Irony of Chance (after O. W.)' in his *Unpath'd Waters* (1913).

49 *Lady Brooke [the Ranee of Sarawak]*: Margaret, Lady Brooke (1849–1936), queen-consort of the White Rajah of Sarawak, Charles Anthony Johnson Brooke. Wilde dedicated his story 'The Young King' (published in *A House of Pomegranates*, 1891) to her. She became a close confidante of Constance Wilde's in exile.

50 *Bobbie*: Robert Ross.

51   *I thank you very much for writing to the Home Secretary*: More
     Adey's petition to the Home Secretary (which is believed to have
     been partly drafted by George Bernard Shaw) urging a remission
     of Wilde's sentence, though printed and ready, was never sent,
     since almost immediately Adey received a letter from the Home
     Office saying that the Home Secretary 'has come to the conclu-
     sion that no grounds, medical or other, exist which would justify
     him in advising any mitigation of the sentence'.

52   *I was allowed to become insolvent when there was no reason*:
     Wilde was taken from prison for his public examination in
     the Bankruptcy Court on 24 September 1895 and again on 12
     November. The *Labour Leader* on 16 November reported: 'They
     have cut his hair in a shocking way and parted it down the side
     and he wears a short, scrubby, unkempt beard.'

53   *I would feel quite safe if Arthur . . . it would be a great thing*:
     On 8 October 1895, Arthur Clifton wrote to Carlos Blacker: 'I
     was very much shocked at Oscar's appearance, though scarcely
     surprised. Fortunately he had his ordinary clothes on: his hair
     was rather long and he looked dreadfully thin. You can imagine
     how painful it was to meet him: and he was very much upset and
     cried a good deal: he seemed quite broken-hearted and kept on
     describing his punishment as savage.'

54   *the Florentine Tragedy*: A fragment of a play that was never
     completed. The German translation of the text was made into
     an opera by the Austrian composer Alexander Zemlinsky, first
     performed in 1917.

55   *I am so glad Pierre Louÿs has made a great name for himself*:
     Pierre Louÿs (1870–1925), French poet and writer, whose novel
     Aphrodite (1896), a depiction of courtesan life in ancient Alex-
     andria, was a phenomenal success in France.

56   *In what a mire of madness I walked!* . . . : All the ellipses in this
     letter are Wilde's.

57   *Poor Aubrey*: Aubrey Beardsley (1872–98), English illustrator
     and artist; a leading figure in the Aesthetic Movement, he con-
     tributed to the development of Art Nouveau. At this point, he
     had already begun to suffer from the terminal effects of his child-
     hood consumption which would kill him on 16 March 1898.

58   *To the Home Secretary*: See note 38 on p. 238. This petition,
     like its predecessor (see note 41 on p. 239), was forwarded to
     the Home Office with a medical report. It was rejected almost
     immediately.

59   *To Robert Ross*: Attached to this letter is a note in Ross's hand:

'The front sheet of this letter which dealt with business matters was forwarded to Hansell or Humphreys [lawyers] and was not returned to me.'

60 *There is a thorn . . . that I must pluck out of my flesh in this letter*: 2 Corinthians 12: 7.

61 *terrible thoughts that gnaw me . . .* : All the ellipses in this letter are Wilde's.

62 *being no 'winged living thing', as Plato feigned it*: Phaedrus 246A–249B.

63 *I believe that my letter . . . cut out by a pair of scissors*: See letter of Saturday 30 May 1896 (p. 14).

64 *Charley Parker*: One of the young men who gave evidence at Wilde's trials.

65 *Infant Samuel . . . Malebolge*: The 'Infant Samuel' refers to how Samuel was called by God as a child (1 Samuel 3). The reference here may also recall the famous painting from 1776 of the same subject by Sir Joshua Reynolds. 'Malebolge' is the eighth circle of Dante's *Inferno*.

66 *Gilles de Retz and the Marquis de Sade*: Gilles de Laval, Sire de Retz or Raiz (1404–40), the comrade-in-arms of Joan of Arc, turned to debauchery, devil-worship and child murder, for which he was finally executed. The Marquis de Sade (1740–1814), author of *Justine* (1791) and other novels of cruelty, was sentenced to death for various offences but escaped the scaffold and died in a lunatic asylum.

67 *the wonderful story of the little restaurant with the strange dish of meat served to the silent clients*: Max Meyerfeld, in his annotations to *Letzte Briefe* (Berlin: 1925, see p. 164) suggests that this is a reference to a story told by Robert Ross about an archbishop who relishes a dinner at a Wardour Street restaurant, only to discover that it was made of human flesh.

68 *my wife's offer*: Constance Wilde's advisers wished her to buy Wilde's contingent life interest in her marriage settlement from the official receiver.

69 *(2) It would be a great thing for me to see you (or Arthur Clifton) some time next month, and at intervals, on my affairs. I hope permission will be granted*:

70 *Stevenson's memoirs etc.*: There was no such book. Wilde must have confused it with Stevenson's *Vailima Letters* (see note 35 on p. 238).

71 *Ollendorff*: Heinrich Gottfried Ollendorff (d. 1865) produced 'a new method of learning to read, write and speak a language in

six months'.

72 *Arthur*: Wilde accidentally wrote 'Charles', with his now-despised solicitor in mind.

73 *I wait them eagerly*: Humphreys had sent Wilde a present of books.

74 *the French translator of my novel should be considered*: In the spring of 1895, Albert Savine published a French translation of *The Picture of Dorian Gray* by Eugène Tardieu and Georges Maurevert. It went through four editions in 1895.

75 *The mischief of Lady Windermere's Fan . . . no use bothering*: Presumably a reference to the French translation rights, although in a letter of June 1897 to William Rothenstein (see note 45 on p. 247) Wilde refers to a possible translation of the play.

76 *an old family name on her side*: Constance Wilde changed her, Cyril and Vyvyan's last name to Holland.

77 *October year last*: Actually 21 September.

78 *She also on the death of my mother . . . to me here in person*: On 19 February 1896. She travelled from Genoa.

79 *Charles Wyndham*: The actor-manager Charles Wyndham (1837–1919) originally owned the rights to *The Importance of Being Earnest*, which he gave to George Alexander when Alexander's production of Henry James's *Guy Domville* failed and he was in need of a new production. One of the conditions, it seems, was that Wyndham should have Wilde's next play.

80 *Miss Napier . . . Mrs Napier*: Mary Eliza Napier (known as Eliza) was Constance Wilde's first cousin. After Constance's death she became to some extent a foster-mother to Wilde's sons. Mrs Napier (Louisa Mary Napier, mother of Eliza) did lend Constance £100.

81 *I am still at work at the letter*: For this letter, known as *De Profundis*, see pp. 45–161.

82 *Mr Grain*: John Peter Grain (1839–1916), barrister, was Charles Humphreys's brother-in-law. He appeared as counsel for Alfred Taylor in both Wilde's trials and for Wilde in the Bankruptcy Court.

83 *He need not have been . . .* : Wilde's ellipsis.

84 *People, as somebody in one of Ibsen's plays says, don't do these things*: The last line of *Hedda Gabler* (1890), spoken by Judge Brack after Hedda's suicide.

85 *from the bottom of page one*: i.e. from 'As regards the Queensberry family . . .', paragraph three of this letter.

86 *Mr Stoker*: Presumably a partner in Messrs Stoker and Hansell, solicitors.

87 *For the list of books . . . la Sainte Bible:* On 10 March 1897 a list of books was submitted to the prison governor, who approved all of them, except the periodical the *Nineteenth Century*, which he thought unsuitable. The other books included volumes by Dante, Goldoni, D. G. Rossetti, Stevenson, Meredith and Hardy as well as a French Bible and a German grammar.

De Profundis

1 *To Lord Alfred Douglas:* This long letter is known as *De Profundis*. On 2 April 1897, the prison governor wrote to the Prison Commission to ask whether this letter, 'written during the last three or four months', might be sent out. He informed them that there were twenty folio sheets, each of four pages. 'Each sheet,' he wrote, 'was carefully numbered before being issued and withdrawn each evening and placed before me in the morning with the usual papers.' This is unlikely; it is more probable that the governor allowed Wilde greater freedom to revise and correct. On 6 April the Commission wrote to say that sending the letter was impossible; instead it could be kept and handed to the prisoner on his release. This was done on 19 May and Wilde, in turn, handed it to Robert Ross at Dieppe when he landed there the next morning. Ross had two typed copies made. According to him, he sent Douglas one of these copies. In 1905 Ross published extracts, as *De Profundis* (a title he chose – see note 43 on p. xxxii), amounting to less than half the letter, and a slightly fuller version in 1908. Neither of these contained any reference to Douglas. In 1909 Ross presented the original copy to the British Museum on condition that no one be allowed to see it for fifty years. The second typescript, kept by Ross and eventually bequeathed by him to Vyvyan Holland, supplied the 'first complete and accurate version' which Holland published, again as *De Profundis*, in 1949. There were, however, considerable differences between the manuscript and the typed copy. Some of these were caused by errors in the typing and dictating; others were caused by Ross, who, for example, removed more than a thousand words, almost all of them fiercely critical of Douglas and his father. Wilde's letter is printed here exactly as he wrote it, except that it has been divided up into more paragraphs than his ration of paper allowed him.

2 *without ever having received a single line from you . . . except such as gave me pain:* Wilde's indictments of Douglas in this

letter need to be approached with caution. Some of them are both inaccurate and unfair.

3   *in my letter to Robbie*: See letter of 30 May 1896 (p. 14).

4   *such an artist as I am*: Wilde originally wrote 'was'.

5   *John Hare*: (1844–1921), actor and manager of the Garrick Theatre 1889–95.

6   *John Gray*: (1866–1934), poet of the Aesthetic Movement often suggested to be the inspiration for Dorian Gray.

7   *I had succeeded in inducing your mother to send you out of England*: Wilde wrote to Lady Queensberry on 8 November 1893.

8   *the Florentine Tragedy and La Sainte Courtisane*: Like *The Florentine Tragedy* (see note 54 on p. 240), *La Sainte Courtisane* is an unfinished play, begun by Wilde in 1894.

9   *'Plain living and high thinking'*: William Wordsworth's sonnet 'Written in London, September 1802'.

10   *Out of my dinner with Robbie came the first and best of all my dialogues*: Almost certainly Wilde's essay 'The Decay of Lying' (published with other essays in *Intentions*, 1891), in which two characters, Vivian and Cyril, debate the values of Aestheticism.

11   τερπνὸν κακόν: Euripides, *Hippolytus* 384; literally, 'delightful wickedness'.

12   *you at that time . . . elements or its expression*: In March 1893, Wilde wrote to Douglas: 'Bosie – you must not make scenes with me – they kill me – they wreck the loveliness of life – I cannot see you, so Greek and gracious, distorted by passion...'

13   *'the only tyranny that lasts'*: *A Woman of No Importance*, Act 3.

14   *Pater says that 'Failure is to form habits'*: In the 'Conclusion' to Walter Pater's *Studies in the History of the Renaissance* (see note 79 on p. 249).

15   *your place is with the Infant Samuel . . . Marquis de Sade*: See notes 65 and 66 on pp. 241.

16   *In the most wonderful of all his plays . . . all that he possesses*: Aeschylus's *Agamemnon*; the words quoted occur in lines 717–28.

17   *my pointing out the schoolboy faults of your attempted translation of Salomé*: It seems that Wilde insisted on changes in Douglas's translation. The volume is dedicated to Douglas – it reads 'To my friend Lord Alfred Bruce Douglas, the translator of my play' – but Douglas's name does not appear as the translator on the title page.

18   *one of my own friends*: Wilde originally wrote 'Robbie'.

19   *family*: Wilde originally wrote 'wife'.

20 *candidissima anima*: 'purest [literally 'whitest'] soul'.

21 *try and get you connected with some Embassy abroad*: When Douglas left Egypt in March 1894, he was appointed honorary attaché to the British ambassador at Constantinople, but did not take up the appointment.

22 *bad line from which you come*: The 7th Marquess of Queensberry (1818–58) died in a shooting accident. His youngest son, Lord James Edward Sholto Douglas (1855–91), cut his own throat in the Euston Hotel.

23 *your father ... that afternoon, through a letter addressed to you, began his first attack on me*: This would have been *circa* 1 April 1894.

24 *I was trying to finish my last play at Worthing by myself*: Wilde wrote The Importance of Being Earnest in Worthing in August 1894.

25 *the influenza, your second, if not third attack*: On 6 October 1894, Wilde sent a telegram to Ada Leverson reporting the state of health of Lord Alfred Douglas: 'Much better, temperature gone down, is to be allowed chicken to the sound of flutes at 7.30. Many thanks for kind enquiries.'

26 *Wednesday was my birthday*: In 1894 Wilde's birthday (16 October) was a Tuesday, and Ross changed this sentence accordingly in the typescripts.

27 *in a public restaurant*: The Berkeley, in Piccadilly.

28 *on the Friday*: 19 October 1894.

29 *the heir to the title ... his gun lying discharged beside him*: Viscount Drumlanrig was killed by the explosion of his gun on 18 October 1894 (see also note 39 on p. 246).

30 *lacrimae rerum*: Literally, 'tears of things' – Virgil, *Aeneid* 1: 462.

31 *It is not of our vices only they make instruments to scourge us*: Shakespeare, *King Lear* V. iii. 181–2: 'The gods ... of our pleasant vices / Make instruments to plague us.'

32 *I reply by a letter of fantastic literary conceits*: Letter written probably in January 1893. It began: 'My Own Boy, Your sonnet is quite lovely, and it is a marvel that those rose-leaf lips of yours should have been made no less for music of song than for madness of kisses.'

33 *I compare you to Hylas, or Hyacinth, Jonquil or Narcisse*: In Greek mythology, Hylas, Hyacinth and Narcissus were young men all noted for their beauty. Narcissus and jonquil are both common names for flowering plants of the *Narcissus* genus,

named after the flower that supposedly sprang up in the spot where the eponymous youth fell in a pool and drowned, so intently was he gazing at his own reflection.

34 *the manager of the theatre where my work is being performed*: Herbert Beerbohm Tree (1853–1917), actor-manager. As manager of the Haymarket Theatre, he produced two of Wilde's plays – *A Woman of No Importance* and *An Ideal Husband*.

35 *I sent him a page of paradoxes destined originally for the Saturday Review*: Thirty-five aphorisms of Wilde's were published in the first and only edition of the *Chameleon*, an Oxford undergraduate magazine published in December 1894. Much play was made with them at the trial and also with two other items in the magazine – a poem of Douglas's called 'Two Loves' and an anonymous story called 'The Priest and the Acolyte', attributed to Wilde but in fact written by the magazine's editor, John Francis Bloxam.

36 *'the Love that dares not tell its name'*: The last lines of Douglas's poem 'Two Loves' are: '"I am true Love, I fill / The hearts of boy and girl with mutual flame." Then sighing said the other, "Have thy will, / I am the Love that dare not speak its name."'

37 *on that fatal Friday*: 1 March 1895.

38 *some £700*: This (or rather £677) was the amount of Queensberry's taxed costs in Wilde's unsuccessful action against him. The total of Wilde's debts was £3,591 (see PRO b9–429), but Queensberry was the petitioning creditor whose action made Wilde a bankrupt.

39 *Secretary for Foreign Affairs at Homburg*: In 1893 Queensberry's eldest son, Drumlanrig (see also note 29 on p. 245), was then private secretary to Lord Rosebery, Foreign Secretary in Gladstone's last government. Queensberry, who began to quarrel with his son, followed Rosebery to Homburg, threatening to horsewhip him because he suspected his son of a homosexual relationship with the Foreign Secretary, and was only persuaded to desist by the Prince of Wales.

40 *a foolish and vulgar telegram*: This telegram (dated 2 April 1894) read: 'WHAT A FUNNY LITTLE MAN YOU ARE.'

41 *The faculty 'by which, and by which alone . . . as in their ideal relations'*: Quoting a passage from earlier in *De Profundis* (p. 74).

42 *scies*: 'irritating things'.

43 *a letter you had published in one of the halfpenny newspapers about me*: In April 1895, when Wilde was awaiting trial, the

Marquess of Queensberry replied to a letter in support of Wilde published in the *Star*. Lord Alfred Douglas, in turn, replied to his father.

44 *you wrote other letters to other newspapers that they did not publish*: In June 1895 Douglas also wrote to Henry Labouchère's *Truth* and to T. W. Stead, editor of *Review of Reviews* (see also note 18 on p. 258).

45 *my Monticelli: my Simeon Solomons*: A picture by the French painter Adolphe Joseph Thomas Monticelli (1824–86) was sold in the Tite Street sale of Wilde's goods to the artist William Rothenstein (1872–1945), who bought it for £8 and later sold it for Wilde's benefit. Simeon Solomons (1840–1905) was an English painter and illustrator.

46 *more summarily than even wretched perjured Atkins was*: Frederick Atkins was at different times a billiard-marker and a bookmaker's clerk. When he gave evidence for the Crown at Wilde's first trial, he perjured himself so flagrantly that the judge described him in his summing up as 'a most reckless, unreliable, unscrupulous, and untruthful witness'. Wilde, who admitted having taken Atkins on a trip to Paris with him, was acquitted of the charges brought in respect of this witness.

47 *the arrow had pierced a King between the joints of the harness*: 1 Kings 22: 34.

48 *the entire chrysolite of the whole world*: Shakespeare, *Othello* V. ii. 143–4: 'If heaven would make me such another world / Of one entire and perfect chrysolite'.

49 *I was greatly taken aback . . . stopped at once*: See note 12 on p. 236.

50 *feuilletoniste*: Newspaper columnist.

51 *I think they love not Art . . . glare or gloat*: The closing lines of the octave of Wilde's sonnet 'On the Sale by Auction of Keats' Love Letters' (1886), although the printed version has 'glare and gloat' (Wilde was quoting from memory).

52 *Lombroso*: See note 39 on p. 239.

53 *I am told that Henri Bauër had already done it extremely well*: See note 29 on p. 238.

54 *Infant Samuel . . . Gilles de Retz and the Marquis de Sade*: See notes 65 and 66 on pp. 241.

55 *the leper of mediaevalism, and the author of Justine . . . Sandford and Merton*: The first two refer back to Gilles de Retz and the Marquis de Sade of four sentenced earlier (see previous note). *The History of Sandford and Merton*, an improving and immensely

popular book for children by Thomas Day (1748–89), was origi-
nally published 1783–9.

56   *I would readily consent to be 'blackmailed by every renter in
     London'*: What he actually wrote was: 'I'd sooner be rented all
     day, than have you bitter, unjust, and horrid – horrid – '.

57   *The faculty 'by which, and by which alone . . . as in their ideal
     relations'*: See note 41 on p. 246.

58   *Suffering is one long moment*: It was with this sentence that
     Robert Ross's 1905 edition of *De Profundis* started (see note 1
     on p. 243).

59   *A week later*: Wilde originally wrote 'On the 13th of
     November'.

60   *lord of language*: Tennyson, 'To Virgil' (1882).

61   *'Non ragioniam di lor, ma guarda, e passa'*: 'Let us not speak of
     them, but look, and pass on', Dante, *Inferno* 3: 51.

62   *thin beaten-out leaf of tremulous gold ... eye cannot see*: A ref-
     erence to the gold leaf used by bookbinders with which Wilde
     would undoubtedly have been familiar. The slightest, almost
     imperceptible disturbance in the air would cause it to fly off the
     cutting cushion on which it was being prepared for tooling on
     the book.

63   *why I wrote . . . such scorn and contempt of you*: Referring to his
     letter of 30 May 1896 (see p. 14).

64   *the soul of Branca d'Oria in Dante*: *Inferno* 33: 135–47.

65   *Edwin Levy*: It seems possible that Levy was some kind of
     moneylender or private inquiry agent.

66   *causerie intime*: Intimate chat.

67   *Alfred Austin*: (1835–1913), succeeded Tennyson as Poet Laure-
     ate in 1896.

68   *Street*: George Slythe Street (1867–1936), journalist and author
     of *The Autobiography of a Boy* (1894) and other books.

69   *Mrs Meynell had been pronounced to be the new Sibyl of Style*:
     In December 1895, Coventry Patmore (1823–96) had written
     to the *Saturday Review*, advocating the claims of the popular
     columnist and poet Alice Meynell (1847–1922) to the vacant
     Laureateship.

70   *When I wrote . . . the feet of clay that made the gold of the image
     precious*: A reference to *The Picture of Dorian Gray*, chapter 15.
     This chapter first appeared in the book edition in April 1891.

71   *my two children are taken from me by legal procedure*:
     Constance Wilde's summons was heard on 12 February 1897.
     The resulting order gave her custody of the children, with
     herself and Adrian Hope (1858–1904) as the guardians. Hope,

who was Secretary to the Hospital for Sick Children from 1888, continued as guardian after Constance's death, but, according to Vyvyan Holland, they hardly ever saw him.

72 *To revisit the glimpses of the moon*: Shakespeare, *Hamlet* I. iv. 53:"Revisit'st thus the glimpses of the moon'.

73 *It was simply that 'one really fatal defect ... lack of imagination'*: Referring to two earlier passages in *De Profundis* (see pp. 74 and 77).

74 *I was no longer the Captain of my Soul*: An echo of W. E. Henley's poem 'Invictus' (1875).

75 *Suffering ... And has the nature of Infinity*: Wordsworth, *The Borderers* (written 1795-7; published 1842), Act 3; 'has' in the second line should be 'shares'.

76 *Vita Nuova: The New Life* (1295), Dante's treatise on the art of poetry with a commentary on the emotions – his unrequited love for Beatrice – that gave rise to his verse.

77 *'where I walk there are thorns'*: *A Woman of No Importance*, Act 4.

78 *'the world is shrivelled to a handsbreadth'*: Ibid; followed in the play by 'and where I walk there are thorns' – see previous note.

79 *reading in Pater's Renaissance ... those who wilfully live in sadness*: Walter Pater's essay 'The Poetry of Michelangelo' (1871), collected in *Studies in the History of the Renaissance* (1873).

80 *Tristi fummo / nell' aer dolce che dal sol s'allegra*: 'Sad once were we, / In the sweet air made gladsome by the sun', *Inferno* 7: 121-2 (H. F. Cary's translation).

81 *accidia*: Sloth, one of the Seven Deadly Sins.

82 *'sorrow remarries us to God'*: *Purgatorio* 23: 81.

83 *the delight I really felt at our meeting*: This probably refers to Saturday, 27 February 1897, when Ross and Adey paid Wilde a visit.

84 *Who never ate his bread ... ye Heavenly Powers*: Carlyle's translation of a verse in Goethe's *Wilhelm Meister's Apprenticeship* (1795-6), book 2, chapter 13, where 'midnight' is 'darksome', 'waiting' is 'watching', and 'Heavenly' is 'gloomy'.

85 *that noble Queen of Prussia ... humiliation and exile*: Louisa (1776-1810), wife of King Frederick William III. She is said to have copied these lines when she and her husband were in flight after the Battle of Jena (1806). After the total defeat of Prussia in 1807, she went to Tilsit to plead, unavailingly, for generous terms from Napoleon, who had consistently but vainly tried to blacken her character.

86 *'a month or twain to feed on honeycomb'*: Swinburne, 'Before

Parting' (published in *Poems and Ballads*, 1866); 'feed' should be 'live'.

87 *one of the most beautiful personalities I have ever known*: Adela Schuster.

88 *'heights that the soul is competent to gain'*: Wordsworth, *The Excursion* (1814), 4: 139.

89 *'gate which is called Beautiful'*: Acts 3: 2.

90 *The Soul of Man*: 'The Soul of Man under Socialism', Wilde's essay from 1891, expressing an anarchist worldview.

91 *in the prose-poem . . . it is incarnate*: A misquotation of Wilde's prose poem 'The Artist', which first appeared in the *Fortnightly Review* for July 1894. Here the images are reversed, which perhaps suited both his mood and his argument better. Whether the reversal was deliberate or not is uncertain.

92 *Marius the Epicurean*: Walter Pater's historical and philosophical novel (1885), set in ancient Rome.

93 *which Wordsworth defines as the poet's true aim:* Wilde must have been thinking of Walter Pater's essay on Wordsworth in *Appreciations* (1889). After quoting Wordsworth on 'the operations of the elements and the appearances of the visible universe, on storm and sunshine, on the revolutions of the seasons, on cold and heat, on loss of friends and kindred, on injuries and resentments, on gratitude and hope, on fear and sorrow', Pater comments: 'To witness this spectacle with appropriate emotions is the aim of all culture.'

94 *'When you are not . . . go away at once'*: Referring to an earlier section of *De Profundis*, p. 65.

95 *'the secret of Jesus'*: 'But there remains the question: what righteousness really is. The method and secret and sweet reasonableness of Jesus', *Literature and Dogma* (1873), chapter 12.

96 *Caesar Borgia, of Alexander VI*: Rodrigo Borgia (1431–1503), who purchased his own election as Pope in 1492 and whose pontificate as Alexander VI is commonly regarded as the nadir of papal morals, but who, in sheer depravity, was outdone by his own son Cesare (1475/6–1507).

97 *Emperor of Rome and Priest of the Sun*: The effeminate, homosexual Roman emperor Heliogabulus or Elagabulus, whose rule from 218 to 222 was of legendary immorality and who was only eighteen at the time of his assassination.

98 *the sufferings of those . . . whose dwelling is among the tombs*: Mark 5: 5 and 9.

99 *'pity and terror'*: Aristotle, *Poetics* 13.

100 *'Thebes and Pelops' line'*: Milton, *Il Penseroso*, line 99; 'and' should be 'or'.

101 *it would be impossible . . . one blameless in pain*: Poetics 13.

102 *'musical as is Apollo's lute'*: Milton, *Comus*, line 478.

103 *Renan in his Vie de Jésus . . . as he had been during his lifetime*: 'S'être fait aimer, "à ce point qu'après sa mort on ne cessa pas de l'aimer," voilà le chef-d'œuvre de Jésus et ce qui frappa le plus ses contemporains' (chapter 28). Joseph Ernest Renan (1823–92), French philosopher and writer, best known for his *Vie de Jésus* (1863), which presents Jesus as an historical figure.

104 *'The body of a child . . . I am not worthy of either'*: An allusion to the prayer said at Mass before Communion: *'Domine, non sum dignus . . .'* ('Lord, I am not worthy . . .').

105 *It is tragic how few people . . . before they die*: 'And see all sights from pole to pole, / And glance, and nod, and bustle by – / And never once possess our soul / Before we die', Matthew Arnold, 'A Southern Night' (1861).

106 *'Nothing is more rare . . . an act of his own'*: Ralph Waldo Emerson, in his lecture 'The Preacher', published posthumously in *Lectures and Biographical Sketches* (1883).

107 *'Forgive your enemies' . . . 'Sell all that thou hast and give it to the poor'*: Matthew 5: 44 ('Love your enemies') and Luke 18: 22.

108 *how salt is the bread of others and how steep their stairs*: Dante, *Paradiso* 17: 58–60: *'Tu proverai sì come sa di sale / Lo pane altrui, e com'è duro calle / Lo scendere e il salir per l'altrui scale.'* See also the opening of Wilde's sonnet 'At Verona', published in *Poems* (1881): 'How steep the stairs within Kings' houses are / For exiled-wearied feet as mine to tread, / And O how salt and bitter is the bread / which falls from this Hound's table.' He had already used the first line in his poem 'Ravenna' (1878).

109 *O Seigneur, donnez-moi la force . . . sans dégoût*: From 'Un Voyage a Cythère' in *Les Fleurs du mal* (1857). The quotation is marginally incorrect: it should read *'Ah! Seigneur!'* and *'mon cœur et mon corps'*.

110 *'whose silence is heard only of God'*: Quoting a passage from earlier in *De Profundis* (p. 115).

111 *but he himself had been cruel to Marsyas and had made Niobe childless . . . Pallas there had been no pity for Arachne*: For Marsyas, see note 141 on p. 253. In boasting of her many children, Niobe is made childless by Apollo and his sister Artemis, who kill all of them. Arachne claimed to be a better weaver than Pal-

las Athena, her arrogance eventually causing the goddess to punish her by turning her into a spider.

112 *mother of Proserpina ... son of Semele*: Demeter and Dionysus.

113 *Cithaeron or at Enna*: Mount Cithaeron was the scene of the Bacchic orgies in honour of Dionysus. It was from the flower-filled meadows of Enna that Proserpina was seized by Pluto and carried off to the underworld.

114 '*He is despised and rejected of men ... from him*': Isaiah 53: 3.

115 *Christ found the type ... the world was waiting*: Cf. Virgil's fourth *Eclogue*: '*Jam redit et virgo*', translated literally as 'Now the Virgin returns' and meaning 'Now the good times are coming back', a reference to the goddess Astraea, who fled the earth but will one day return, signalling a new golden age.

116 '*His visage was marred ... the sons of men*': Isaiah 52: 14.

117 '*that in which ... in which Form reveals*': Quoting a passage from earlier in *De Profundis* (p. 110).

118 *Chatterton's 'Ballad of Charity'*: 'An Excellent Ballad of Charity', one of the poems composed by Thomas Chatterton (1752–70) under the pseudonym of Thomas Rowley, an imaginary monk from the fifteenth century.

119 '*some strangeness of proportion*': Francis Bacon, 'Of Beauty' (from *Essays*, 1597).

120 '*bloweth where it listeth ... whither it goeth*': John 3: 8.

121 '*of imagination all compact*': Shakespeare, *A Midsummer Night's Dream* V. i. 8.

122 *I said in Dorian Gray ... take place in the brain*: In chapter 2.

123 *Charmides*: The central character of Plato's dialogue *Charmides*, where he appears as a beautiful young man typifying the central theme of moderation. Wilde's long poem of the same name is about an imaginary character.

124 ἐγώ εἰμι ὁ ποιμὴν ὁ ὀ ὁ καλός: 'I am the Good Shepherd', John 10: 11 and 14.

125 καταμάθετε τὰ ... κοπιᾷ οὐδὲ νήθει: 'Consider the lilies of the field, how they grow; they toil not, neither do they spin', Matthew 6: 28.

126 τετέλεσται: 'It is finished', John 19: 30.

127 *I love the story St Mark tells us ... that the children let fall*: Mark 7: 26–30.

128 *it is by love and admiration that we should live*: Wordsworth, *The Excursion* 4: 763: 'We live by Admiration, Hope and Love'.

129 *Domine, non sum dignus*: See note 104 on p. 251.

130 '*a guisa di fanciulla ... e ridendo pargoleggia*': *Purgatorio* 16: 86–7.

131 *'The birds didn't . . . Is not the body more than raiment?'*: Matthew 6: 26, 34 and 25.

132 *with Ruth and Beatrice . . . snow-white Rose of Paradise*: Cf. Dante, *Paradiso* 30–32.

133 *'Even the Gods cannot alter the past'*: Cf. Aristotle, *Ethics* 6: 2 and Pindar, *Olympia* 2: 15–17.

134 *the Liber Conformitatum*: A massive compilation illustrating the similarities in the lives of Christ and St Francis, written by Fr Bartholomaeus de Pisa in the fourteenth century and first printed in 1510.

135 *as the Greek oracle said, to know oneself*: 'Know thyself', in Greek letters, was inscribed over the entrance to the temple of Apollo at Delphi.

136 *When the son of Kish . . . already the Soul of a King*: The 'son of Kish' is Saul; see 1 Samuel 9.

137 *Verlaine and of Prince Kropotkin . . . passed years in prison*: Paul-Marie Verlaine (1844–96) was imprisoned for wounding Rimbaud with a revolver shot. Prince Peter Alexeievitch Kropotkin, Russian author, geographer and anarchist (1842–1921), was imprisoned for his political views and actions.

138 *this new personality*: Major James Osmond Nelson took over the governorship of Reading Gaol in July 1896.

139 *'my brother the wind' and 'my sister the rain'*: 'The Canticle of the Sun' (*c.* 1224).

140 *dalla vagina delle membre sue*: Dante, *Paradiso* 1: 20–21.

141 *I hear in much modern Art the cry of Marsyas*: In his review of W. E. Henley's *A Book of Verses* (1888), Wilde wrote: 'To me there is more of the cry of Marsyas than of the singing of Apollo in the early poems of Mr Henley's volume, "Rhymes and Rhythms in Hospital" as he calls them. But it is impossible to deny their power.' Marsyas was a mortal who challenged Apollo to a musical competition and was flayed alive for his pains. References to this myth recur often in Wilde's later letters.

142 *Even Matthew Arnold . . . has not a little of it*: 'Oh! that Fate had let me see / That triumph of the sweet persuasive lyre, / That famous, final victory, / When jealous Pan with Marsyas did conspire', *Empedocles on Etna* (1852), Act 2.

143 *the Phrygian Faun*: 'Marsyas, that unhappy Faun', ibid.

144 *I remember I used to say . . . a mask of noble sorrow*: Cf. 'Some noble grief that we think will lend the purple dignity of tragedy to our days', 'The Critic as Artist', part 2. Wilde uses similar imagery – the wearing of stately purple to denote a sad dignity – throughout the letters.

145 *It is said that . . . mean to the looker-on*: 'It is said all martyrdoms
     looked mean when they were suffered', Ralph Waldo Emerson,
     'Experience', published in *Essays: Second Series* (1844).

146 *On November 13th 1895 . . . from London*: It was actually 21
     November.

147 *I say, in Dorian Gray somewhere, that 'a man . . . choice of
     enemies'*: Chapter 1.

148 *It was like feasting with panthers*: An echo from Balzac's *Illu-
     sions perdues* (1837–43): '*Aussi, ce soir me semble-t-il que je
     soupe avec des lions et des panthères qui me font l'honneur de
     velouter leurs pattes*', part 2, chapter 18.

149 *Clibborn and Atkins*: Clibborn, referred to in the Queensberry
     trial as 'Cliburn', was a professional blackmailer who failed to
     extort any money from Wilde in respect of the letter to Lord
     Alfred Douglas, written probably in January 1893, which had
     been stolen from Douglas by an agent of the blackmailing gang.
     Clibborn was later sentenced to seven years' penal servitude for
     blackmailing offences. 'Atkins' (see note 46 on p. 247), is prob-
     ably a slip for 'Allen', a blackmailing associate of Clibborn's.

150 *Voilà où mènent les mauvais chemins!*: The last five words are
     the title of the third part of Balzac's *Splendeurs et misères des
     courtisanes* (1838–47), in which the misguided life of Lucien de
     Rubempré comes to its pitiful and tragic end. Vincent O'Sullivan
     records Wilde's saying: 'When I was a boy my two favourite
     characters were Lucien de Rubempré and Julien Sorel [in Stend-
     hal's *Le Rouge et le Noir*]. Lucien hanged himself, Julien died
     on the scaffold, and I died in prison', *Aspects of Wilde* (London:
     Constable, 1936), p. 36.

151 *But what a trade! What a competition!*: For Queensberry's letters
     to his son, see Merlin Holland, *Irish Peacock and Scarlet Mar-
     quess: The Real Trial of Oscar Wilde* (London: Fourth Estate,
     2003), pp. 214–8.

152 *Alfred Wood*: A blackmailer who gave evidence at Wilde's trials.

153 *Madame Roland*: Marie-Jeanne 'Manon' Phlipon (1754–93),
     bluestocking and hostess, married (1781) Jean-Marie Roland
     (1734–93), who later held office in the revolutionary govern-
     ment. Eventually, they fell foul of Marat, Madame Roland was
     arrested, wrote her *Mémoires* in the Conciergerie and was guillo-
     tined, after exclaiming, 'O Liberty! What crimes are committed
     in thy name!' Her husband killed himself two days later.

154 *George Wyndham*: The Right Honourable George Wyndham
     (1863–1913), son of the Honourable Percy Scawen Wyndham

and grandson of the 1st Baron Leconfield. He had been MP for Dover since 1889 and private secretary to Mr Balfour in 1887–92. He later reached the Cabinet. He wrote a number of books on literary subjects and was a relation of Lord Alfred Douglas.

155 *the small notoriety of a second divorce suit*: Queensberry, having been divorced by his first wife in 1887, remarried in 1893 a Miss Ethel Weeden, who obtained a decree of nullity against him on 24 October 1894.

156 *Of this public I have said . . . Tartuffe for the other*: There is no such remark in any of Wilde's published plays, but it was part of a long speech at the beginning of Act 3 of *A Woman of No Importance* which the actor-manager Herbert Beerbohm Tree (see note 34 on p. 246) persuaded Wilde to omit.

157 *a silly question asked . . . the Crown and by the Judge*: On 25 May 1895, the sixth and last day of Wilde's final trial, the foreman of the jury asked the judge if a warrant had been issued for the arrest of Lord Alfred Douglas or if it had been contemplated. The judge replied: 'Not to my knowledge.' He then instructed the jury to deliberate on the case in question without considering the case against Lord Alfred Douglas. In fact, the Director of Public Prosecutions had taken advice from the Senior Treasury Counsel, who wrote on 19 April 1895, a week before Wilde's first trial, that the evidence against Douglas was too slim and that it would be 'undesirable to start such a prosecution unless there was a strong possibility that it would result in a conviction'. See Merlin Holland, *Irish Peacock and Scarlet Marquess: The Real Trial of Oscar Wilde* (London: Fourth Estate, 2003), pp. 294–6

158 *She has chosen Adrian Hope . . . and with him Cyril and Vyvyan have a good chance of a beautiful future*: See note 71 on p. 248.

159 *delightful as cynicism is . . . man who has no soul*: Diogenes, the Cynic philosopher (419–324 BC), lived in a tub.

160 *a friend of ten years' standing*: It was Frank Harris, according to himself, but more likely R. H. Sherard.

161 *listening to Lockwood's*: The Solicitor-General, Sir Frank Lockwood (1847–97), who led for the prosecution in Wilde's second trial.

162 *like one of Savonarola's indictments of the Popes at Rome*: Girolamo Savonarola (1452–98), Dominican friar who called for reformation of the Church, defying the ban on preaching placed on him by Pope Alexander VI, which led to his excommunication and execution.

163 *Emotional forces, as I say somewhere in Intentions . . . forces of physical energy*: See 'The Critic as Artist', part 2.

164 *The martyr in his 'shirt of flame'*: Alexander Smith, 'A Life-Drama' (published in *A Life-Drama and Other Poems*, 1853), scene ii: 'Like a pale martyr in his shirt of fire'.

165 *Brutus used madness . . . the dagger of his will*: Not the Brutus of Shakespeare's *Julius Caesar*, but Junius Brutus who expelled Tarquin, the last king of Rome.

166 *'the contemplation of the spectacle of life with appropriate emotions'*: See note 93 on p. 250.

167 *'report Hamlet and his cause aright to the unsatisfied'*: Shakespeare, *Hamlet* V. ii. 334–5 ('Hamlet' and 'his' should be 'me' and 'my').

168 *Absents him . . . draws his breath in pain*: Ibid., 345–6 ('Absents him' and 'Absent his' should be 'draws thee' and 'draw thy').

169 *Angelo*: A character in Shakespeare's *Measure for Measure*.

170 *He who writes a new De Amicitia . . . in Tusculan prose*: A reference to Cicero, author of *De Amicitia* (*On Friendship*) and *Tusculanae Disputationes* (*Tusculan Disputations*), the latter believed to have been written at his villa in Tusculum – hence 'Tusculan'.

171 *the special cuvée of Perrier-Jouët reserved always for us*: Evidently a favourite with Wilde as Perrier-Jouët makes another appearance at the end of Act 3 of *The Importance of Being Earnest*.

172 Θάλασσα κλύζει πάντα τ'ἀνθρώπων κακά: *Iphigenia in Tauris*, line 1193.

173 *Linnaeus fell on his knees . . . blossoms of the common furze*: Carl Linnaeus (1707–78), the Swedish botanist and zoologist who established the principle of the two-part naming of species, visited England in 1736 where he passed on his system of classification, as laid out in his recently published *Systema Naturae* (1735).

174 *Like Gautier . . . pour qui le monde visible existe*: 'Critiques et louanges me louent et m'abîment sans comprendre un mot de ce que je suis. Toute ma valeur, ils n'ont jamais parlé de cela, c'est que je suis un homme pour qui le monde visible existe', the French poet Théophile Gautier (1811–72), quoted in the *Journal des Goncourt* for 1 May 1857. Wilde used the phrase in chapter 11 of *Dorian Gray*, to describe Dorian.

175 *'because of his importunity'*: Luke 11: 5–8.

176 *Miser of sound and syllable, no less / Than Midas of his coinage*: Keats, 'On the Sonnet' (1819) ('Misers' in original).

177 *'Where others . . . the sons of God shouting for joy'*: '"What," it will be Questioned, "When the Sun rises, do you not see a round Disk of fire somewhat like a Guinea?" O no, no, I see an Innumerable company of the Heavenly host crying, "Holy, Holy, Holy is the Lord God Almighty"', William Blake's commentary on his painting *A Vision of the Last Judgment* in the second edition of the *Descriptive Catalogue* (1810). See also Job 38: 7.

Letters of April 1897–March 1898

1 This letter to Ross, clearly intended to be dispatched to him at the same time as the MS of *De Profundis*, may well have been held back by the authorities for similar reasons (see note 1, p. 243). It resulted in Wilde repeating some of the contents of this letter in the subsequent one of 6 April.

2 *It is not unlikely that you may help me*: The letter, from which extracts were later published under the title *De Profundis* in 1905, was handed by Oscar Wilde to Robert Ross, who had remained loyal to him, on the day after Wilde left prison. Ross had two typed copies made, one of which was sent to Lord Alfred Douglas, although he denied receiving it. A fuller version was published in 1908, and in 1909 Ross presented the original to the British Museum. For more detail, see note 1 on p. 243.

3 *Mrs Marshall*: The owner of a typing agency on the Strand to whom Wilde had previously sent the manuscripts of *An Ideal Husband* and *The Importance of Being Earnest*.

4 *Hornton Street or Phillimore Gardens*: More Adey and Robert Ross shared lodgings at 24 Hornton Street, Kensington, and Ross's mother lived nearby at 11 Upper Phillimore Gardens.

5 *from 'and the end of it . . . I must forgive you' . . . page 4*: Most of these two passages were included in the 1905 edition of *De Profundis* (see note 1 on p. 243).

6 *Frankie Forbes-Robertson*: Frances ('Frankie') Harrod (1866–1956), painter and novelist; sister of Sir Johnston Forbes-Robertson (see note 27 on p. 237). They were among eleven children of John Forbes-Robertson, a theatre critic and journalist, and his wife Frances.

7 *'Habet Mundus Epistolam'*: 'The world has the letter'.

8 *Epistola: In Carcere et Vinculis*: 'Letter: In Prison and in Chains'.

9 *'cleansed my bosom of much perilous stuff'*: Shakespeare, *Macbeth* V. iii. 46: 'Cleanse the stuffed bosom of that perilous stuff'.

10   *the poet whom . . . rescuing from the Philistine*: Max Meyerfeld
     says that this refers to Ross's joking suggestion of founding an
     Anti-Shakespeare Society to combat exaggerated Bardolotry and
     that Douglas's sonnet 'To Shakespeare' (published in *The City of
     the Soul*, 1899) was written in anger at the suggestion. Douglas,
     it seemed, missed the joke, or misunderstood that the idea of
     the society was to rescue Shakespeare from the masses. See Max
     Meyerfeld, *Oscar Wilde: De Profundis* (Berlin: 1909), p. 184.

11   *20th March 1896*: Actually 10 March.

12   *She warned me . . . she will do so*: On 26 March, Constance
     Wilde wrote from Italy to her brother: 'I have again had pressure
     put upon me to persuade me to go back to Oscar, but I am sure
     you will agree that it is impossible. I am told that I would save a
     human soul, but I have no influence over Oscar. I have had none,
     and though I think he is affectionate I see no reason for believing
     that I should be able now to perform miracles, and I must look
     after my boys and not risk their future.'

13   *But surely you were something better / Than innocent!*: From
     Swinburne's 'Adieux à Marie Stuart' (published in *Tristram of
     Lyonesse and Other Poems*, 1882).

14   *damnosa haereditas*: A legal term for that portion of the prop-
     erty of a bankrupt that constitutes a charge to the creditors.

15   *£50 conveyed through Leverson*: This must refer to Wilde's
     brother and sister-in-law, since Mrs Willie Wilde was the only
     recipient of £50 from Leverson.

16   *a letter I am sending to More Adey at the same time as this*:
     See the letter that follows. Although this letter repeats much of
     the proceeding one, it is included for the extra matter which it
     contains.

17   *But surely you were something better / Than innocent!*: See note
     13 above.

18   *Labouchère, Stead*: Henry Du Pré Labouchère (1831–1912),
     Radical MP for Northampton 1880–1906, introduced Clause
     11 to the Criminal Law Amendment Act of 1885 outlaw-
     ing male homosexuality. William Thomas Stead (1849–1912),
     editor of the *Pall Mall Gazette* 1883–9, launched a campaign in
     1885 against the white slave traffic and organized vice. He was
     drowned on the *Titanic*.

19   *Meredith's novel*: George Meredith, *The Amazing Marriage*, first
     published on 15 November 1895.

20   *Rossetti's letters are dreadful*: *Dante Gabriel Rossetti: His
     Family-Letters, with a Memoir by William Michael Rossetti*,

published in two volumes in 1895.

21   *my grand-uncle's Melmoth and my mother's Sidonia*: For *Melmoth*, see note 46 on p. 261. *Sidonia the Sorceress*, Lady Wilde's translation of the Gothic romance *Sidonia von Bork* by Wilhelm Meinhold, was published in 1849.

22   *As regards the conspiracy . . . The conduct of a thrush in Cheyne Walk*: This incident in fact took place at Broadlands in Hampshire. W. M. Rossetti wrote: 'I remember there was once a thrush hard by, which, to my hearing, simply trilled its own lay on and off. My brother discerned a different note, and conceived that the thrush had been trained to ejaculate something insulting to him. Such is perverted fantasy – or I may rather infer such is an outcome of chloral-dosing', *Dante Gabriel Rossetti: His Family-Letters* (London: Ellis and Elvey, 1895), volume 1, p. 339. The poet Dr Thomas Gordon Hake (1809–95) was one of D. G. Rossetti's closest friends. His son Alfred Egmont Hake, author of *Free Trade in Capital* (1891) and other books, invented a new system of banking which had amused Wilde.

23   *Stevenson letters most disappointing also*: Robert Louis Stevenson, *Vailima Letters* (1895) – see note 35 on p. 238.

24   *En Route is most over-rated*: This novel by J.-K. Huysmans (1848–1907) was first published in 1895.

25   *It is worse French than Ohnet's*: Georges Ohnet (1848–1918), prolific and popular French novelist.

26   *Huysmans tries not to be, and is . . .* : All ellipses in this letter are Wilde's.

27   *Hardy's novel is pleasant, and Frederic's*: Thomas Hardy, *The Well-Beloved*, published 16 March 1897, and *Illumination* by the American novelist Harold Frederic (1856–98).

28   *Stanley Weyman*: Stanley John Weyman (1855–1928) had already published nine historical novels, including *Under the Red Robe* (1894) and *Memoirs of a Minister of France* (1895).

29   *You mentioned Henley had a protégé*: Probably H. G. Wells, whose first novel, *The Time Machine* (1895), had been serialized by W. E. Henley (see notes 74 and 141 on pp. 249 and 253) in the *New Review*.

30   *the 'Anthony Hope' man*: Pen-name of Anthony Hope Hawkins (1863–1933), author of many books. In 1894 he scored a double success with *The Dolly Dialogues* and *The Prisoner of Zenda*.

31   *Cosmo Lennox . . . Gilbert Burgess, Max*: Cosmo Charles Gordon-Lennox (1869–1921), actor, playwright and adapter. He played the part of the Vicomte de Nanjac in the original

production of *An Ideal Husband*. Gilbert Burgess (1868–1911), author and journalist. The writer and caricaturist Max Beerbohm (1872–1956) responded to Wilde's appeal and sent four books, including his own *Works* and *The Happy Hypocrite* (both 1896).

32   *Miss Siddal is fascinating, and her poem A1*: This poem, 'A Year and a Day' by Rossetti's wife Elizabeth Siddal, is printed on pp. 176–7 of the first volume of *Dante Gabriel Rossetti: His Family Letters* (see notes 20 and 22 on p. 259).

33   *French Books*: Some of the items on the list that follows have been scored through lightly in ink or pencil. This may conceivably have been done by the prison authorities (as has been suggested), but it looks much more as if Ross had struck out, at different times, in different ways, and with different pens and pencils, those items he obtained. Moreover, the publication dates of some of the books, and the objects at the end of the list, make it clear that these were the books and objects that Wilde hoped would be waiting for him when he left prison, so that the authorities cannot have been concerned.

34   *Translated by Father [H. S.] Bowden*: There exists a letter from Father Bowden to Wilde, written from the Oratory, London, on 15 April 1878, from which it is clear that Wilde had visited him on the previous day to ask for advice about the possibility of joining the Roman Catholic Church.

35   *Arthur Morrison . . . Criminology series*: Wilde was confusing the novelist Arthur Morrison (1863–1945), author of *Tales of Mean Streets* (1894), with the Reverend William Douglas Morrison (1852–1943), a prison chaplain and author of *Crime and its Causes* (1891) and *Juvenile Offenders* (1896).

36   *Humphreys*: Almost certainly Arthur Humphreys, the bookseller, who provided Wilde with books while in prison and whom Wilde thanked personally at Hatchards on the day of his release.

37   *Mr Horatio Lloyd*: John Horatio Lloyd, Constance's grandfather, a former MP and lawyer.

38   *Sporus*: The young boy whom the emperor Nero had castrated and later married, making him appear in public as his wife.

39   *my own portrait*: By the American artist Robert Goodloe Harper Pennington (*c.* 1854–1920).

40   *Will Rothenstein . . . Shannon's pastel of the Moon*: For Rothenstein, see note 45 on p. 246. Charles Shannon (1863–1937), artist and illustrator well known for his portraits.

41   *promises me ginger biscuits!*: At the bottom of this note Martin
     wrote in pencil: 'Your ungrateful I done more than promise.'
     This and the three short pieces that follow are examples of sur-
     reptitious notes, written on odd scraps of paper, which Wilde
     passed to him in prison.

42   *You must get me his address some day*: On the back of the note
     Martin wrote: 'However to compromise matters I will ask him
     [A.3.2] verbally for his address if that would suit you as well. Do
     you think you could pass the *Chronicle* under the door. Today's
     very easy for him to know who give it as there is no one in the
     prison at present but your humble servant.'

43   *To the Home Secretary*: Like Wilde's previous letters to the
     Home Secretary, this was written on an official form – see note
     38 on p. 238.

44   *20th May, 1895*: Actually 25 May, but Wilde's sentence ran,
     as the custom was, from the first day of the Sessions (20 May
     1895). Remission for good conduct was allowed only to prison-
     ers undergoing penal servitude (three years or more).

45   *A.2.11*: A.2.11 was a half-witted soldier called Prince. By paying
     their fines Wilde secured the release of these three children, who
     had been convicted of snaring rabbits. Warder Martin gave a
     biscuit to one of the children who was crying, and was dismissed
     in consequence.

46   *Mr Melmoth*: From the 'Wandering Jew' hero of *Melmoth the
     Wanderer* (1820) by the Irish writer Charles Robert Maturin
     (1782–1824), who was Wilde's great-uncle. Robert Ross and
     More Adey had collaborated in an anonymous biographical
     introduction to a new edition of the novel in 1892, and Ross
     suggested this alias to Wilde. The Christian name Sebastian was
     probably in memory of the martyred saint.

47   *Stewart Headlam's*: The Reverend Stewart Duckworth Headlam
     (1847–1924) had been for many years a vicar in the East End of
     London, but his socialism and religious unorthodoxy cost him
     his position in the Church. He was now living at 31 Upper Bed-
     ford Place, Bloomsbury. He had private means and, although he
     scarcely knew Wilde, had gone bail for him in 1895 because he
     thought the case was being prejudged and now offered his house
     as temporary asylum.

48   *To the Editor of the Daily Chronicle*: This letter was thus dated
     when it appeared in the *Daily Chronicle*, under the heading 'THE
     CASE OF WARDER MARTIN, SOME CRUELTIES OF PRISON
     LIFE', on 28 May, but it was presumably begun on or soon after

the 24th, when the *Daily Chronicle* printed a letter from Warder Martin recounting the circumstances of his dismissal (see note 45 on p. 254) and added an editorial comment: 'We are, of course, unable to verify our correspondent's statement, but we print his letter.' On the 28th, Wilde's letter was backed up by two leading articles, and another letter from Martin, discussing the Home Secretary's denial (in reply to a question from Michael Davitt, MP – see note 56 below) that the facts were as Martin had stated them.

49   *Eccelino da Romano*: Ghibelline leader (1194–1259) whose cruelties earned him a place in Dante's *Inferno*.

50   *'the silent rhythmic charm of human companionship'*: Carlyle, *Shooting Niagara: and After?* (1867), section IX: 'the silent charm of rhythmic human companionship'.

51   *to see that the lunatic prisoner is properly treated*: For earlier reference to Prince, see note 45 on p. 261.

52   *To an Unidentified Correspondent*: This was one of a number of letters Wilde enclosed in a letter to Robert Ross for sending on to the individuals in question, in this case one of three prisoners Wilde had known in Reading Gaol – either 'Ford', 'Bushell' or 'Millward', as identified in the letter to Ross – and to whom he felt himself indebted and hence was sending money via Ross.

53   *Massingham*: H. W. Massingham (1860–1924), editor of the *Daily Chronicle* 1895–9.

54   *I have also asked him ... outcasts and beggars*: The only further prose-writing of Wilde's about his prison experiences was a second letter to the *Daily Chronicle* in March 1898.

55   *I have heard from my wife ... I want my boys*: On 24 May, Constance Wilde wrote from Italy to her brother: 'O has written me a letter full of penitence and I have answered it' and on 5 August: 'Oscar wanted me to bring the boys to Dieppe, and then wanted to come to me, but I think Mr [Carlos] Blacker has persuaded him to wait and come to me at Nervi when I am settled.'

56   *Michael Davitt*: Irish writer and socialist politician (1846–1906) who suffered frequent imprisonment for Fenian, Land League and similar activities; he was several times elected to Parliament. His published work includes *Leaves from a Prison Diary* (1885). He had already, on 25 and 27 May, asked two questions in the House of Commons about the dismissal of Warder Martin (see note 48 on p. 262).

57   *You suffered for what was done by someone else*: In 1870 Davitt had been sentenced to fourteen years' imprisonment for treason.

The 'someone else', Arthur Forrester (1850–95), seems to have been anxious to murder a supposed traitor in the Fenian ranks. Davitt wrote him a letter which the jury took to be an incitement to murder, though modern historians disagree. Davitt served seven years and was then released on a ticket-of-leave, which was several times withdrawn when his political activities became troublesome.

58 *To the Editor of the Daily Chronicle*: This letter appeared in the *Daily Chronicle*, under the heading 'DON'T READ THIS IF YOU WANT TO BE HAPPY TODAY', on 24 March 1898, when the House of Commons began the debate on the second reading of the Prison Bill. This, which introduced some of the improvements suggested by Wilde, became law in August as the Prison Act.

THE BALLAD OF READING GAOL

1 *THE BALLAD OF READING GAOL*: After his release from prison on 19 May 1897, Wilde went to France where he began work on this poem, finishing a first draft in August. In October, as he worked on revisions, he wrote to Robert Ross: 'The poem suffers under the difficulty of a divided aim in style. Some is realistic, some is romantic, some poetry, some propaganda.' The poem was first published on 13 February 1898 by Leonard Smithers. Wilde's prison number, C.3.3., rather than his name appeared on the title page until the seventh edition when it was placed in brackets below his number. The poem tells the story of a trooper of the Royal Horse Guards, Charles Thomas Wooldridge, who was awaiting execution for the murder of his wife. On 7 July 1896 he was hanged. Wilde included this dedication in the book: 'In Memoriam C.T.W. Sometime Trooper of the Royal Horse Guards. Obiit H.M. Prison, Reading, Berkshire, July 7th 1896.'

2 *He did not wear his scarlet coat*: Wilde adapts facts to suit his poem here. Trooper Wooldridge's coat was actually blue, the colour of the Royal Horse Guards. When taxed by a correspondent with using the wrong colour, Wilde is said to have replied that he could hardly have opened his poem 'He did not wear his azure coat / for blood and wine are blue' (Hesketh Pearson, *The Life of Oscar Wilde* (London: Methuen, 1946), p. 350.)

3 *The poor dead woman ... murdered in her bed*: Wooldridge's wife was, in fact, murdered on the road near her home.

4   *a suit of shabby grey*: Wooldridge, as a remand prisoner, wore the clothes in which he was arrested.

5   *I walked . . . / Within another ring*: Prisoners took exercise by walking single file in a ring.

6   *Yet each man kills the thing he loves*: Shakespeare, *The Merchant of Venice* IV. i. 66: 'Do all men kill the things they do not love?'

7   *silent men / Who watch him night and day*: Those condemned to death were placed under continuous observation.

8   *The shivering Chaplain robed in white*: The Chaplain was the Reverend Martin Thomas Friend (1843–1934), who was appointed to Reading Gaol in 1872. He served there for forty-one years.

9   *the Governor all in shiny black*: Henry Bevan Isaacson (1842–1915), a retired lieutenant-colonel, was governor of Reading Gaol from 1895 to 1896.

10   *binds one with three leathern thongs*: A prisoner awaiting execution was bound at wrists, knees and elbows.

11   *Caiaphas*: The high priest who paid Judas for betraying Jesus.

12   *peek*: Presumably means 'peak'.

13   *green or dry*: Luke 23: 31: 'For if they do these things in a green tree, what shall be done in the dry?'

14   *At last the dead man walked no more / Amongst the Trial Men*: Wooldridge's final sentencing took place on 17 June 1896. Condemned men were kept away from the rest of the prisoners.

15   *the iron gin*: A snare or trap.

16   *The Regulations Act*: A law, considered inadequate by prison reformers, that placed prisons under government supervision and prescribed humane treatment for prisoners.

17   *The Doctor*: The prison medical officer Dr Oliver Maurice.

18   *We tore the tarry rope to shreds*: Prisoners like Wilde who were sentenced to hard labour had to unravel the loose fibres, called oakum, from old ships' rope. This work caused the skin to dry and split and was very painful. Wilde performed such work at the beginning of his sentence, 28 May–4 July 1895.

19   *we soaped the plank*: The plank bed.

20   *We turned the dusty drill*: One of the tasks assigned to prisoners was the crank, a narrow drum with a long handle that raised and emptied cups of sand.

21   *sweated on the mill*: The treadmill, used to pump water. Both the treadmill and the crank were abolished in 1898.

22   *bitter wine upon a sponge*: Jesus on the cross was given a sponge full of vinegar to assuage his thirst.

23   *The grey cock crew, the red cock crew*: When Peter denied Christ,

a cock crowed (Matthew 26:34).

24 *rigadoon*: A dance for two people.

25 *mop and mow*: Grimaces.

26 *gyves*: Shackles.

27 *demirep*: A woman with a doubtful reputation.

28 *seneschal*: The person in charge of domestic arrangements in a noble house.

29 *the Herald came*: The executioner was called Billington.

30 *running noose*: A rope running through an eyelet to ensure a strong jolt and a quick death.

31 *to wait for the sign to come*: The tolling bell of St Lawrence's Church, Reading, fifteen minutes before the hanging and continuously thereafter.

32 *Strangled into a scream*: In fact, the prisoner seems to have died without a struggle and without a word.

33 *in monstrous garb / With crooked arrows starred*: Marks on the prison uniform in the shape of arrows.

34 *the burning lime / Eats flesh and bone away*: Executed prisoners were buried in lime, so the corpse would quickly dissolve.

35 *the barren staff . . . / Bloomed in the great Pope's sight*: Tannhäuser asked the Pope for forgiveness for having sinned with Venus, but the Pope declared it as impossible as the idea that roses might bloom on the pilgrim's staff. Soon, the staff burst into bloom.

36 *The shard, the pebble, and the flint*: Shakespeare, *Hamlet* V. i. 239: 'Shards, flints and pebbles should be thrown on her.'

37 *Life's appointed bourne*: Ibid., 77–9: 'The undiscover'd country, from whose bourn / No traveller returns.'

38 *And alien tears . . . outcasts always mourn*: These four lines were inscribed on Jacob Epstein's monument over Wilde's grave in Père-Lachaise.

39 *straws the wheat and saves the chaff / With a most evil fan*: Matthew 3: 12: 'Whose fan is in his hand, and he will thoroughly purge his floor, and gather his wheat into the garner: but he will burn up the chaff with unquenchable fire.'

40 *Till it weeps both night and day*: See letter to the *Daily Chronicle* of 27 May 1897 (p. 188).

41 *broken box . . . scent of costliest nard*: See Mark 14: 3–9, where Christ, dining with Simon the leper, is approached by a woman carrying an alabaster box of ointment. She breaks it open and pours the precious oils upon his head. For this, her sins are forgiven.

42 *The Thief to Paradise*: See Luke 23: 39–43, where Christ says

to the thief who repents: 'Today shalt thou be with me in Paradise.'

43   *a broken and a contrite heart ... not despise*: Psalm 51: 17: 'a broken and a contrite heart, O God, thou wilt not despise.'

44   *The man in red who reads the Law / Gave him three weeks of life*: The judge who sentenced Wooldridge to death was Mr Justice Henry Hawkins (1817–1907) at the Berkshire Assizes on 17 June; the execution took place three weeks later.

45   *the crimson stain that was of Cain ... snow-white seal*: Cain, who killed his brother, was marked by God lest he be killed in return. See also Isaiah 1: 18: 'Come now, and let us reason, saith the Lord: though your sins be as scarlet, they shall be as white as snow; though they be red like crimson, they shall be as wool.'